HOLYOKE PUBLIC LIBRARY

KFVS
St825

SEXUAL
HARASSMENT
AND BULLYING

DISCARD

HOLYOKE PUBLIC LIBRARY
250 CHESTNUT STREET
HOLYOKE, MA 01040

Sexual Harassment and Bullying

A GUIDE TO KEEPING KIDS SAFE AND HOLDING SCHOOLS ACCOUNTABLE

SUSAN L. STRAUSS

ROWMAN & LITTLEFIELD PUBLISHERS, INC.
Lanham • Boulder • New York • Toronto • Plymouth, UK

Published by Rowman & Littlefield Publishers, Inc.
A wholly owned subsidiary of The Rowman & Littlefield Publishing Group, Inc.
4501 Forbes Boulevard, Suite 200, Lanham, Maryland 20706
www.rowman.com

10 Thornbury Road, Plymouth PL6 7PP, United Kingdom

Distributed by National Book Network

Copyright © 2012 by Rowman & Littlefield Publishers, Inc.
First paperback edition 2013

All rights reserved. No part of this book may be reproduced in any form or by any electronic or
mechanical means, including information storage and retrieval systems, without written
permission from the publisher, except by a reviewer who may quote passages in a review.

British Library Cataloguing in Publication Information Available

Library of Congress Cataloging-in-Publication Data
The hardback edition of this book was previously
cataloged by the Library of Congress as follows:
Strauss, Susan 1946-
   Sexual harassment and bullying : a guide to keeping kids safe and holding schools accountable
/ Susan L. Strauss.
      p. cm.
Includes bibliographical references.
(ebook)
1.Bullying. 2. Sexual harassment in education. 3. Bullying—Prevention.
4. Sexual harassment—Prevention. I. Title.
BF637.B85S77 2012
302.34'3—dc23
                               2011031731

ISBN: 978-1-4422-0162-0 (cloth: alk. paper)
ISBN 978-1-4422-0164-4 (electronic)

♾™ The paper used in this publication meets the minimum requirements of American National
Standard for Information Sciences—Permanence of Paper for Printed Library Materials,
ANSI/NISO Z39.48-1992.

Printed in the United States of America

Dedicated to my precious grandchildren, Chase and Reese:

My wish is for your school days to be filled with curiosity, awe, fun, and friendships; and may you and your generation know a new consciousness of gender and gendered norms, social justice, and a peaceful world.

CONTENTS

ACKNOWLEDGMENTS

This book would probably not have been written if Suzanne Staszak-Silva from Rowman Littlefield would not have invited me to do so. I'm indebted to her for igniting my energy to write this guide to assist parents and other concerned adults who want to help reduce children and teens' victimization in schools. Suzanne has been a tremendous support along the writing journey, answering my numerous questions and prodding me along the way. A big "thank you" to production editor Elaine McGarraugh and other staff at Rowman & Littlefield for editing, for creating a wonderful cover design, and for all the other elements required to publish this book.

When I think back to the beginning of my involvement in sexual harassment in the 1980s, there are numerous people that deserve recognition. Kudos to my former students at the Carver Scott Educational Cooperative Center in Chaska, Minnesota, who completed one of the first national surveys on sexual harassment in schools, and stimulated my interest in the problem. These same students provided assistance and feedback when my colleague Marcie Combs and I designed sexual harassment curriculum for high school students. Two Minnesota Department of Education sex equity specialists, Laura Kiscaden and Sue Sattel, were pioneers in recognizing the need for sexual harassment curriculum, and hired me to develop the curriculum for all Minnesota schools.

Elsa Kircher Cole, general counsel for the Michael & Susan Dell Foundation and contributing editor for the *Educator's Guide to Controlling Sexual Harassment*, provided necessary feedback on the chapters related to the law. I know I was a pest with all of my e-mails asking questions to ensure I explained the laws accurately. Her patience and legal eye in reviewing the chapters on the law are greatly appreciated.

Connie Anderson reviewed drafts of the manuscript and provided invaluable editing to improve my writing. She was also a great support in my frustrations about being able to express myself so the reader would understand.

And, always, I thank my wonderful family. Though my dad, Dr. Ken Strauss, is no longer with me, I could feel his spirit and love during the writing of the book. My mom, Jean, is always one of my cheerleaders, along with my sister, Julie. My beautiful daughters, Amy and Jill, continue to instill beauty in my life in ways they could never fully understand. It is because of my daughters and my precious grandchildren, to whom the book is dedicated, that I both work and write in this field.

FOREWORD

Paul Kivel

Over my years of talking with young people I have heard very few express fear of being killed at school. That is realistic on their part because in any year they are more likely to be struck by lightning than die from violence. What they do express, almost without exception, is fear of being bullied, harassed, excluded, marginalized, teased, discriminated against, or humiliated. This everyday, all-to-often taken-for-granted violence shapes their behavior, relationships, and future opportunities. The abuse from teachers, administrators, and other students is devastating and the indifference and lack of effective response from adults demoralizing.

Susan Strauss's book is a much needed antidote to such indifference, and offers many valuable suggestions about effective responses. As important, she takes the current popular attention on bullying and provides a broader social and political framework for understanding bullying as one of the often legally prohibited forms of sexual, gender-based, racial, or other kind of harassment and discrimination from which schools are mandated to protect students. The book is both a wake-up call and a prescription for responding to the serious levels of daily abuse that so many students face.

Adults have many questions about why students fail to thrive and succeed in school. Inadequate funding, run-down facilities, unequal opportunities, standardized tests, and low-paid and poorly prepared teachers are certainly some of the causes. But contributing to the high youth suicide and drop-out rates, poor performance, drug use, and destructive behavior are the common forms of abuse that young people experience from classmates at school, at school-related events, in non-school settings, or over the Internet. This book does an excellent job of documenting the many forms that such harassment takes and the impact it has on students.

Recent youth suicides linked to bullying and harassment have highlighted the costs of our neglect of students' health and safety. So far the response from adults has been ambivalent, confused, and legalistic. Laws, by themselves, will not protect students. Neither will curricula that are limited in scope, don't involve teachers, other school personnel, and parents, or are poorly or irregularly implemented. Dr. Strauss highlights effective programs, and points the way to integrated, school-wide interventions that have been shown to make a difference. But it is up to adults to demonstrate the commitment, resourcefulness, and courage to challenge the "it's just something you have to put up with—it will get better" approach that most adults still adopt.

One of the core values in U.S. culture and law is equal opportunity for all. Nowhere is that principle more seriously compromised than in our schools. We can ensure that every student is provided safety, respect, and dignity at school. This book is a call to action and a practical guide to making it happen.

Paul Kivel, violence prevention educator, activist, and writer and co-author of *Helping Teens Stop Violence, Build Community and Stand for Justice*. www.paulkivel.com.

INTRODUCTION

If you are holding this book, you are probably a parent, youth minister, scout leader, youth advocate, or a concerned member of the community. Or, maybe you are a teacher or school administrator. The book's message is for those concerned about sexual harassment and bullying occurring daily in our schools, and about the lack of responsibility by some schools to stop this hurtful and abusive behavior that has resulted in school shootings, youth suicides, and psychological distress lasting into adulthood.

The book's purpose is to inform you about sexual and gender-based harassment and about bullying, including students' rights and the law. The book will give you the tools needed to partner with your school district to keep kids safe. You will also learn how to effectively advocate for your child if she or he has been sexually harassed or bullied, and how to hold schools accountable to stop the misconduct.

The book will not tell you how to become an activist or a consumer advocate. However, when you read the chapter on causes and contributing factors of sexual harassment and bullying, you may just decide to become an outspoken critic about pornography, sex trafficking of children, violence toward women, and about advertisers and media moguls. A side effect of the book may be your boycott of specific brands, retailers, or movies, but that is not the intent.

I am writing this book from a number of perspectives: as a parent of a former victim of sexual harassment; a former teacher of high school students; and a sexual harassment and bullying consultant, trainer, and investigator for schools and workplaces as well as an expert witness for sexual harassment lawsuits.

My daughter was sexually harassed in her high school many years ago. I know the pain a parent experiences when the school is not responding to protect your child and other children from behavior that interferes with your child's right to an education. As a former high school teacher, I know the culture of schools, and that most teachers are caring, compassionate, and committed professionals who enjoy their students and teaching. As a consultant to schools and workplaces and an expert witness for lawsuits, I see the full gamut of sexual harassment and bullying, how schools respond (or not), and the consequences of their actions. My nursing and public health background provide a health and healing viewpoint to the misconduct—the health and healing of victims, and of a school's climate. My doctorate in education, with an emphasis in organizational leadership, adds yet another dimension to the book. My experiences and education bring together these complementary points of view for a balanced and honest book to guide you in keeping kids safe and holding schools accountable.

Perhaps you are worried about your child's change in behavior and appearance—she doesn't want to ride the bus or go to school, his grades have dropped, she isolates herself from the family by heading for her bedroom right after school. Maybe he's gained weight, and doesn't go out with his buddies. She's become so angry. Or he complains of headaches, stomachaches, and generally of not feeling well. Plus, you're not sure, but, for the first time, you think you've smelled alcohol on her breath when she's been out with her friends.

You may be wondering if these changes are a result of your child's sexually harassment or bullying at school based on overhearing her phone conversation with a friend. But, if so, why hasn't she told you about it? Maybe he thinks he needs to tough it out—after all, boys don't cry. Maybe he blames himself. She might not want to rat on her classmates, and fears what would happen if she did; and, besides, isn't that just the way boys are anyway?

In every school district, every day and in innumerable ways, children and youth are harassed and bullied when they receive damaging messages about their gender, their sexuality, their race, their disability, and even their weight and how they wear their hair. These messages are compounded when billboards, television programs, newscasts, magazines, lyrics to music, and the toys children play with continually deliver these same points.

While writing this book in the fall of 2010, the national media told stories of nine gay, lesbian, bisexual, and transgender (GLBT) young people who committed suicide after experiencing sexual and gender-based harassment at their schools. Many of the victims were boys unmercifully harassed because they didn't fit the stereotype of masculinity. They were not protected by teachers and district administrators who held a set of values and beliefs about gender expression, violence, and human sexuality that didn't include the safety and dignity of GLBT students. Is it any wonder that a segment of youth, who are demeaned and badgered, would begin to see themselves as unworthy, and become so depressed that they didn't want to continue their lives of victimization?

Schools are microcosms of society, representing a system rich in gendered hierarchy and patriarchy with norms of sexism, heterosexism, oppression, exploitation, and aggression. Recognizing this requires an acknowledgement that school administrators, teachers, staff, and students, as well as you and I, are creators and sustainers of this system and society's norms. Research on sexual and gender-based harassment and bullying suggests that it is patriarchy and sexism that normalizes these forms of misconduct in our schools.

This book deals with sexual harassment, gender harassment, and bullying. However, the U.S. Department of Education, Office for Civil Rights (OCR), is responsible for enforcing harassment based not only on sex but also on race, color, national origin (Title VI for the Civil Rights Act of 1964) and disability (Section 504 of the Rehabilitation Act of 1973 and Title II of the Americans with Disabilities Act), when it creates a hostile environment that is not adequately addressed by school officials. The discrimination and harassment of these other protected classes are not included in this book.

OVERVIEW OF THE BOOK

Chapter 1 provides a definition of sexual harassment using Title IX, OCR regulations, and emerging Title IX case law. Several sexual harassment cases are discussed to demonstrate how sexual harassment looks and feels and how it impacts the victim. The chapter provides an examination of sexual harassment research studies with an emphasis on research completed by the American Association of University Women. Their study asked students how often they experienced sexual harassment, how it affected them emotionally and behaviorally, and what impact the misconduct had on their school performance and activities. A discussion of Title IX law will show the difficulty in bringing a lawsuit. Whereas Title IX is the legal arm of sexual harassment, OCR is the regulatory branch. The two work in tandem but have different responsibilities, which are discussed in detail.

Though most of us have difficulty even thinking sexual harassment occurs to elementary students and special education students—it does. Chapter 2 is about those two groups. Early elementary grade students don't conceptualize sexual harassment the same as do older high school students. They do, however, recognize that certain behaviors don't feel "right," and little girls (in many cases) know they are being mistreated just because they are girls. One of the country's first sexual harassment cases occurred to a first grade girl on her school bus. Sexual aggression is occurring at younger and younger ages. The chapter discusses specific examples of elementary sexual harassment and how, in a few cases, schools overreacted to innocent curiosity by very young school children. Special education students may be more vulnerable to sexual harassment from their classmates, as well as to more likely sexually harass. Special education laws create challenges in responding to their victimization and perpetration.

Harassment of GLBT youth has received a great amount of recent press and other media attention while I was writing this book. Chapter 3 discusses the harassment, often incorrectly labeled bullying, of GLBT students. For some of you reading this book, you may have strong feelings against GLBT issues in school, and are disgusted that it is included here. Despite what your values and beliefs may be, I believe that you do care about kids and that, no matter what, recognize that they deserve to be treated with respect and dignity. So, I encourage you not to skip this chapter. When you read the stories about these kids' experiences, I think you will be shocked and saddened.

The fourth chapter explores the many aspects of bullying, including the bullied victim and the witnesses. The definition of bullying often differs depending on who is conducting the research, so it is difficult to compare studies about bullying. However, the prevalence of bullying in different grades is addressed, as well as how the misconduct hurts the target and the witnesses of the behavior. Bullying is less common than sexual harassment. The chapter looks at risk factors in schools that might precipitate bullying, and briefly addresses state bullying laws.

One of the primary reasons I wrote this book was for parents, guardians, youth advocates, the media, community members, and others to learn the difference between sexual and gender-based harassment compared to bullying. The media and schools seem to have forgotten about sexual (and other protected class) harassment of students and frequently mislabel sexual and gender-based harassment as bullying. Chapter 5 compares the two types of misconduct to help clarify the distinctions. The distinctions are important because sexual harassment is a violation of civil rights laws, and requires enforcement based on Title IX. Therefore, as a parent or other concerned adult, if a student is being sexually harassed there are additional steps you can take to work with the school to compel them to stop the harassment, as required by law. Those same legal protections do not exist for students who are bullied.

Chapter 6 incorporates social networking and its role in cyberharassment and cyberbullying. New words such as "sexts," "tweets," and "friend" are part of new everyday verbiage and behavior for our young people. Some negative social networking behavior is finding its way into the courts and students are being criminally charged, for example, for sending pornographic pictures of their friends via their iPhone, Facebook, and MySpace. Schools are struggling to find ways to deal with the new technology while maintaining students' rights to free speech. When is it okay, if ever, for a student to post nasty comments about a teacher, for example, on an imposter Facebook page?

While the bullying chapter discusses how bullying impacts kids, chapter 7 details the multitude of ramifications to students directly targeted by or a witness to sexual harassment. Victims' parents may also be the brunt of retaliation if they have filed a formal complaint with OCR or their state's agency or filed a lawsuit. Student victims may be diagnosed with post-traumatic stress disorder (PTSD), commit suicide, and drop out of school. Often they are not believed, are blamed, and receive no support from school officials or the community, even when sexually abused by a favorite teacher.

Chapter 8 expounds on a school's actions and inactions when confronted with students' complaints about sexual and gender-based harassment and bullying. Regrettably, numerous studies show that schools are remiss in protecting students from harassment and bullying, intervening on incidents when they occur, remedying the situation, and making necessary changes within the school system to prevent future occurrences. Often districts do not conduct necessary sexual harassment training for faculty and staff or have educational programs for students, as required by OCR. Those tasked with conducting investigations have not been trained in how to do so, resulting in an inadequate, if any, investigation. Teachers who harass are often transferred to other school districts or are allowed to resign rather than be fired. I think you'll find the information in this chapter alarming.

There are a myriad of causes and contributing factors regarding why sexual and gender-based harassment and bullying exists, as discussed in chapter 9. The root cause is something called *hegemonic masculinity*, sometimes also referred to as *patriarchy*, a system that often unconsciously establishes a gender hierarchy with heterosexual males on top, and females and males who don't meet traditional masculine norms, below. Patriarchy is played out in our media, clothing, movies, sports, television programs, and aggression, to name a few.

A number of other laws, in addition to Title IX, are important for you to be aware of as a parent, guardian, or youth advocate when advocating for a student. Chapter 10 explains many of these laws. For example, often when parents contact me, they want to know what discipline the perpetrator received and are angry the school won't disclose that information. The Family Educational Rights and Privacy Act (FERPA) prevents schools from providing that information. Sometimes students can personally sue individual school officials under the 14th ammendment Section 1983. Hazing and the First Amendment are also discussed.

And finally, chapters 11 and 12 contain information on keeping kids safe and holding schools accountable. Chapter 11 provides opportunities to partner with schools to keep kids safe, by identifying specific actions school districts should implement and listing elements of effective sexual harassment and bullying policies. Chapter 12 discusses how to advocate for a child when she or he has been the target of sexual harassment or bullying. The chapter provides clear steps to take to hold schools accountable in stopping the misconduct and what to do when they fail to do so.

And last, there are a myriad of resources including a glossary of terms and helpful websites and organizations.

I hope this book will be a useful tool for you to understand the complexity of sexual and gender-based harassment and its relationship with bullying. Our society has become less civil, respectful, and empathetic, and it is especially evident in our youth. As adults, we have a responsibility to leave the world a better place than we found it. I'm hopeful this book provides you with some tools to use in doing just that.

✿   ✿   ✿   ✿

This book uses the term "sexual harassment" to encompass (1) male to female; (2) female to male; (3) same-sex (non-homosexual); and (4) GLBT harassment. Some experts and researchers refer to same-sex sexual harassment, and harassment of GLBT youth, as gender harassment, and others name it gender bullying, but I will use the term "sexual harassment."

Throughout the book, the terms "victim" and "target" will be used interchangeably when referring to the individual who has been sexually harassed or bullied. The harasser and bully may be referred to as "offender," "bully," "harasser," or "perpetrator."

Some information is repeated in different sections of the book. Due to the complexity of sexual harassment, it was necessary to include aspects of the misconduct in more than one chapter. I am hoping that by doing this it allows you to use chapters as a "stand-alone" reference.

SEXUAL HARASSMENT, TITLE IX, AND THE U.S. DEPARTMENT OF EDUCATION, OFFICE FOR CIVIL RIGHTS

Boys say, "Oooh, look at those jugs, look at this, look at that," and you may laugh or something cuz you're nervous and people are looking at you and stuff but it does bother you—it affects your self-esteem."

—Traci, a high school girl[1]

"Mom, I'm coming home from school and I'm never going back again—I've had it! Why don't they make it stop?" Deena, an eighteen-year-old senior high school girl, spoke these words, after she discovered her name was on a despicable list entitled the "The 25 Most Fuckable Girls" at her high school. "The list," as it became known, was posted on bathroom walls and circulated in classrooms. To call it simply "The list" is a bit of a misnomer that minimizes the definition and the intent of the document. Under each girl's name was written sexually vile and offensive comments. Some comments used derogatory language to refer to girls' genitals, while other comments claimed to know which girls would enjoy being tied down and "taken." The list was discovered and confiscated by a teacher before Deena did not know what was written about her, but she knew her name was on it. (As egregious as the list was, some of her female classmates felt slighted that their names were not included because, sadly, they viewed inclusion on the list as a compliment.) Deena was livid; it was yet another act of sexual harassment in her school, and she was going to do what needed to be done to get the school to change its culture. As a result of the list and numerous other sexual harassment incidents, Deena filed formal sexual harassment charges with her state's civil rights department. In one of the nation's first sexual harassment cases in education, her state's civil rights department found probable cause against her school district, and Deena was awarded financial compensation.

Milburn High School in New Jersey made *Newsweek*'s list of the top two hundred schools in the nation and, unfortunately, was also newsworthy because of the "slut list."[2] Twenty years after Deena's case in 1990, popular senior girls created a similar list with vulgar comments written about twenty-one incoming freshman girls. Things haven't changed. Apparently this activity has been ongoing for ten to fifteen years. In addition to the list, on the first day of school the freshmen girls were shoved into lockers and were subjected to loud whistles. Stickers were placed on their backs labeling them "sluts" and "whores." Over the years parents had complained, yet others said it's been blown out of proportion; and like the list Deena was on, some girls felt snubbed when they were not included on the slut list. Some girls say it is all in good fun, and those on the list as freshmen will be the senior girls doing the same in a few years.

Students may be targets of sexual harassment by other students, teachers, administrators, coaches, bus drivers, and other school staff such as janitors, cooks, and secretaries, or non-school employees such as a visiting speaker or athletes. What is actually meant by the term sexual harassment? If a student calls another student a bitch, is it sexual harassment? If a boy tells a girl he wants to have sex with her and she is offended, is it sexual harassment? And what if the harasser and the target of the behavior are the same sex—does that make any difference? Defining sexual harassment is difficult and elusive. What is flirting to one person may be offensive and harassing to another. Males and females often perceive sexual behaviors differently, with females feeling more threatened and intimidated by the misconduct. Because sexual harassment deals with both overt and subtle/covert behavior, it is even more difficult to define. Some of the behaviors may be acceptable in some circumstances, such as when interacting socially, but are not appropriate behavior in school. And, as our world continues to shrink and the U.S. population is more diverse, cultural differences add even more challenges.

WHAT IS SEXUAL HARASSMENT?

There are a couple of ways to think about sexual harassment; and not all sexually harassing behavior constitutes sexual harassment from a Title IX and legal perspective. One way, with which most are familiar, is to conceptualize sexual harassment from a practical, *behavioral perspective* and the second is from a *legal perspective*. A simple, practical definition of sexual harassment is any unwanted sexual or gender-based behavior by a person who has power over another. Sometimes that power is formal, such as a teacher or coach over a student; yet other times the power is informal, and may be more subtle because the two individuals may be peers. For example, perhaps the harasser has informal power because she is a popular girl, or he is the quarterback on the football team, or a chemistry partner who gets all "As." In the behavioral definition, the targeted student may define her or his experience as sexual harassment, yet it doesn't fit the legal definition based on the Civil Rights Act, Title IX. In order for the behavior to constitute illegal sexual harassment, it must be sexual and/or gender-based and severe, persistent, pervasive, and offensive enough to create a hostile educational environment, and to interfere with the student's ability to learn and engage in school activities.[3] Even with these required legal elements—severe, persistent, pervasive, and offensive—the definition is confusing because of the ambiguity surrounding the definition of these terms.

Let's examine the U.S. Education, Office of Civil Rights (OCR) definition of sexual harassment to begin understanding this complex behavior.

> Sexual harassment is any unwelcome conduct of a sexual nature. Sexual harassment can include unwelcome sexual advances, requests for sexual favors, and other verbal, nonverbal, or physical conduct of a sexual nature. Sexual harassment of a student can deny or limit, on the basis of sex,

the student's ability to participate in or to receive benefits, services, or opportunities in the school's program. Sexual harassment of students is, therefore, a form of sex discrimination prohibited by Title IX.[4]

Still a bit confusing, isn't it? A number of words in the definition are not clear—for example, hostile environment, sexual advances, and sexual favors. *Sexual advances* refers to a "come on" or an attempt by a teacher, classmate, or others to lure a student into a short-term or long-term sexual liaison. It may be an attempt to kiss, touch, or date the target, for example. *Sexual favors* are acts performed in return for an award such as having a "date" with a teacher in exchange for a higher grade. *Verbal, nonverbal, or physical conduct of a sexual nature* recognizes that sexual harassment takes many forms such as comments, ogling, or touch, for example. In order for sexually harassing behavior to be considered sexual harassment according to Title IX and the courts, however, the behavior must be unwelcome to the student targeted; be sexual and/or gender-based; and it must interfere with the student's ability to get an education (to attend classes and learn), and to participate in programs such as sports, debate, and band, to name a few. In other words, if a teacher or a classmate in a particular class is sexually harassing a student to the point that the victimized student doesn't want to attend class, is emotionally distraught, is not doing the assigned work, or is receiving lowered grades because of his or her refusal to go along with the harassment by, say, a group of classmates—then it is interfering with the student's ability to get an education.[5] Other examples of sexual harassment that may interfere with a student's ability to get an education or to participate in school programs include the following:

- A teacher refuses to provide a college reference unless the student gives in to the teacher's sexual demands.
- A student has difficulty working with a specific classmate on a project due to the sexual harassment by that classmate.
- A student drops out of football because of the sexual harassment by his team members.

Another form of sexual harassment that is not captured in the definition above is what is referred to as gender-based sexual harassment, which is a non-sexual form of sexual harassment. Gender-based harassment may include both verbal and non-verbal behavior, aggression, bullying, and any other type of hostility directed towards a student because of the student's gender or because the student doesn't fit the stereotype of being male or female. Because gender harassment is sex discrimination, the school must respond as it does with what is traditionally thought of as sexual harassment. Additionally, if students are targets of gender harassment in addition to sexual harassment, a hostile environment may exist even if the gender-based harassment or the sexual harassment, separately, would not be ample enough to do so. Some researchers use another term—"sexist harassment," which is generalized sexist remarks and behaviors, not necessarily designed to elicit sexual cooperation, but rather to convey insulting, degrading or sexist attitudes.[6]

Sexist harassment, also called *gendered bullying* by some researchers (defined as *sexual harassment* for this book), is often directed to girls as a group or individually and can include subtle physical intimidation such as blocking the way or invading personal space. It is sex-based—directed to girls because they are girls.[7] It may begin as fun and joking, and turn into harassment. When a girl doesn't like it and tells the boys to stop, she often, hears: "Oh we were just joking" or "Can't you take a joke?"[8] Sex-based harassment is still a form of having power "over" another student.

When teaching students about sexual harassment, boys often said they felt pressured by their male classmates to harass girls because, if they did not, they were ostracized and/or became vulnerable to male classmates sexually harassing them by, for example, using homophobic taunts. They were called names like "queer" and "fag," and were the brunt of jokes implying they weren't heterosexual. The harassment of girls by boys was an expected rite of passage, used to assure their sexual masculine identity and to generate acceptance by their male classmates within the male hierarchical power relationships (not just in terms of gender, but race and class as well).[9] The sexual harassment of their female classmates represents hegemonic masculinity or patriarchy (see chapter 9 on causes and contributing factors for further discussion). [Hetero]sexual sexual harassment is a way to demonstrate dominance towards females, not just for the sake of the behavior itself, but to ensure acceptance in the male group. When boys are harassed, it is often because they don't portray themselves as the "right" kind of boy, not being male enough, thereby building hierarchy and enforcing heterosexual masculinity.[10] Sexual harassment can act as a way to police and maintain gender boundaries and hierarchy.[11] It is also a way to put a girl in her place when boys are angry and want to reinforce their own power. Girls are used to enhance a boy's rank in masculinity.[12]

Many girls, however, ignore the boys' behavior or even play along in hopes that it will stop. They often don't want to make a big deal of it if it is only a one-time incident; of course, that enhances the normalization of the behavior. For some boys, their behavior toward girls is rarely given a second thought because of its normalization and acceptance by the school and by society.[13] Some boys see sexual harassment as something required to attract girls and prove their masculinity. The sexual harassment of girls by boys becomes invisible because it is a natural part of everyday male-female interaction. Some girls believe the sexual harassment is just part of being female.

Sexual harassment can be very aggressive, as in a sexual assault or rape, or subtle, such as sexual graffiti on the bathroom wall. Sexual harassment victimizes not only the direct target of the misconduct, but bystanders as well. Examples of sexual harassment *may* include any or all of the following unwelcome behaviors:

- Scoping—obvious leering at students and loudly rating their appearance and sexual attributes so the targeted student is aware of the behavior
- Sexual gossip/rumors
- Sexual innuendo
- Sexual name calling such as "sluts," "ho," "lesbo," "whores," "cows" to girls and "pussy," "fags," and "queer" to boys
- Stalking
- Graffiti
- Giving neck and/or shoulder massages
- Grabbing a female's breasts
- Grabbing either gender's genitals, inner thigh, or buttocks
- Kissing
- Sexually suggestive sounds and gestures, such as winking, sticking out one's tongue in a suggestive manner, sucking sounds, throwing kisses, whistling, "pretending to sex" (pelvic thrusts)

- Touching, pinching, rubbing, patting, hugging, tickling, humping
- Touching oneself in a sexual way, for example on the genitals
- Comments because a student doesn't fit a gender stereotype such as "mama's boy" and "sissy"
- Sexist comments and jokes
- Ridicule, jokes, and sexual remarks—"Give me some booty," "Give me a blow job," "Give me a lap dance"
- Sexually offensive/demeaning atmosphere created by sexist or offensive posters, cartoons, and pictures
- Cornering/blocking a student's movement—"hold them down to get booty or pussy"
- Propositions
- Pornography
- Spiking—one or more students either pulls down another student's pants (sometimes referred to as "pantsing" or "de-pantsing") or pulls up the pants so the pants are uncomfortably tight on the genitals and/or into the buttocks (sometimes called a "wedgy")
- Mooning and/or flashing—students pull down their pants and show their buttocks or boys will expose their genitals
- Flipping—boys pull girls' skirts up above their waists—usually occurs in elementary school
- Repeatedly asking for sex
- Sexual assault (including grabbing breasts and genitals) and rape.
- Cyberharassment

WHAT THE RESEARCH SAYS

The American Association of University Women (AAUW) conducted the only nation-wide sexual harassment in schools studies in 1993, 2001, and 2011. The research methods and results in the 1993 and 2001 years are similar. The 2011 study asked different questions. I discuss elements of both study results since each provides different information. The 2011 study showed that 48 percent of students, including 56 percent of girls and 40 percent of boys, were sexually harassed with 87 percent of students indicating that it negatively affected them.[14] Twenty-nine percent of students who were sexually harassed admitted to sexually harassing others. Thirty percent of students, more girls than boys, experienced sexual harassment through electronic media such as text, e-mail, Facebook, and other forms. The most common forms of sexual harassment for both sexes were sexual comments (calling someone gay or lesbian was more common), jokes, and gestures. Girls experience more physical sexual harassment than do boys. Both sexes equally (18%) experience being called gay or lesbian in a negative way.

The 2001 study showed that students are sexually harassed in the hallways and classrooms in front of teachers.[15] Thirty-eight percent of students were sexually harassed by teachers or other employees. The 2011 study found most students were sexually harassed by one male student (54%) or a group of male students (12%). Fourteen percent of students indicated they were harassed by one female student and five percent were harassed by a group of females. The majority of male harassers admitted to sexually harassing their male classmates (72%) and 50 percent of female harassers told of sexually harassing a boy. Nineteen percent of boys and 41 percent of girls admitted to sexually harassing a girl. Only 9 percent of students reported their sexual harassment to an adult at school, 27 percent told a family member, 23 percent told a friend, but 50 percent of students did not discuss their victimization with anyone.

INTERNATIONAL LAWS AND REGULATIONS REGARDING SEXUAL HARASSMENT IN K–12 SCHOOLS

Schools are a microcosm of society, complete with the same gendered dynamics where the inequality between the sexes is as ripe for exploitation as it is in the larger society. Unfortunately, schools are not a safe haven for children, particularly girls who are deluged with sexual violence.[16] Schools that condone and approve of other types of violence, such as bullying, will also support sexual violence.[17] Sexual harassment in schools does not occur in a vacuum; it is influenced by both sexual and non-sexual violence and the specific culture in which it resides.

Sexual harassment in schools is not unique to the United States. Other locations in the developed world, specifically Canada and Europe, also have laws against the behavior. The United States and other countries, including those countries with no specific laws against sexual harassment in education, are bound under a number of international laws, treaties, declarations, and conventions that the majority of countries have ratified that do outlaw the behavior. There are twenty-eight international and regional treaties addressing human rights, women's rights, children's rights, sexual violence, and the right to an education.[18] Treaties carry legal weight, and declarations are a political catalyst for remedying a variety of abuses against women and children.[19] International human rights law requires countries to prevent and to intervene against human rights violations including sexual assault and rape. Additionally, monitoring of any government treaty is required to ensure implementation of the treaty and compliance with its requirements.[20]

Sexual harassment in U.S. schools and schools around the world includes a progression of behaviors, from sexist and misogynist comments, verbal sexual comments, and physical fondling, to sexual assault and rape. According to the World Health Organization (WHO), "for many young women, the most common place where sexual coercion and harassment are experienced is in school."[21] Gendered violence against girls in education is a pandemic that transcends race, culture, geography, religion, and class.[22]

Most of the research on gendered violence of girls in and around schools has approached the issue from a heterosexual perspective, and ignored girl-to-girl violence and student-to-teacher violence.[23] Both genders can be victims of sexual violence at school, but the research demonstrates that girls are the more likely targets of sexual assault and heterosexist sexual harassment.[24]

In 1995 the United Nations implemented The Convention on the Elimination of All Forms of Discrimination Against Women (CEDAW), which all countries have ratified except eight, including the United States.[25] CEDAW requires that women and men receive equal treatment, including the right to an education. Because gender-based violence is considered a form of discrimination it is outlawed by CEDAW. Violence against women is defined by CEDAW as "any act of gender-based violence that results in, or is likely to result in, physical, sexual or psychological harm or suffering to women."[26] The declaration recognizes the vulnerability of girl children and specifically singles out schools as a location of gender violence. Why hasn't the United States ratified this important convention?

Governments worldwide have ratified the 1989 Convention on the Rights of the Child (CRC), with two exceptions, Somalia and the United States![27] CRC requires countries to protect children from sexual abuse and sexual exploitation, and to provide equal education to both genders.[28] Again, why hasn't the United States ratified such an essential convention to protect our children? Is there even a credible excuse for such a lack of leadership?

The right to education is also proclaimed in the International Covenant on Economic, Social and Cultural Rights (ICESCR) and the Universal Declaration of Human Rights, with both ensuring equal education to both males and females.[29] Additionally, the International Covenant on Civil and Political Rights (ICCPR) requires equal rights for men and women and effective compensation for abuse.

In 1996, the WHO created two resolutions recognizing that gender violence to women and children was a public health priority.[30] In 2000, the United Nations Millennium Summit announced eight UN Millennium Development Goals. Goal number three requires gender equality in all levels of education by 2015.[31] It doesn't look like the world is going to come close to meeting WHO's goal.

The right to education is also proclaimed in the ICESCR and the Universal Declaration of Human Rights, with both ensuring equal education to both males and females.[32]

As important as these international statues are, we've learned, unfortunately, that laws and regulations are sometimes an ineffective way to deal with sexual harassment because it is so deeply rooted in a country's culture, gender norms, and gender hierarchy.[33] Women's human rights and respect for women are lacking; as a result sexual harassment will continue despite legal attempts to stop the behavior.

Both boys and girls can be victimized by sexual harassment and assault. However, most of the research in the United States and around the world demonstrates that girls are the most likely target and face obstacles in overcoming their victimization. The sexual harassment of girls by boys and male teachers at school is a worldwide issue studied by numerous non-governmental organizations (NGOs) and by a two-year worldwide United Nations (UN) *Study on Violence Against Children*.[34] Sexual violence is a violation of the rights of girls and boys, threatening their right to achieve an education, and injuring their psychological and physical well-being.[35] Sexual violence to girls in schools has far-reaching consequences to society.[36]

U.S. SEXUAL HARASSMENT LAWS
AND THE OFFICE FOR CIVIL RIGHTS

Sexual harassment is an age-old behavior but a relatively new legal phenomenon, and continues to develop in definition based on new case law. Law professor and author, Catharine MacKinnon, was one of the first authors to conceive of sexual harassment as a form of sex discrimination in 1979. It wasn't until 1986 that the U.S. Supreme Court, in *Meritor Savings Bank v. Vinson,* identified sexual harassment as a form of sex discrimination in the workplace.[37] In 1992, six years after *Meritor,* the U.S. Supreme Court, ruled that schools may be liable for teacher to student sexual harassment in the landmark case of *Franklin v. Gwinnett Public School District.*[38] In 1999, the U.S. Supreme Court ruled in *Davis v. Monroe School District* that students could sue the school district for student to student sexual harassment.[39]

Sexual harassment is a form of sex discrimination, which is a violation of the Civil Rights Act, Title IX of the Education Amendments of 1972, the Equal Protection Clause of the Fourteenth Amendment to the United States Constitution, 42 U.S.C. § 1983 (Section 1983), as well as state and local human rights laws. Title IX is modeled after the Civil Rights Act, Title VII of 1964, which outlaws sex discrimination in the workplace (chapter 10 discusses the Equal Protection Clause and Civil Rights Title VII); however, the standard to incur Title IX liability is higher than Title VII liability because, according to various courts, schools are a place where students test out behaviors, some of which are unacceptable elsewhere.

Title IX, spurred by a presidential order amended by President Johnson, developed out of both the civil rights and feminist movements and is supported by the Vocational Equity Act of 1963. It wasn't until 1972 that Title IX was enacted. Title IX lawsuits may rely on Title VII case law, if pertinent, when deciding a case. Under Title VII, a plaintiff must demonstrate that: (1) she or he was subjected to unwelcome harassment, (2) such harassment was sexual and/or gender based, and (3) it was suffi-

ciently severe and/or pervasive that it interfered with the victim's ability
to work and created a hostile or abusive work environment.[40] Title IX is
comparable to Title VII but more rigid, indicating that the harassment
has to be so severe, pervasive, *or* persistent that it interferes with a student's ability to participate in or benefit from the services, activities, or
opportunities offered by a school.[41] Under the Supreme Court's *Davis*
opinion, harassment of students must also be objectively offensive.[42]
Additionally, under Title VII, the organization has liability if it "should
have known" if harassment is occurring, whereas, under Title IX, there
is liability only if the school official who has the power to intervene had
"actual knowledge" of the misconduct and was "deliberately indifferent"
to the complaint.[43]

The OCR is the regulatory agency that is responsible for schools'
compliance with Title IX. OCR enforces discrimination laws intended to
protect students from discrimination based on sex, race, national origin,
and disability. Any educational institutions that provide federally funded
educational programs, and other organizations where students receive
federally funded financial aid, are required to abide by OCR's regulations or risk losing federal funding. This includes all public schools (and
universities and colleges) and any private schools that receive federal
funds or whose students receive federal aid.[44]

The federal courts and OCR are each responsible for the enforcement of Title IX but through different roles and compliance standards,
which is sometimes confusing. However, the distinction in their roles
and responsibilities is an important one, because it has resulted in the
courts and OCR exercising different criterion for liability.

OCR's role is to provide technical assistance to correct sexual harassment issues, whereas the courts' role is to offer compensation and other
forms of redress to student victims when the school district has failed to
protect student civil rights in incidents of sexual harassment.

OCR identifies three elements for a violation of Title IX to have occurred: (1) there is a hostile environment; (2) the school had "actual
knowledge" or "should have known" sexual harassment occurred; and
(3) the district failed to take prompt and effective action to intervene
and stop the hostile environment and to prevent a recurrence. In contrast, the courts require the following elements as a violation of Title
IX: (1) the sexual harassment occurred in a location within the control

of a school; (2) an appropriate person had "actual knowledge" of the harassment; (3) the school acted with "deliberate indifference"; and (4) the harassment was so severe, pervasive, and objectively offensive that it effectively created obstacles for the victimized student to receive an educational opportunity or benefit.[45] A discussion about these differences and what it means is later in the chapter.

OCR was authorized by Congress to enforce Title IX.[46] They do this by issuing the *Sexual Harassment Guidance: Harassment of Students by School Employees, Other Students, and Third Parties*, conducting investigations, consulting with schools in their prevention and intervention strategies, providing compliance reviews, and providing an avenue to resolve student complaints. OCR does not determine damages under Title IX; only the courts have that power. However, OCR can cut off federal funding to a school or school district that does not comply with Title IX. OCR clearly spells out compliance standards required of schools by law which include the following:[47]

1. To take *prompt and effective* action to stop the harassment, to prevent further victimization, and, when appropriate, to provide redress to the victim. These steps, which include conducting a fair and impartial investigation, are required even if a student has not complained about sexual harassment but the school becomes aware of the behavior.

2. To establish, publish, and distribute to students, parents, staff, and faculty a sex discrimination policy and grievance procedure for students to know how and to whom to report complaints. The policy and procedure should be written in age-appropriate language. A specific sexual harassment policy and procedure is not required. However, the district is required to have a sex discrimination policy and procedure that clearly indicates that it includes sexual harassment. Failure to enact a policy and procedure is a violation of Title IX, and may put the school at risk to receive federal funding even if sexual harassment hasn't occurred. Timeframes for policy review and revision must be incorporated. When new policies and procedures have been created, they must be published in the student handbook and the district's website, and students and parents need to be informed.

3. To name a school employee as the coordinator/administrator of Title IX standards and regulations and to coordinate investigations and other required steps when responding to a complaint of discrimination. This individual's name, school address, and school phone number must be communicated to all students, staff, and faculty. The coordinator should maintain a record of complaints, which can be used to monitor repeated behavior, and ensure all employees are trained on sexual harassment including their obligation to report any alleged or observed sexually harassing behavior to the appropriate school official. If an internal trainer is used, that trainer must be qualified and competent in sexual harassment.
4. To educate students about sexual harassment including the policy and grievance procedure.
5. To ensure that all employees who are aware of harassment recognize their obligation to report the behavior to the appropriate school official who can correct the behavior.
6. If harassment is out in the open and pervasive (widespread, occurs in public places such as the school bus, recess, classrooms, hallways, and bathroom walls, and is known by students and staff), the school *should* know it is occurring and conduct an investigation. (This is a major distinction between OCR and the courts; the courts do *not* stipulate the schools "should know" but that the school must have actual knowledge.)[48] In these cases, the obvious signs of the harassment are sufficient to put the school on notice. In other situations, the school may become aware of misconduct, triggering an investigation that could lead to the discovery of additional incidents that, taken together, may constitute a hostile environment.
7. To conduct a fair and impartial investigation of sexual harassment complaints and any observations of potential harassment. Additionally, OCR requires that a school district investigate all complaints of potential harassment, even if the student does not complain, or if they suspect the misconduct is a violation of Title IX. Investigations may be challenging if the victimized student requests confidentiality—it is difficult to investigate an allegation under those circumstances—yet the district is required to take reasonable steps to do so. All alleged sexual assaults must be

investigated by the district, as required by Title IX, even though law enforcement will be conducting its own criminal investigation. Each Title IX coordinator, and any other individuals responsible for conducting investigations, needs to be trained in how to do so. Investigations conducted by law enforcement or insurance companies do not negate the school's responsibility to conduct its own investigation.

8. To provide information regarding the outcome of the investigation to all parties involved. Both the target of the harassment and the accused have the right to know the investigator's conclusions.

THE INVESTIGATION

The investigative process may vary somewhat depending upon the nature of the student's complaint, and the age(s) of the student(s) involved. Merely disciplining a harasser does not reduce the potential liability if the harassment has been pervasive. Failure of schools to stop repeated sexual harassment may be considered *unreasonable* and therefore *deliberately indifferent*. School officials must ensure that the discipline stops the harassment, and, if it fails to do so, the district must take additional steps, such as stricter disipline or suspension of the offender.

The investigator must examine the type of misconduct that occurred—was it a one-time event of graffiti or name calling, and did it occur privately, or were there witnesses? A single incident, unless it is severe, is unlikely to constitute a hostile environment based on federal and state laws. If the single incident was a sexual assault, for example, then one incident may constitute a hostile environment because it is severe. If misconduct is persistent, such as daily sexual comments or taunts, it may create a hostile school environment. To determine if a hostile environment exists requires an examination of all relevant facts—the who, what, where, and when of the behavior. In determining whether sexual harassment occurred, the law, school policies, and a full examination of the behavior, including the essence of the harassment, the relationship between the perpetrator and the target, and the circumstances or context surrounding the behavior need to be examined. All of these issues are important in determining if the behavior was sexual harassment and/or a violation of the school's policy. It is possible the behavior may *not* constitute illegal harassment because it was not severe, persistent, pervasive, or offensive enough, yet be a violation of the school's policy and thus require discipline. The standard to determine if the behavior is illegal harassment is that there must be a *preponderance of evidence.* Sexual harassment is against civil law and not criminal law, which requires the standard of *beyond a reasonable doubt.*

If the investigation determines that sexual harassment occurred, the district is required to take "prompt and effective steps reasonably calculated to end the harassment, eliminate any hostile environment and its effects, and prevent the harassment from recurring."[49] These responsibilities are required of all schools, even if the misconduct is covered by an anti-bullying policy. This follow-up must occur regardless of whether or not a student complained, asked the school to take action, or identified the harassment as a form of discrimination.[50]

If OCR conducted an investigation in response to a student complaint of sexual harassment and found a violation of Title IX, its role is to provide technical assistance to the district so that it is in compliance with the law. If the district fails to take the necessary steps required by OCR, then a formal finding of a violation would be filed and the district risks losing federal funding. To my knowledge no district has ever lost federal funding. Most complaints are resolved by schools by creating and disseminating comprehensive policies and procedures, training staff and students, and thereby resolving the complaint.

When OCR becomes involved in a complaint, they approach it from one of two perspectives: *quid pro quo* or *hostile environment. Quid pro quo* is a Latin term meaning "this for that." An example is when a district employee communicates to a student (either directly or indirectly) that the student might get a "benefit"—such as a better grade, not flunking a test, a reference for college—if the student engages in some sort of sexual activity with the employee—such as sex, dating, viewing pornography, or coming to the employee's house. *Hostile environment sexual harassment* occurs by a classmate, but could also be by a school employee, when the individual asks the student for a "sexual favor"—date me, kiss me, view pornography with me, let me touch you, sends sexual texts or sexts, or follows the student from class to class. It is a hostile environment if the harassing behavior is sexual and/or gender-based and is severe, persistent, pervasive, and offensive enough that it interferes with the student's ability to get an education (learn and study) or take part in school activities (sports, band, debate) and creates a hostile educational environment.[51]

A hostile environment is based on both the "totality of circumstances," and the context in which the sexual harassment occurred. The investigator needs to examine the behavior from both a subjective (how the victim feels) and objective (how a "reasonable" victim would feel) perspective to determine if the behavior created a hostile environment. A student does not need to experience actual harm, such as failing a test or emotional trauma, to experience a hostile environment, though continuing to go to school and maintaining good grades may still be a challenge for the victim.

TITLE IX AND THE COURTS

The courts are responsible for interpreting either federal or state laws, depending on the court in which the complaint was filed. The sexual harassment landscape changes often, and rulings from Title VII workplace case law play a significant role in defining Title IX law as well. Each state's laws, assuming the state's legal statues include harassment in schools, may vary somewhat, but most follow the federal law. If a student does not feel satisfied with the school's response to her or his complaint, and OCR has conducted an investigation and found the district was in non-compliance with Title IX, the student may choose to file a lawsuit or claim in federal court or in state court with the state's human/civil rights department. However, students may also choose to file a lawsuit concurrently with filing a formal claim with OCR.

A 1998 precedent-setting ruling by the U.S. Supreme Court in *Gebser v. Lago Vista Independent School District* (*Gebser*) found that a student-victim harassed by a teacher could not collect any financial award if she (in this case) sued the school district with the following exception: A school would be found liable if a school official who had the authority to take action to "correct" the harassment has actual knowledge that it occurred and failed to respond appropriately.[52] In *Davis v. Monroe County Board of Education* (*Davis*), the Court announced that a school may also be liable for monetary damages for student-to-student harassment if a school official who has the authority to take action to "correct" the harassment had actual knowledge that it occurred and failed to respond appropriately,[53] the same standard established in *Gebser*. Both the *Davis* and *Gebser* courts continued to say that the district's response to the student's complaint of sexual harassment must be so minimal that it amounts to "deliberate indifference." In other words, the only time a student can receive any monetary award for damages is if the school official failed to take reasonable steps to correct the harassment and demonstrated a deliberate indifference to the harassment complaint. The Supreme Court's opinions in both cases result in only minimal protection to harassed students.

OCR uses a stricter standard than the *Gebser* ruling and requires that districts must respond to any allegation of educator-to-student sexual harassment. OCR stated that "actual knowledge" occurs if a responsible employee knows or "should have known" (because the harassment occurred in public such as the hallways or classrooms and was known by students). OCR asserts that a complaint of harassment may be communicated to the school district by using the grievance procedure, or by contacting any school employee such as a teacher, security person, or even the bus driver. Additionally, if school staff, faculty, and administration observe harassing behavior, it requires following through with an investigation. The legal standard for Title IX, however, is that a school official with the *power to intervene* must know of the harassment. The law does not recognize liability for harassment about which the official "should have known."

Confusion about the *Davis* ruling centered on what job position/title has the authority to correct the harassment of a student by a teacher, or a student by another student, and what "deliberate indifference" means. The Supreme Court justices did not indicate who must have knowledge, who qualifies as a school official to correct the behavior, or what constitutes "actual knowledge" or "deliberate indifference." Court opinions have not helped in clearing up the confusion as to "actual knowledge" and "deliberate indifference," with different courts interpreting the U.S. Supreme Court's ruling very differently in cases that are almost mirrors of each other.

The legal issues of "deliberate indifference" and "actual knowledge" represent a major difference between OCR's requirements and the federal courts' requirements. First, the courts, as mentioned above, require "actual notice"; OCR requires "constructive notice," meaning that a school official either "knew" or "should have known" about the harassment. A second difference between OCR and the courts is that the U.S. Supreme Court indicated that an "appropriate person" must be informed of the misconduct but did not identify what position was an "appropriate person." OCR identifies an appropriate person as a principal, security officer, teacher, affirmative action officer, Title IX officer, or bus driver. A principal may constitute an appropriate person according to the U.S. Court of Appeals for the Eighth Circuit, but a guidance counselor cannot be considered an appropriate person because they lack the power required to take corrective action against a perpetrator. And, finally, a third difference between the federal courts and OCR is the degree or level of misconduct required to violate Title IX. In *Davis*, the Supreme Court ruled that sexual harassment must be "so severe, pervasive *and* objectively offensive" that it bars the victim's access to an educational opportunity or benefit. The Court concluded that teasing and name calling alone are not enough for liability.

In addition, the Court ruled that schools can only be held liable for that which they can control, which translates into liability for school officials' responses to student misconduct, not for the misconduct itself. *A common misperception with parents and others is that the school is liable for the behavior of the harassing student—it is not.* In contrast, OCR is less strict, saying the harassment must be "severe, pervasive *or* objectively offensive."

The elements that determine whether the sexual misconduct is severe, pervasive, and objectively offensive[54] are: (1) the degree to which the conduct affected one or more students' education; (2) the duration, type, and frequency of the behavior; (3) the relationship between the target of the harassment and the harasser; (4) the number of students (or teachers, staff, or administrators) involved; (5) the sex and age of the target and the harasser; (6) the size of the school, the location of the harassment, and the context in which it occurred; (7) any other school incidents; and (8) occurrences of gender-based non-sexual harassment. These legal elements have led many to believe that Title IX sexual harassment is far too narrow to provide meaning and effectiveness to victims of sexual harassment in schools.

When a student and his mother reported a teacher's abuse to Barbara Patrick, a principal at Dallas Independent School district and she didn't believe them, the Fifth Circuit Court of Appeals said the teacher only showed poor judgment.[55] Though she erred in not believing the student's complaint, the court found that her actions did not constitute deliberate indifference, and, because she didn't believe the complaint, the court determined that she didn't have actual knowledge. This ruling is in stark contrast to the U.S. District Court of Eastern Virginia's opinion that principal Catherine Malone demonstrated deliberate indifference when failing to believe a student's complaint of teacher abuse. She was ordered to pay $350,000 to the student.[56]

Defining "deliberate indifference" is a challenge. According to the U.S. Supreme Court, if the school's actions (or inactions) to the student's suffering from harassment and vulnerability were "clearly unreasonable," it is deliberate indifference. Even within the Court's attempt to assist in defining the term, we are left with confusion. To confound the problem, if schools attempt to end the misconduct, and their attempts are unsuccessful, that alone cannot establish deliberate indifference, according to some but not all courts.

REAL CASES

In the sexual orientation sexual harassment of Theno, a student enrolled in the Unified School District in Kansas, the court found that the district was guilty of deliberate indifference because the school's punishment of the harassers was ineffective.[57] The court identified a minimum of twenty-four harassers during the four years Theno was victimized before he quit school. His harassment consisted of being kicked, having objects thrown at him, and called names such as "fag," "queer," " jack-off kid," and "flamer," to name a few. Over the years, Theno's parents repeatedly complained to a counselor, principal, superintendent, and the school board. The district's response was to only warn the student harassers, and very few were suspended or disciplined. The district had actual knowledge that its meager attempts to curtail the harassment were ineffective, yet they continued to employ those same inept methods to no avail.

In a student-to-student incident of harassment, the *school official* may vary depending on the specific district—principal, vice principal, superintendent, or school board. However, in a teacher-to-student harassment incident, it *may* be either a principal, superintendent, or the school board who has the authority to take whatever corrective measures would be required. If the teacher needs to be terminated, that can only be an action taken by the school board. I highly recommend that you inform the school board, along with the superintendent, if a teacher or staff member is alleged to have engaged in sexual misconduct. Courts have indicated that a teacher or guidance counselor may be the appropriate person for students to report student-to-student harassment, but not so with teacher-to-student sexual harassment. That's not to say that either the principal or superintendent shouldn't take immediate steps to intervene to protect the student(s), but, most often, the corrective discipline is the school board's responsibility. It is important that the school board is directly informed of a teacher's sexual misconduct, because not all superintendents take corrective action.

The following lawsuit was brought against a teacher by a former high school girl alleging sexual comments and touch. The girl's mother contacted the superintendent with her daughter's allegation, and the superintendent immediately contacted the police and advised the girl's mother to do the same, which she did. When the police officer arrived at the school, the superintendent accompanied the officer to the teacher's classroom, and told the teacher he was suspended with pay pending the outcome of an investigation of an allegation of a violation of the district's sexual harassment policy. The teacher was escorted out of the school immediately. The police criminal investigation followed, in which the superintendent observed the interview with the alleged perpetrator. Even though the teacher was found not guilty in a court of law, the school board believed there was enough suspicious evidence that it merited the teacher's termination of employment. In this case, the superintendent did exactly what he should have done, which played a role in the district *not* being liable.

If both male and female students are harassed by either a student or a teacher, the conduct may not necessarily qualify as illegal discrimination because the misconduct was directed towards both genders. In the case of the perpetrator being a teacher, however, it may be illegal under criminal law. If the teacher's wrongdoing was not based on a student's sex, then the school district is not liable under Civil Rights, Title IX. An Illinois court stated that, "Harassment is not discriminatory simply because it has sexual content or connotations. . . . It is only discriminatory if it causes disadvantageous terms or conditions of employment or education to one sex but not the other."[58]

Illegal retaliation is also outlawed under Title IX. Retaliation consists of any negative behavior that occurs to any student who brought a sexual harassment complaint to the attention of school officials, or to any other student who was part of a harassment investigation as a witness. Claims of retaliation require an investigation using the standard of "preponderance of the evidence" in determining if retaliation occurred.

When students sue their school districts under Title IX, they often also sue using 42 U.S.C. Section 1983, known as Section 1983. Chapter 10 explains Section 1983 in more detail. However, briefly, Section 1983 allows students the opportunity to sue not only the school district but also individual school employees for punitive damages.[59]

Sixth grader B. G. experienced daily harassment from three boys in her Frick Middle School in Pittsburgh. Unfortunately, she and the three boys shared most of their classes, where the boys called her names, told her she was overweight and ugly, and made sexual comments based on sex stereotyping. Despite complaints to school officials, the harassment continued throughout the school year and into seventh grade, with additional boys joining in the abuse. At lunch, when they would call her fat, she moved instead of eating in front of them, and then threw her food away. The result—B. G. developed anorexia nervosa. School officials knew of the harassment but failed to inform B. G.'s mother. Finally, school administrators suspended the boys for one day, but the harassment continued, so B. G. left school. Because the school was uncooperative in providing B. G.'s education record to her new school, her mother filed complaints with the board of education and also contacted local politicians. The principal, in response, filed a disorderly conduct charge against Mary, B. G.'s mother, which was dismissed as groundless. Mary sued the school district under Title IX, sued the principal under Section 1983, and also sued the principal for retaliation. At the time of this writing, no settlement or court opinion is available.[60]

Some state courts differ from federal courts in protecting GLBT youth from discrimination and harassment. Presently, twenty-three states recognize the GLBT community (youth and adults) as a protected class, but the federal government does not. However, if students are harassed because of their sexual orientation or gender identity, their harassment may be actionable as a gender stereotype, which is prohibited by the federal courts under Title IX. The *Price Waterhouse* Title VII case provided that the sex stereotype claim may be appropriate in that homosexuals, by definition, don't conform to traditional gender norms—at least in their sexual practices.[61] Some judges have disagreed, indicating that a gay man *may* conform to what is viewed as a stereotypical man, who is not effeminate, and therefore would not be protected.

Title IX prohibits sexual and gender-based harassment of students regardless of their real or perceived sexual orientation or gender identity of either the harasser or the target.[62] Title IX does not prohibit harassment based on sexual orientation but does protect GLBT students from sex discrimination—very confusing! As with other sexual harassment complaints, OCR requires that schools investigate and remedy real and perceived sexual orientation or gender-based harassment. Even though OCR does not have the authority to investigate complaints alleging sexual orientation harassment, it must investigate complaints of misconduct that is based on a student's sex rather than on sexual orientation. For example, if a GLBT student is targeted with verbal, physical, or sexual advances, it may be sexual harassment. In contrast, if a GLBT student is subjected to abusive comments or name calling due to the student's sexual orientation or gender identity, then it is not sexual harassment under Title IX law. If your state's human rights/civil rights laws recognize discrimination to include sexual orientation and gender identity protections, however, then sexual orientation and/or gender non-conformity is a protected class based on your state laws.

In the 2011 legislature, two bills in Congress are intended to provide GLBT students additional protection, based on sexual harassment or gender stereotyping—the Student Nondiscrimination Act (SNDA) and the Safe Schools Improvement Act (SSIA). SNDA would prohibit harassment based on real or perceived sexual orientation or gender identity in any school/program receiving federal funding. SSIA requires schools that receive federal funding to implement and report on GLBT anti-bullying programs.[63]

Defining and understanding the complexities of sexual harassment under both Title IX and OCR is difficult. Sexual harassment is a form of sex discrimination that is a violation of the Civil Rights Act, Title IX of the Education Amendments of 1972, however, not all sexually harassing behavior constitutes sexual harassment from a Title IX and legal perspective. Some state courts differ from federal courts in protecting GLBT youth from discrimination and harassment. Bottom line: If the harassed student is emotionally distraught, skipping school, not doing the assigned work, or denied other benefits of learning, then it is interfering with the student's ability to get an education, and prohibited by Title IX.

2

SEXUAL HARASSMENT OF ELEMENTARY AND SPECIAL EDUCATION STUDENTS

The fact that neither the boys nor the girls were sufficiently mature to realize all of the meanings and nuances of the language that was used does not obviate the findings that sexual harassment occurred. . . . In this case, there is no question that even the youngest girls understood that the language and conduct being used were expressions of hostility toward them on the basis of their gender.

—Kenneth Mines, OCR Letter of Finding[1]

When eleven-year-old Tianna Ugarte was in sixth grade, one of her male classmates sexually jeered and threatened her for ten months. She was plagued by name calling such as "whore," "slut," "bitch," and other sexual slurs, and in front of her classmates he asked her why she didn't have larger breasts. Her father reported the behavior to Tianna's teacher, principal, and superintendent, as well as to the boy's parents. The superintendent failed to follow through on the complaints because, as he told Tianna's parents, he didn't have the power since there was no proof that the boy had committed these acts. Her parents sued, and during the four-week trial the school district attempted to blame Tianna for her own victimization by proclaiming that she was too sensitive. Despite the district's attempts at blame, however, Tianna was awarded $500,000

in damages in 1996—and her former principal was required to personally pay $6000 of the amount.[2]

You may be wondering why this book has a chapter on sexual harassment of elementary students. I first heard about sexual harassment occurring in the early elementary grades twenty years ago and I thought,
"No way! It must be just innocent behavior from curious children."
Then, the stories became obvious—some of the behaviors were un-
questionably sexual harassment. Still, it took a while for me to readily
acknowledge that sexual harassment was occurring at earlier and earlier
ages. I really believed that the early elementary–aged student was just
too young to be involved in this kind of misconduct, let alone understand what the behavior means. Early elementary students obviously
don't have the same conceptual framework and sophistication as older
students. Yet, as discussed in this chapter, sexual harassment is occurring in this age group; it has been said that sexual harassment has its
roots in the primary grades.[3]

Scarce research has been conducted on sexual harassment of elementary students. The AAUW 2001 study found that 35 percent of students
had their first sexual harassment experience by sixth grade or before.[4]
The Minnesota Attorney General's office studied 651 elementary and
69 middle schools from 1993 to1994.[5] Seventy percent of schools responded to the survey, reporting 2,081 sexual harassment incidents and
377 sexual assaults. The Minnesota Department of Education believed
that was a conservative response, which was supported by many comments by districts such as "there were too many [incidents] to report."
In 2007, Maryland's Department of Education reported 166 elementary
students were suspended for sexual harassment, and Virginia reported
255 elementary students were suspended for sexual touching.[6] A Justice
Department survey reported that almost 4 percent of sexual assaults in
the United States were committed by children aged seven to eleven.

Another study of third to fifth grade students found that the majority
of both boys and girls had equally experienced peer sexual harassment.[7]
After viewing twelve different vignettes, the girls were more likely to
perceive some of the sexual harassment in the vignettes as frightening,
yet fewer than 20 percent of the boys indicated they felt the victim in
the vignette would be afraid. Girls' self-esteem lowered in response
to watching the vignettes–but the boys' did not. Though none of the

vignettes included explicit verbal or physical threats, the girls tacitly understood that the boys in the vignette were more powerful and might harm the girls. Even at this young age, girls recognized the power differential due to gender.

The Eden Prairie, Minnesota school district had the distinction of being the first in the country in which an elementary student, first grader Cheltzie Hentz, brought charges of sexual harassment to OCR and the Minnesota Department of Human Rights. OCR ruled in a momentous decision in 1992 that the Eden Prairie School District was in violation of Title IX for failure to intervene with respect to Cheltzie's and other girls' sexual harassment on their school bus. The boys repeatedly chided Cheltzie and her classmates for being girls and not having a penis and aggressively approached the girls with black rubber knives, telling them they had "stinky vaginas" and that they should go home and "suck their daddy's dicks." Cheltzie's mother repeatedly met with school officials, pleading with them to protect her daughter and the other girls and to stop the harassment, but to no avail. Finally, she filed charges and both OCR and the Minnesota Department of Human Rights, separately, determined that Cheltzie had been sexually harassed and her school was noncompliant with civil rights law for not stopping the harassment.

Following OCR's investigation, its Letter of Finding stated "The fact that neither the boys nor the girls were sufficiently mature to realize all of the meanings and nuances of the language that was used does not obviate the findings that sexual harassment occurred. . . . In this case, there is no question that even the youngest girls understood that the language and conduct being used were expressions of hostility toward them on the basis of their gender."[8] The Letter of Finding went on to say that "the failure [by the school district] to recognize the incidents as creating a sexually hostile environment for the students involved was seen by students and their parents as underestimating the injury which they experience."

Jonathan Harms was a first grader at Rice Elementary School in Sauk Rapids-Rice School District in Minnesota when he first learned the pain of sexual harassment. Thirteen of Jonathan's classmates accused him of having sex with his mother, sister, and animals; called him sexually repulsive names; made sexually noxious comments; and pulled down his pants and underwear.[9] The sexual harassment was a daily occurrence on the playground, in the classroom, bathroom, and hallways, and on the bus until well into third grade. When Jonathan reported the abuse to his teachers, he was told to "stay away from them" or "go play somewhere else."

As with most children, Jonathan did not tell his parents until he'd experienced about a year and a half of victimization. When his parents met with school officials to stop the harassment, they were told that it was just squabbles between third grade boys, and the harassment continued unabated.

As a smart boy recognizing that school officials just didn't get it, Jonathan realized he would have to take matters into his own hands. He secretly carried a hidden tape recorder to school to record the disgusting language his classmates spewed at him. Then, his parents provided a transcript of the tape to the district's superintendent of schools. The superintendent wasn't keen on reading the transcript after the first meeting with Jonathan's parents, nor after the second meeting. Finally, at the third meeting, he read the transcript. The superintendent met with the parents of the thirteen boys and suspended five of them, but still the harassment continued.

Jonathan's health began to suffer as a result of the persistent victimization. He developed an involuntary grunt, facial tic, inability to sit still, inability to concentrate, eye twitching, reverting to baby talk, frequent crying, and constant movement.

School officials did not grasp their responsibility for Jonathan's sexual harassment during the approximately twenty times that his persistent and committed parents met with them. "Why do you keep dragging me into this?" the principal reportedly asked Jonathan's parents. School officials suggested that Jonathan's parents bring Jonathan in for psychological help to determine why his classmates would continually sexually harass him. It was obvious that they were blaming Jonathan for his own victimization.

Finally, his parents had reached their limit, and they filed a formal complaint with the OCR and the Minnesota Department of Human Rights. The agencies, separately, ruled in the Harms' favor that Jonathan's civil rights had been violated by the school and that he was sexually harassed.

A school district in Modesto, California was cited by OCR for failure to stop the sexual assault of two elementary school girls by a group of six of their male classmates. The boys had thrown the girls to the ground, fondled them, made sexually repugnant comments, and attempted to remove the girls' clothes while forcing the girls to kiss them. In New York schools, the director of health services found that children as young as six were "molesting" other children.[10]

Some argue that it is inappropriate to label this behavior in the elementary schools as sexual harassment. Failure to define the behavior as sexual harassment, but rather as "teasing," "bullying," "emerging sexuality," "horseplay," "flirting," or "boys will be boys," fails to capture the magnitude of the tragedy for those who experience it. "The question of naming the misconduct is important. The language we use to describe behavior both reflects and affects how serious we perceive that behavior to be."[11]

Another landmark case that was eventually heard by the U.S. Supreme Court involved fifth grader LaShonda Davis against the Monroe County Board of Education.[12] A male classmate persistently assaulted LaShonda over a period of five months by touching her breasts and genitals. Her parents contacted the police when the school district repeatedly failed to protect their daughter and make the sexual abuse stop. The boy pleaded guilty to sexual battery.

In a narrow ruling of 5 to 4, the Court ruled in LaShonda's (and therefore all U.S. students') favor, deciding that school districts could be held liable under Title IX for student-to-student sexual harassment. To be liable, districts would have to be "deliberately indifferent" to complaints of "severe, pervasive, and objectively offensive" sexual harassment. (See chapter 1 for a discussion of the ruling.) Justice Kennedy disagreed with the majority's opinion, and, in writing the dissent stated, "A teenager's romantic overtures to a classmate (even when persistent and unwelcome) are an inescapable part of adolescence. . . . After today, Johnny will find that the routine problems of adolescence are to be resolved by involving a federal right to demand assignment to a desk two rows away."

When Jonathan Prevette was a six-year-old first grader in a school in Lexington, North Carolina, he kissed one of the little girls in his class on the cheek, according to his mother.[13] Much of the media reported that the school principal suspended him for violating the school's sexual harassment policy. But Ellen Goodman's *Boston Globe* column, "The Truth Behind 'The Kiss'" discounted the common theme in other media. Jonathan was not suspended but sent to a different room for unwanted touching that was a violation of the student behavior code."

Shortly after Jonathan's famous kiss, a second grader from Queens, New York, De'Andre Dearinge, was suspended for five days because he kissed one of his female classmates and tore a button off her skirt, which violated the school's sexual harassment policy. The boy admitted his misconduct, explaining that he liked her and that's why he kissed her, and that the button prompted him to think of the missing button on Corduroy's pants, the teddy bear in one of his books. Following the media blitz about De'Andre's behavior, the school board rescinded its five-day suspension and allowed him back to school after three days.

While these two incidents offer an opportunity for the "teachable moment" for teachers and other school officials, both cases represent an overreaction by educators. The responses by school officials demonstrated their lack of understanding as to what behaviors constitute sexual harassment, and how to respond to behaviors such as Jonathan's and De'Andre's. What was missing from the media's stories, however, was the response by the little girls who were targeted by the boys, and whether the boys' behavior was a first-time or repeated event. If the boys' behavior was repetitive, that may require a different response by school officials than if it was a one-time occurrence. The media furor about these two incidents both distracts the public from, and serves to minimize, the epidemic of actual sexual harassment that occurs daily in classrooms, hallways, playgrounds, and busses. Many experts argue that the schools' overreactions were overplayed in the media, when the biggest problem with sexual harassment is failure for educators to intervene when justified.

The sexual harassment discussed here is less common in elementary schools than it is in middle and high schools; nonetheless, the behavior is not isolated and seems to be increasing in severity. Educators, police officers, psychologists, public health professionals, and sociologists assert that the early sexual acting-out by children is a symptom of the increasingly prevalent societal attitudes about violence and sex. Additional examples of sexual harassment among elementary students include:[14]

- "Nutting"—A boy jumping on the back of his female classmate and pressing his genitals onto the girl's buttocks
- Discussions about "finger-raping" a girl
- Pornography with classmates' names on the pictures
- Threatening to rape
- Gender demeaning comments
- Boys exposing their genitals
- Girls attempting to kiss their male classmates' genitals

In addition, group sexual misconduct among youth has become more prevalent, according to Alice Vachss, former chief of the special victims unit in the Queens district attorney's office in New York City.[15] Minneapolis, Minnesota police reported similar group assaults by children. One example included three boys, ages five, seven, and nine, forcing a three-year-old girl to perform oral sex.[16] Other group assaults by elementary school children include the following:

- Eight elementary students "playing rape" by throwing a girl onto the playground and fondling her breasts and genitals.[17]
- An eight-year-old girl sexually assaulted in a locker room by five, eight- to nine-year-old boys; the boys were charged with sexual abuse, false imprisonment, and attempted sodomy.
- Three boys between the ages of eight and ten pulled off the pants of a first-grade girl, inserted a stick into her vagina, and told her that they would "kill her pussy" and that, if she told anyone what they did to her, they would cut off her hands and kill her dog.

Dr. Michael D. Resnick, an expert on youth at the University of Minnesota School of Public Health, stated that "It's a very disturbing trend. . . . We are seeing an earlier onset of behaviors that used to be reserved for late adolescence, then early adolescence, and now late childhood."[18] A national database from the National Center for the Prevention and Treatment of Child Abuse and Neglect of the University of Colorado Health Science Center lists eight hundred programs for adolescent sex offenders with two hundred of these programs treating children below the age of ten. In a study of sixteen hundred young sex abusers, four hundred said they started sexually abusing other children before the age of twelve.

Several years ago I was invited to speak on sexual harassment in education to a large group of educators from K–12, colleges, and universities. Before I began my remarks, I asked the audience to identify by a show of hands which level of education they represented. After hands had been raised for the various levels, I noticed a group in the upper right of the auditorium that had not raised their hands for any level. When I asked them what grade they taught, they responded, "We're preschool teachers, and we're stunned at the increase of sexually aggressive behavior with preschoolers. We're not quite sure what to do! Is it sexual harassment when it occurs in preschool?"

Some curious sex play is normal among preschool toddlers, but how does one know when it has crossed the line from normal to unhealthy? Exhibiting some sexual behavior was found as fairly common in a study of 564 day-care providers in Minnesota. Researchers discovered that approximately one third of the children six years old and younger periodically masturbated, as well as attempted to touch their classmates' genitals.[19] Approximately one-third of four- to six-year-old children used trickery or aggression to manipulate their classmates into sexual activity. As was evident in the preschool teachers' comments at the presentation referenced above, day-care providers grapple with how best to deal with the increase in aggressive sexual behavior. They recognize that it is normal and healthy for children, as sexual beings, to be curious about their bodies, but when the curiosity about their classmates' bodies becomes aggressive, it is no longer healthy.[20]

SPECIAL NEEDS CHILDREN AND YOUTH

Special needs students, those with behavioral, cognitive, or physical challenges, are vulnerable to sexual harassment as both a victim and a perpetrator.[21] However, not all children with physical or mental disabilities are "special education" children. Children whose disabilities involve impairments require that districts provide special education and related services that are covered under federal special education law.

One study suggested that disabled students experienced more sexual harassment incidents than non-disabled students, but there were no significant mental health differences between the two groups.[22] When a student is disabled and sexually harasses another student, teachers must intervene. According to the U.S. Department of Education, Office for Civil Rights, the student's special education status cannot be used as a defense for sexual harassment.[23] Also, if a student "bullies" a special education student because of that student's appearance, behavior, or stereotyped perceptions of the special education student's gender, then the convergence of Title IX, IDEA, Title II of the ADA), and/or Section 504 of the Rehabilitation Act of 1973 may need to be considered.

There have been few studies of special education students and sexual harassment. One study found that harassment was likely to occur in front of others, rather than in private, and that most harassers were boys and the victims were girls.[24] Disabled girls were also sexually harassed by non-disabled boys. This same study showed that adult-to-student sexual harassment was at least as prevalent as student-to-student harassment, and the adult harassers were those who were involved with the special education environment—paraprofessionals, van drivers, and aides. These findings suggested that both girls and boys with disabilities may be at more risk from the adults who care for them than from their classmates.

Another study indicated that disabled girls and boys were sexually harassed more than their non-disabled classmates with 100 percent of the girls and 94 percent of the boys indicating their victimization.[25] These students experienced more negative comments about their appearance, more sexual rumors, and more sexually offensive messages or pictures. Additionally, they were sexually touched and pressured for dates. Boys were exposed to more sexual graffiti and pressure for dates than were their female classmates. Disabled students indicated that their friends, and people they were dating or had formerly dated, were least likely to sexually harass, which coincided with non-disabled students' reports. These results raise concerns that disabled youth may face greater risks to their mental health as a result of their increased victimization.

Disabled students may also be more likely to sexually harass and/or bully since they are more likely to display less impulse control and social skills than their abled classmates.[26] This challenges educators about ways to ensure the rights of both the harassed victim and the disabled harasser. Disciplining a disabled harasser may be complicated when their harassment is considered part of their disability. However, OCR stated in the Eden Prairie (Cheltzie Hentz) case that a student's disability cannot be used as an excuse to ignore the victimization of another student. The student's individual education plan may require a revision to incorporate the misconduct. If the student has a 504 accommodation plan, staff are required to intervene in the event of sexual harassment. If the sexual harassment continues, the disabled harasser may need to be transferred to a more controlled environment to protect the harasser and the harassed students. Disabled students must also, as must their non-disabled counterparts, attend sexual harassment training catered to their emotional and cognitive abilities.

Title II of the ADA and Section 504 require schools to regularly notify students, parents, and employees that the school does not discriminate on the basis of sex and disability. In addition, as with Title IX, the schools are required to implement and disseminate complaint procedures for handling allegations of discrimination, and to designate an employee responsible for coordinating compliance with these laws.[27]

When a special education child is bullied, the school has a responsibility to ensure that the student's right to an education is not jeopardized, or the parents could bring a claim under the IDEA.[28] If a teacher moves the disabled student to a different classroom to prevent further victimization, they could be jeopardizing the student's right to be in the least restricted learning environment.[29]

Sexual harassment of elementary and special education children is difficult to even think about. Yet, *Davis*, one of the nation's precedent-setting sexual harassment cases, dealt with an elementary-aged child. Balancing the rights of the disabled special needs child with the rights of the victim of sexual harassment is an effort for special education teachers. Schools are required to protect their youngest and most vulnerable under Title IX, ADA, and Section 504—an on-going challenge.

3

HARASSMENT OF GAY, LESBIAN, BISEXUAL, AND TRANSGENDER STUDENTS

Nearly 9 out of 10 LGBT students experienced harassment at school in the past year and nearly two-thirds felt unsafe due to their sexual orientation. Nearly a third of LGBT students skipped at least one day of school in the past month because of safety concerns.

—2009 Gay, Lesbian and Straight Education
Network National School Climate Survey[1]

W. W., a student at McNair Middle School in the Fayetteville Arkansas School District, was called "fag" and "homo" by his male classmates.[2] The name calling was reported to Byron Zeagler, school administrator, who failed to intervene. As a result, W. W. experienced repeated offensive name calling, threats of physical assault, and attacks on the school bus throughout the school year. After one such attack, W. W. was suspended before school officials had reviewed the bus tape that clearly showed he was not at fault. When the harassment continued into the following school year, and was again reported to Zeagler, his only response to W. W. was "Well, are you gay?" When Zeagler was informed of another incident, he ridiculed W. W. in front of the harassing student by stating, "So you went to the bathroom and cried like a little baby." The student harasser, who was not disciplined, left the scene, and Zeagler then told W. W. to "toughen up" and not "go to the bathroom and cry." After W. W. was punched by a fellow student, Zeagler refused to contact the police. Zeagler told W. W.'s mother that he got what he deserved because W. W. made comments about the other student's dead mother, which was not true. School officials still did not intervene when W. W. was severely beaten by three of his classmates.

The harassment of W. W. moved to Facebook where he was referred to as "a little bitch and [sic] a homosexual that NO ONE LIKES." Additional anti-gay comments were threatening. W. W.'s mother reported the Facebook activity to Zeagler who responded with, "Well, is he a homosexual?" And still Zeagler did not intervene. A follow-up Facebook post from one of W. W.'s classmates said that he was going to have W. W. beaten up. Again, W. W.'s mother reported the posting to Zeagler who minimized the Facebook post, stating that, "students said things all the time." That afternoon, in front of his teachers, W. W. was punched in the face by one of his classmates. The teachers essentially ignored the assault, merely saying, "Kids, cut it out." Again, Zeagler refused to contact law enforcement about the assault.

When W. W. returned to school following his recuperation from the attack, Zeagler pulled him out into the hallway, did a pat down, and searched his pockets for an iPod. The search violated the school district's policy. The same day, Zeagler contacted the police, telling them that W. W. threatened to get even with the boy who punched him in the face. Later that day, school resource officers were sent to W. W.'s home because they were told that he was threatening to bring a gun to school. Nothing was found to support the report of a threat with a gun.

W. W.'s mother informed the police of the incident in which W. W. was punched in the face. When police met with Zeagler, he stated he did not inform police of the incident because "both parties were involved." Zeagler provided the police officer with his handwritten notes and the unfounded allegation that W. W. threatened to bring a gun to school. Zeagler provided no information to police about the classmates that assaulted W. W.

The year W. W. began high school, Zeagler became the vice principal of the high school—and the harassment continued. While waiting at the bus stop, another student punched W. W. while the student's brother video-recorded the assault, and then showed the recording to other students and posted it on YouTube.

The *New York Times* featured an article about W. W.'s harassment and the failure of the school district to intervene. Zeagler refused to be interviewed for the article other than to claim in a press release that "the whole story can't be told." This phrase was used repeatedly in public discourse. Zeagler, another teacher, various students, and the district's public relations department created a Facebook group called "The Whole Story." The harassing and threatening comments posted on the site were severe enough that Facebook shut it down. At graduation the principal, while referencing W. W., stated that "students and teachers demonstrated their remarkable character" and "in my 31 years as an educator, I've never been more proud."

In 2010, W. W. sued his school district in federal district court and lost his case. The findings are being appealed to the U.S. Court of Appeals, Eighth Circuit. At the time of this writing, no decision about his case has been made.

SAME-SEX, GLBT, OCR, AND TITLE IX

Same-sex harassment may or may not be homosexual in nature. Sexual harassment that is based on whether a student fits the stereotype of her or his gender (masculinity or femininity) is labeled *gender-based* harassment by OCR. OCR states that gender-based harassment, including sex stereotyping, is in violation of Title IX. That said, there is no federal law that distinctly forbids discrimination and harassment based on a student's sexual orientation or gender identity. However, numerous states provide legal redress for discrimination based on sexual orientation. Some states provide anti-discrimination protections for both gender identity and sexual orientation, yet other states and school districts have specifically voted against adding sexual orientation and gender identity to their statues. Many courts and the U.S. Department of Education have adopted same-sex "bullying" as harassment following the U.S. Supreme Court's Title VII decision in *Oncale v. Sundowner Offshore Services,* which is discussed later in the chapter. Both federal laws, Title IX and Title VII, provide limited protection for GLBT students and employees. It would be beneficial to check state and local laws as they may be broader in protection.

OCR does not explicitly address GLBT harassment; however, gender-based harassment directed at GLBT students or those perceived to be GLBT is prohibited. Title IX bans harassment of both genders by either gender—in other words, harassment by the same sex. It also prohibits harassment—aggression, intimidation, and hostility based on one's sex stereotype. This means that, if a student is harassed based on how they express their gender, and their expression is stereotypically uncharacteristic for their gender/sex, or they don't fit the norms of what is masculine or feminine, they are protected from discrimination. In addition, the U.S. Justice Department argued that the federal law against gender-based discrimination applies to gender expression. As a result, a New York teen-age boy harassed and physically accosted because he was perceived as effeminate won an out-of-court settlement for $50,000, legal fees, and the cost of therapy.[3]

While Title IX prohibits sex discrimination against transgender students, it is unclear whether Title IX protects the students from harassment based on their transgenderism. Not all legal issues regarding GLBT students have been resolved. Some courts hold that Title IX safeguards GLBT students.[4] In addition to OCR, lower federal courts and some state courts have unanimously determined that same-sex harassment is protected under Title IX.

According to several courts, the use of words such as "fag" or "homo" may not necessarily be a violation of Title IX or indicative of gender harassment unless it is judged as severe, pervasive, persistent, and offensive, and used in combination with other sexual harassment. The behavior must deny students access to their education and have a negative impact denying students school-related resources.[5]

SAME-SEX HARASSMENT UNDER TITLE VII

Even though Title VII deals with discrimination in employment, rulings under Title VII often are incorporated into Title IX lawsuits. Two specific U.S. Supreme Court rulings have provided support for GLBT employees. *Oncale v. Sundowner Offshore Services, Inc.* determined that it was irrelevant if the harassment was same-sexed. The target of the harassment could still establish that his or her harassment was "because of sex" (a requirement for sexual harassment) if the target was subjected to sex-specific terms that clearly demonstrated hostility toward him or her because of his or her sex. In *Price Waterhouse v. Hopkins*, the U.S. Supreme Court found that a victim could be discriminated against if the discrimination or harassment was directed at the victim because of a failure to meet stereotypical gender expectations. The Court stated that same-sex harassment does not have to be based on sexual desire or attraction but rather is hostility based on the perceived failure of the victim to comply with the stereotype of masculinity or femininity.[6]

TRANSGENDERISM AND GENDER NON-CONFORMITY

The term "sexual," as in "sexual harassment," is often used to refer to "heterosexual." When thinking of sexual harassment, we don't often think of homosexual sexual harassment because we are a heterosexist culture. Plus, we usually think that sex refers only to male or female, yet a very small percentage of babies are born with the external genitals of one sex and the internal genitals of another—a hermaphrodite. Others are born with ambiguous genitals where it is difficult to discern if the baby is a boy or a girl—a pseudohermaphrodite. In both instances, parents feel obliged to do *something* about *it*, so the child is either male or female. In addition, some cultures include other categories of sex. Native American Navahos, for example, recognize and provide legitimate social standing for sexual ambiguity and label the third sex category as *"nadle."*[7] Recently, Australia became the first country in the world to legally recognize a third category of sex they label *intersex*.

Less is known about gender non-conformity or gender expression harassment. Gender expression refers to how students display their masculinity or femininity. The California Safe Schools study showed that 27 percent of students reported being harassed for gender non-conformity, being "not as masculine as other boys" or "not as feminine as other girls."[8] Additionally, 49 percent of students were harassed because of their sexual orientation or gender expression. The term transgender is often used to describe gender non-conforming people. Transgender students are often perceived as gay, but sexual orientation and gender identity are not the same. Transgender refers to people whose gender identity and gender expression differs from what their biological sex (genitalia) was at birth.[9]

Gender identity is an individual's internal sense of being male or female. Sexual orientation is about who someone is sexually attracted to, which may be someone of the opposite sex, the same sex, or either sex. A transgender person may be gay, lesbian, bisexual, or straight. Generally speaking, one's gender identity, not their physical sex, determines their sexual orientation. Transgenderism is becoming more evident in young children.

Society tends to judge males who are gay and gender non-conforming more harshly than how it judges girls who are lesbian and gender non-conforming. Schools, as a microcosm of society, do the same, thereby implicitly and explicitly supporting traditional masculinity and patriarchy. Qualities such as being nurturing and having an interest in the arts are usually attributed to the feminine, and therefore devalued and considered inferior if seen in boys.[10] Patriarchy (discussed in chapter 9) is the social standard of male privilege, entitlement, and power, and places a tremendous amount of pressure on boys to conform to what is expected of heterosexual males. This pressure may limit the school activities that gender non-conforming students, particularly boys, decide to engage in, with them foregoing activities such as the arts, dance, theatre, or even playing the violin in orchestra compared to playing the drums in band. When this happens, the educational system is failing many of its students.

Born as a biological male, Pat Doe identified as a female and dressed accordingly while attending her Massachusetts middle school.[11] She enjoyed wearing female fashions and accessorized with hair extensions, bras, and barrettes. The school district discriminated against Pat by infringing on her freedom of speech and expression and "liberty interest in appearance" rights (her rights to her own appearance) when they sent her home repeatedly for dressing like a girl. Every day, Pat was forced to appear in front of her principal to receive approval—or not—on what she was wearing. By eighth grade, the school recommended to her family that Pat seek therapy.

P. S. was perceived as girlish in elementary school, and, when he began middle school, he was harassed more so than when in elementary school. When he wasn't isolated by his classmates, P. S. was the victim of unrelenting verbal and physical harassment.[12] The taunts focused on his physical appearance, lack of athleticism, and the perception that he was feminine. He was labeled "faggot," "gay," "transvestite," "transsexual," "queer," "loser," "big tits," and "fat ass." Despite reports of the harassment to school officials, the sexual harassment continued, taking a deep toll on him. He was diagnosed with depression, his grades dropped, and he was placed in special education. The harassment continued unabated, forcing his parents to enroll him in another school district. They sued the high school for the cost of out-of-district tuition because the district failed to intervene and stop the harassment, thereby denying P. S. of his right to an education.

WHAT THE RESEARCH SAYS

Comments such as "that's so gay" and "don't be such a fag/queer" and jokes that ridicule and degrade GLBT students about their speech, their mannerisms, or the way they walk are commonplace in California schools.[13] Teachers are less likely to intervene in the event of harassing comments towards GLBT students than other types of demeaning comments to straight students.

A two-year study was conducted in 2001 by Human Rights Watch (HRW),[14] an agency that investigates world-wide human rights abuses, found that GLBT youth in America's high schools were experiencing widespread harassment and discrimination by their classmates. Alarmingly, the study found that educators failed to intervene, thereby colluding with the perpetrators, and in some instances participating as full-fledged offenders in the sexual harassment of their GLBT students.

The study told horrendous and revolting stories of close to three hundred students and educators in seven states. For some of these students, every day they walked through the school door it was like walking into a war zone—some literally feared for their safety and their lives. They were verbally, physically, and sexually assaulted in all areas of the school, and especially in the bathroom. Understandably, many of these GLBT students dropped out of school, became clinically depressed, and some committed suicide.

In 2009, the Gay, Lesbian and Straight Education Network (GLSEN) conducted a national survey of 7,261 middle and high school students from all fifty states, and found that nearly nine out of ten GLBT students were victims of sexual harassment within the year, with one-third of these students skipping at least a day of school per month due to fear for their safety.[15] GLSEN found that the severe harassment of GLBT students over the last ten years had remained fairly constant. There were significant decreases in the frequencies of verbal and physical harassment and physical assault from 2007 to 2009. Homophobic comments decreased in frequency from 1999 to 2003, but from 2005 to 2009 homophobic comments had not significantly decreased. Despite some positive changes over the last ten years, GLSEN refers to their results as a public health crisis.

The key findings from their research were atrocious and dire. The following experiences of GLBT students at school, merely because of their sexual orientation or gender expression, are frightening symptoms of a hostile school environment:

- 85 percent—verbally harassed due to sexual orientation
- 40 percent—physically harassed due to sexual orientation
- 19 percent—physically assaulted due to sexual orientation
- 64 percent—verbally harassed due to their gender expression
- 27 percent—physically harassed due to gender expression
- 13 percent—physically assaulted due to gender expression
- 61 percent and 40 percent felt unsafe at school because of their sexual orientation and gender expression, respectively
- Approximately 30 percent of GLBT students miss a minimum of one class, and another 30 percent miss a full day of school, every month (compared to only 8 percent and 7 percent, respectively, of secondary students nationally)
- GLBT students who were targeted by frequent harassment received a lower grade point average than students harassed less often
- Students experienced depression, anxiety, and low self-esteem when victimized
- GLBT students were more likely to indicate they would not aspire to any post-secondary education

- 63 percent chose not to report their victimization because they did not trust school officials to intervene on their behalf, and/or believed they would be retaliated against
- Of the 34 percent who did report their harassment, school officials failed to intervene
- Specific verbal comments students reported hearing were "gay," "dyke," and "faggot;" hostile comments questioning a student's masculinity or femininity, and cyberharassment using texting, e-mails, or comments on Facebook

On the positive side, there has been an increase in student support groups, gay-straight alliances (GSA), educator support, and GLBT educational materials in school libraries. GLSEN research found that those schools with GSA involvement and inclusive curriculum provided a safer environment for GLBT students. Students heard fewer homophobic name calling and comments, were more likely to report that educators intervened on harassment, felt more connected to the school community, and felt safer because they experienced less harassment. Unfortunately, only about 45 percent of schools provide GSAs, and only 13 percent of schools provided curriculum that included GLBT people in history.

A Yale University study found that GLBT students were about 40 percent more likely than their heterosexual classmates and peers to be punished by schools, courts, and the police, with girls at particular risk for unequal treatment for any type of misconduct.[16] Lesbian and bisexual girls were two to three times more likely to be punished.

Several GLBT students have successfully sued their school districts:[17]

- Dylan Theno, heterosexual but perceived as gay, was targeted by rumors and name calling such as "bitch," "fag," and "homo" from seventh grade until his junior year when he dropped out of school. He sued the Tonganoxie School district in Kansas and was awarded $440,000.
- Joseph Ramelli and Megan Donovan, two gay high school students from Poway High School near San Diego, were spit on, kicked, punched, and threatened and were awarded $300,000 by a jury.

- Alana Flores, Freddie Fuentes, and four other students were victims of anti-gay harassment in their Morgan Hill Unified School district in California. They sued their district, and after a five-year battle were awarded a little over $1 million in damages and attorneys fees.
- Derek Henkle, a gay student at Washoe County School district in Nevada, was awarded $451,000 in damages.

A trailblazing gay man, Jamie Nabozny from Ashland (Wisconsin) school district, decided to fight back after years of severe victimization that began when he was in seventh grade and continued until he ran away at seventeen.[18] Jamie's case was precedent setting. He completed his General Educational Development (GED), and at the age of seventeen he sued his school district, accusing administrators and teachers of failing to keep him safe and failing to intervene on his discrimination. Jamie was awarded close to a $1 million settlement!

Jamie's harassment began in response to gossip that he had been sexually assaulted by a local minister. He was labeled the "class faggot" and classmates wrestled him to the floor, simulated sex, and chanted "You know you want it," while other students stood by watching. Throughout the years he was grabbed in his genitals, spit upon, and called queer, faggot, and other names. He was jeered and taunted, knocked down, and urinated upon, and classmates threw pencils at him. His algebra teacher called him a "fag," and encouraged him to switch to another math class. The worse abuse occurred when several male classmates encircled him, kicked the books out of his hands, and said, "Fight, faggot." Jamie said he would not fight and to leave him alone. Then, one male classmate, wearing cowboy boots, kicked him with such force that Jamie required abdominal surgery to repair the internal damage. He was diagnosed and hospitalized for depression, and attempted to kill himself three times before he ran away in his junior year of high school.

Jamie persistently informed school officials of his repeated victimization by his classmates. Administrators failed to intervene, thereby revictimizing him. The middle school principal colluded with the perpetrators by condoning their behavior with the adage, "Boys will be boys—if you are going to be gay, you have to expect that to happen." The boys tormenting Jamie received no repercussions from school officials, thus receiving unspoken approval for their continued abusive behavior.

Interviewing Jamie for this book, he said the school's vice principal burned his school records to prevent them from being used in his lawsuit. His family suffered retaliation from the community with threats to burn down their house, among other actions. Jamie spoke fondly of his school guidance counselor, Lynn Hanson, who was the one person who supported him throughout his ordeal. Lynn had made copies of Jamie's school record before the vice principal burned them, making them available for his lawsuit. While the jury for Jamie's lawsuit found no liability on the part of the school district, the school administrators were found to have discriminated against him.

Jamie now lives in Minneapolis, Minnesota with his partner of three years. As a result of the fall 2010 media coverage of GLBT student suicides around the country, and specifically in response to an article in the Minneapolis, Minnesota newspaper *Star Tribune* about schools struggling with gay policies, he wrote a letter to the editor of the newspaper. His letter expressed that he is "tired of having to justify why we should be teaching kids to respect GLBT youth in our schools. We are all human beings, and we are all worthy of respect. . . . All kids should be safe in school."

Jamie is now a thirty-five-year-old, successful, well-spoken advocate for GLBT youth. He graduated from the University of Minnesota with a degree in GLBT Youth in Schools, a personal degree he created. Jamie says the verbal abuse has been more difficult to get over than the physical abuse he experienced. He still cringes when he hears someone in a mall yell out "fag" to one of their friends. Jamie travels the country speaking to school districts about sexual abuse and harassment of GLBT students. He is using his horrendous experience to help others.

In a 2006 case, seventh grader Doe was harassed by a group of boys who repeatedly called him "faggot," frequently asked him for a "blow job" or to "make out," pretended to masturbate in front of him, sent him a note that said, "Die, faggot," touched him inappropriately, and exposed their genitalia to him.[19] The teachers allegedly ignored the reports of the behavior. When Doe's mother told the school district that girls were being victimized by the same group of boys, the district's response was quick and strong, expelling one of the boys and suspending two others. When the school district argued that Doe was not protected from sexual orientation harassment under Title IX, the court disagreed, citing *Bibby v. Philadelphia Coca Cola Bottling Co.*, a Title VII (workplace) case in which Bibby was sexually harassed because he failed to conform to the male stereotype. Even though some of the conduct directed at Doe was couched with homophobic remarks, his harassment was based on his sex, as was Bibby's. This is an example where Title VII case law was used in a Title IX case.

October 2010 national news included suicides of several teens victimized by harassment because of their perceived sexual orientation or gender identity:

- Tyler Clementi, an eighteen-year-old college freshman at Rutgers University, jumped off the George Washington Bridge three days after images of him having sexual relations with another male surfaced on the Internet shortly after college began.
- Billy Lucas, fifteen years old, hung himself in a Greensburg, Indiana barn.
- Asher Brown, age thirteen, shot himself in the head.
- Seth Walsh, a thirteen-year-old from Tehachapi, California, hung himself from his backyard tree.
- Four high school students and one middle school student from Anoka Hennepin school district, the largest in Minnesota, plus two other students with a relationship to the district, killed themselves within a year. At least four of those students were tormented because of their perceived GLBT orientation.

In addition, the Anoka Hennepin district and two of their teachers were the focus of a complaint to the Minnesota Department of Human Rights by a male high school student, Alex Merritt, and his parents. In 2008, the two teachers, one male and one female, were accused of harassing Alex because of his perceived sexual orientation. Alex was straight, however. The district did not terminate the teachers' employment and they are on an unpaid leave of absence. The student was awarded a $25,000 settlement from the district.

The Anoka Hennepin school district has what is referred to as a curriculum neutrality policy requiring staff to remain neutral about sexual orientation. As a result, many teachers are grappling with how to respond to GLBT issues, and how to acknowledge their personal beliefs, while at the same time meeting student needs and following district policy. This is compounded when some parents fear that homosexuality indoctrination is the school's agenda. In the summer of 2011 the district received notice that two lawsuits had been filed by numerous students and their parents for failing to intervene on harassment of the students based on their sexual orientation. Many Minnesota schools do not include sexual orientation in harassment policies even though Minnesota lists sexual orientation and gender identity as a protected class. Whether Minnesota schools, or schools in any state that legally protect GLBT people's civil rights, include GLBT discrimination and harassment in their policies has no bearing as to whether those students are protected from discrimination—they are.

Every day in school, GLBT youth face harassment. As well, straight youth who do not fit the stereotype of masculinity or femininity are harassed because of their style of dress, the way they walk, or their general demeanor. It is all about fitting into the patriarchal norms of the school's culture, and of society. Sadly, teachers and other staff often witness the name calling and other physical and verbal assaults—but fail to intervene. Other times, teachers are the harassers, further jeopardizing these students' safety. GLBT youth are protected under civil rights laws in some states, but there is a lack of consistency for protection. When these youth are harassed and fear for their safety, they cannot participate fully in the learning opportunities, resulting in long-lasting consequences.

4

BULLYING

Bullies are always cowards at heart and may be credited with a pretty safe instinct in scenting their prey.

—Anna Julie Cooper (Teacher and Writer)[1]

The practice of violence, like all action, changes the world, but the most probable change is to a more violent world.

—Hannah Arendt (U.S. Political philosopher)[2]

Marty, less confident than his male classmates, was bullied by Gary, a popular football captain who played cruel jokes and tricks. He hid Marty's possessions and stole his cell phone, selling it for less money than it was worth.[3] Gary then tossed the phone money at Marty, letting him know it was a worthless piece of trash and not worth the money he sold it for. Marty's classmates thought Marty should stick up for himself, and they were also uncomfortable with Gary's bullying. Marty attempted suicide. When his classmates heard about Marty's suicide attempt, they felt guilty for not helping him that lasted into adulthood.

Bullying is a form of school violence that is on a continuum from mild to severe, and includes verbal, physical, and relationship aggression.[4] It does not include aggression towards someone due to their gender, their sexual orientation, gender identity, sex, or sex stereotypes, those behaviors are sexual harassment, or harassment based on sexual orientation or gender identity, depending on federal and state laws. The term *bullying* is a gender-neutral reference. Bullying research often mislabels harassment of GLBT teens as bullying, which it is not.[5]

Much of the bullying research includes aggression due to gender, sex stereotypes or GLBT status, which confuses the definition of bullying. Bullying is not illegal, however, whereas sexual (and other protected class) harassment is illegal based on federal and state laws. Many researchers will define sexual harassment as a form of bullying. They may or may not use the term sexual harassment when discussing it as a bullying behavior. I do not. It is confusing. Bullying is status blind; in other words, it doesn't occur because one is female, or Black, or disabled, for example—that is illegal harassment, not bullying.

Bullying is a complex behavior with various causes and contributing factors. It is a tapestry of interactions among society, parents, the school, peers, and the media, to name a few. (See chapter 9 on causes and contributing factors.) Whether a bully is male or female, they are more likely to use alcohol and drugs, and receive less support from their parents than non-bullies. Both bullies and their victims are more likely to either experience or witness abuse at home.[6] If parents know their children's friends, the child is less likely to bully; children tend to hang out with students like themselves, meaning bullies hang out with other bullies and reinforce each other's misconduct.[7] Most bullying occurs on the playground, during recess, and at lunch, and is less likely to occur in the classroom if the teacher is warm and responsive to students. Bullying is a public performance with other students as observers, and therefore as secondary victims. As a result, it creates a school culture of hierarchy through dominance and aggression.[8]

Some experts believe bullying is a social issue because it does not occur in a vacuum but, rather, is a behavior influenced by the bully's family, friends, school climate, and even the community. Children receive approximately two hundred jeers or taunts weekly from their classmates.[9] Bullying is associated with later more serious forms of violence. A new element to bullying is cyberbullying, which is discussed in detail in chapter 6.

The U.S. Department of Education sponsored the first ever Bullying Prevention Summit in August of 2010 in response to the widespread suicides of GLBT students, and those perceived to be GLBT.

WHAT IS BULLYING?

With no consistent definition of the misconduct, it makes it difficult to measure. According to Dan Olweus, the Scandinavian "father" of bullying research, bullying is defined as repeated, aggressive behavior in which there is an imbalance of power or strength between the parties.[10] Bullying may directly target a child such as name calling, kicking, grabbing, hitting, wrestling, and taunting. Or, it can be indirect such as isolating someone and not including them in activities or discussions, spreading nasty rumors or gossip, or manipulating them. Some will argue that bullying does not need to be repeated if it is severe enough. Others believe that the use of the word "repeated" is from an adult's perspective and fails to recognize the impact of even one bullying incident on a child.[11] The definitions by authors and researchers are mercurial and ambiguous, implying that it can be any behavior, from a child sticking his or her tongue out at another child to more severe behaviors such as physical assault, sexual harassment, and hazing.[12] Bullying has been defined as a conscious, willful, and deliberate hostile activity intended to harm, to create terror, and to induce fear through the threat of further aggression.[13] Bullying, according to some, always includes an imbalance of power and the intent to harm and to instill fear of further aggression, and, if it continues, it creates terror, causing the victim to feel powerless. When children define bullying, it is often a definition of behaviors, such as "he's kicking me." Other children's examples include: upsetting someone, scaring, teasing, picking on, making fun of, calling names, getting into a physical fight, pushing, shoving, slapping, kicking, threatening to hurt or hit, or excluding someone from their group of friends during the school year.[14] Even the forty-five states that have passed anti-bullying legislation do not agree on the definition. In a recent U.S. Departments of Education and Justice biannual survey of 3,500 school administrators, *Indicators of School Crime and Safety*,

there is no definition of bullying, it is up to each principals' own definition of bullying.[15]

Without a consistent definition of bullying, research results are inconsistent and faulty. As you read this chapter, it is apparent how the
rate of bullying varies, sometimes drastically, because of the different
definitions and other aspects of the research. Some studies estimate that
anywhere from 30 percent to 85 percent of middle and high school kids
are bullied. It is unknown if that statistic means daily, weekly, monthly,
yearly, or throughout their time in school. One study found that, in a
year's time, 22 percent of children and youth between the ages of two
to seventeen had been physically bullied, and 25 percent had been
emotionally bullied.[16] Six- to twelve-year-olds experienced the most bullying. Another set of studies suggested that anywhere from 10 percent
to 75 percent of students were bullied. Thirty percent of sixth through
tenth graders of over fifteen thousand public and private students reported moderate to frequent involvement in bullying with 13 percent as
bullies only and 11 percent as victims only.[17] Bullying occurs in urban,
suburban, and rural communities at the same rate.[18] It is estimated that
15 percent to 20 percent of kids will be bullied sometime during their
school years.[19]

We can't trust the bullying data as well because much of it includes
bullying behavior due to a student's sex or because a student is gay, lesbian, bisexual, or transgender, and therefore the behavior is harassment,
a violation of Title IX and state civil rights laws, not bullying. We don't
know how many kids are bullied. Additionally, most of the research has
been done in the Scandinavian countries that have a much more homogenous population and will, therefore, have different results. According
to the U.S. Department of Education, almost one-third of all students
experience bullying a minimum of once a month, and one out of every
ten high school dropouts is due to bullying.

The inconsistent bullying definition skews the research results because the misconduct is not examined from a cultural and social perspective. In other words, the role of traditional masculinity, sexism, homophobia, oppression, and patriarchy are excluded. While bullying may
include abuse of power, the bullying studies typically explore the power
from an individual perspective rather than examining social groups and
their dominance. Examples of bullying include:[20]

- Name calling, for example: "dalmatian," because of a girl's freckles; "fat," "ugly," dirtbag (names Dylan Klebold and Eric Harris, the Columbine student killers, were called by classmates), "Pillsbury," to a boy who was overweight; "stupid," "shorty," "midget," and "smurf"
- Exclusion/ignoring
- Nasty comments: rumors, and mocking one's clothing
- Nasty behavior: graffiti, hate notes, drawing pictures of a girl showing her hair spiked and with fangs and passing it around the room, giggling when a student speaks
- Physical aggression: hitting, pushing, tripping, and stuffing classmates into lockers

Defining bullying is often helped by defining behaviors that are *not* bullying; not all aggression is bullying, for example two kids getting into a fight.[21] Bullying does not include criminal assaults, threats with a weapon, or hate crimes. And bullying is not harassment of a student based on their protected class, such as gender, race, sexual orientation, disability, or religion, which is harassment based on Title IX and other state and federal laws.

There are three types of bullying—relationship, physical, and verbal.[22] Verbal bullying is the most common and both boys and girls verbally bully equally. Boys are more likely to engage in physical bullying, and girls are more likely to use relationship bullying. The differences between boys' and girls' usual styles of bullying are attributed to each gender's socialization process. Boys use competition and hierarchy to determine who is dominant. That's not to say that girls do not use physical bullying, or that boys do not use relationship bullying. Girls are more adept at using social or relationship bullying to harm their classmates, and girls know that the mere exclusion of another girl is harmful. Boys are beginning to engage in relationship aggression almost equally to girls.[23] Most research has been done on physical aggression and less on relationship aggression.

The term "hazing" has also been referred to as bullying, even though it has its own set of laws in forty-four states.[24] Hazing is abusive and humiliating behavior used as a type of ritual to initiate a person into a group such as an athletic team or fraternity. It often incorporates sexual harassment and assault as its more common misconduct (see chapter 10 for more information on hazing).

WHAT THE RESEARCH SAYS

Bullying has most often been researched from a psychological perspective, by identifying the psychology of why the bully perpetrates, how it psychologically impacts the victim, and the role of the bystander.[25] Missing from bullying research and bullying curriculum is discussion into the role of gender, particularly masculinity and heterosexuality. Gender is not included in most of the bullying research, yet bullying is one way boys police each other to conform to stereotypical notions of masculinity.[26]

The first studies on bullying took place in the 1980s with Norwegian and Swedish children between the ages of eight and fifteen after several youth committed suicide.[27] Fifteen percent of these children experienced bullying two to three times a month. The United States began to recognize bullying as a dangerous behavior in 1999, with the tragic Columbine shootings. Following the shootings, it became clear that the rampage by the two student killers was a display of vengeance for having been bullied and harassed by their classmates. As a result of the Columbine tragedy, research began in earnest, and showed that American children have higher rates of bullying than those in Scandinavia.[28] And there seems to be no difference in the amount of bullying based on urban, suburban, town, or rural communities.[29]

One of the first studies in the United States found that 17 percent of children and teens had been bullied "sometimes" or more during the school year, and 19 percent bullied others "sometimes" or more often.[30] The most common types of behaviors students experienced were: (1) belittling comments about their looks or the way they spoke (this was the most common bullying behavior), (2) being hit, slapped, or pushed, (3) being the brunt of rumors, and (4) being taunted with sexual comments and gestures (which is sexual harassment). Another study showed that 22 percent of kids aged two to seventeen had been physically bullied, and 25 percent emotionally, bullied within the year.[31] Many children have said they are afraid that "Columbine" will be a reality in their school because of school bullying and violence.

THE BULLY

When a student bullies those who do not fit into the mainstream, they are carrying out the work of the school and society by enforcing conformity and social norms.[32] In other words, bullying is a way to pressure kids that don't fit in because of their style, dress, or speech, for example. This may be one reason teachers and school officials do not intervene. Lack of intervention helps maintain social homeostasis (the status quo). School conformity is an avenue to safety and security because it is predictable and easier to deal with. Bullying helps to limit student behaviors that are not predictable, are not the norm, and therefore pose a potential safety and security risk. While bullying is about power over classmates, the power is not the consummate goal, but rather the power is used to get students to conform and be predictable.[33]

Some students say they bully because having a sense of power over their classmates makes them feel good, that they are better than others which impresses their friends.[34] These same kids will express some sadness about the victim, but then turn around and blame the victim because they are annoying and therefore bring it on themselves. While some studies show that the bully is deficient in social skills, others link bullying to popularity, attractiveness, school leadership, and social intelligence.[35] For example, sixth grade boys who bully are popular boys.[36]

If a bully is a star student because of athletic prowess, academic elitism, or some other school star ability, he is less likely to be disciplined and criticized because, as mentioned earlier, he is carrying out the work of a school by ensuring students adhere to social norms.[37] The bully evokes fear in her classmates which is one avenue of control.[38]

Elementary school children bully more than middle school children, who bully more than high school teens, according to one study.[39] Yet, other studies showed that bullying peaked in middle school, a vulnerable time of development when children are permitted more independence, puberty is booming, and they experience more freedom in the school environment when changing classes.[40] Bullying in elementary school is starting at earlier ages with more of it seen in kindergarten and first grade.[41] One study found that six- to twelve-year-olds experienced the most physical and emotional bullying. Preschool-aged kids experienced the second highest physical bullying, followed by children aged thirteen to seventeen. Weekly physical bullying tended to decrease, and verbal and emotional bullying increased, from sixth grade to tenth grade.[42] Another study found that, if a child was bullying at the age of eight, it was likely that the bullying would continue throughout school and the student would be taking part in criminal activity as a young adult.[43] If a child bullied through K–12, that child was five times more likely than his or her classmates to be convicted of a crime while a juvenile and, when the bully reached adulthood and fatherhood, to have children with aggression problems.[44]

Boys are the most likely to bully,[45] and the most likely to be bullied.[46] Yet other research shows that whether the bully is a girl or a boy, girls are the most likely victim, whereas boys are most often bullied by other boys. Other studies showed that there isn't any difference in who is the bully's favorite target, boys or girls.[47] Boys are more likely to be physically bullied, and girls are bullied by being excluded from their peer group, or being the target of rumors or gossip, and subjected to sexual comments and gestures, which is sexual harassment.[48] Even though bullies behave as though they are better than their classmates, they are often creating that masquerade to hide their feelings of inadequacy and emotional pain.

Caroline Port's victimization began as a seven-year-old in first grade, and caused the little girl to awaken with night terrors and sleep walking.[49] Her mother met with Caroline's teacher and discovered that Caroline, new to her school, was ostracized by her female classmates. She wasn't invited to birthday parties; her female classmates wouldn't play with her and she ate with the boys. No one from the school had informed Caroline's mother. Caroline was clearly experiencing the most common type of bullying among girls—relationship aggression, which until the mid-1990s was not recognized as enough of a problem to study.

Girl-to-girl bullying, sometimes portrayed as "mean girls," can be motivated by a variety of causes:

- Girls may bully other girls due to jealousy over a boy, or because they see a girl as being very attractive and therefore a threat in the competition for boys' attention.[50]
- The bullying could be misplaced anger about the discrimination, mistreatment, sexual objectification, and sexual harassment they experience in school and in society.[51]
- Girls may bully and harass other girls as a way to gain popularity.

Girls are more likely to feel sorry for their victims, and sad about the outcome of the bullying. They are less likely to bully impulsively and will give their bullying more thought. Girl bullies are often viewed as nice girls and are not necessarily aggressive to adults.[52]

ROLE OF RACE AND ETHNICITY IN BULLYING

Many of America's schools have a rich ethnic diversity of the student population. With the diversity comes communication challenges. Students from other countries often dress differently, speak differently, and use different body language and gestures. Any of these differences may be a trigger to bully these students because a bully doesn't understand the cultural differences and is afraid. The fear of classmates who are different and therefore not predictable can result in the bully feeling less in control of a situation. As a result, the bully may fear that school life might change. Unfortunately, even school employees can be guilty of believing and reinforcing negative or unrealistic stereotypes, and making bullying comments to students from various ethnicities.[53]

Studies show that African American students tend to be more direct, challenging, loud, aggressive, and animated when they argue, whereas Mexican American elementary students and Asian American students are viewed as amenable and tranquil.[54] Black students were less likely to be bullied than their Caucasian or Hispanic classmates,[55] and more likely to be identified as aggressive by their peers.[56] Hispanic students were more likely to bully compared to Caucasian or African American students. Teachers and other school officials may be more likely to be threatened by the African American communication style, and misconstrue the students' messages, resulting in unfair discipline to African American students. If African American students are academically gifted and/or behave like "White" kids, they may be harassed for "acting White."

WHY DO CHILDREN BULLY?

Why do children bully? Why are some kids bullied and not others? What role does the bystander play in the bulling incidents? These questions need to be asked so effective, purposeful, and deliberate prevention and intervention strategies can be designed and implemented within the school environment. With that in mind, it is critical to remember that the behavior patterns of bullies, victims, and bystanders may not fit for every child and teen, but rather are those characteristics identified as the most common.

While there is no bully profile,[57] researchers have found a number of common personality characteristics of those children and youth who bully, including:[58]

- Impulsive
- Dominant
- Aggressive
- Easily make friends (are not loners)
- Popular
- Comfortable with violence
- Socially adept (however, may be cold and subtly manipulative)

In addition, bullies tend to be involved in more defiant, violent, and rebellious behaviors than their peers. Some students refer to the bullies as "Goths," "druggies," and "athletes."[59] They may vandalize, own weapons, engage in fights, smoke and use alcohol and other drugs, and do poorly in or drop out of school.[60] Boys who were identified as bullies in elementary school and the beginning of middle school were more likely to sexually harass classmates by the end of middle school. Researchers have questioned what role, if any, the family plays in promoting a child to bully. Family characteristics, including the following, may increase the risk of a child to bully:[61]

- Lack of warmth and emotional support
- Rigid enforcement of rules
- Use of threats and bribes
- Uninvolved parents
- Lack of supervision
- Inconsistent and corporal punishment
- Poor moods
- Bullying of siblings
- Maltreatment by a parent
- Use of humiliation
- Violence—either exposed to or engaged in; nearly twice as likely to have been exposed to domestic violence

THE VICTIM OF BULLYING

Bullied children tend to fall into one of two categories—"passive victims," who comprise the largest group, or "bully victims."[62] Teachers more often describe passive victims as the unpopular kids who are typically submissive to their classmates and may be described as loners.[63] Understandably, then, they report feeling lonely and anxious. The bully is able to pick up on their vulnerability when looking for an easy target. Victims also experienced the following psychological effects:[64]

- Depression—victims were three times more likely to show signs of depression and four times more likely to say they were unhappy.
- Suicidal thinking—those who were bullied a minimum of once a week were twice as likely to admit to thinking of suicide or wishing they were dead. Depression and suicidal thinking were more common with children who were indirectly bullied (ignored or isolated), than those who were directly bullied (being hit or more aggressive actions).

- Low self-esteem—which may have existed prior to or is the result of their victimization.
- Negative health impact—headaches, bedwetting, insomnia, lethargy, abdominal pain, anorexia.
- Negative school impact—avoid school, dislike school, lowered grades.

If students have friends, lots of friends in particular, and their friends are popular and strong, they are less likely to be bullied.[65] Those children most likely to be targeted are those that are perceived as "different" from their classmates in terms of their appearance—hair, glasses, teeth, fat, skinny, their speech, dress, socioeconomic status, or if they behave in ways that irritate or annoy other children. Some children are at a higher risk of bullying than others, such as those with physical, emotional, or learning disabilities, chronic diseases such as diabetes, medical conditions that are evident in their appearance such as cerebral palsy, or paralysis, and being overweight. Students that are autistic or have other mental or emotional problems tend to be excluded and abused. Children are not very accepting and forgiving of those who walk to a different drummer and who express themselves differently than mainstream kids.

Brain science has demonstrated that children who were persistently verbally bullied show the same brain abnormalities as kids who were physically harmed.[66] Those students who were taunted or belittled tended to be more susceptible to drug abuse. Another study found that memory and other cognitive skills of boys eleven to fourteen were impaired when bullied, potentially minimizing their academic achievement. Bullied teens achieved poorer scores on verbal memory tests than did their non-bullied peers. These are all short-term consequences to victimization. Long-term outcomes may include post-traumatic stress disorder (PTSD) into adulthood, depending on the severity and persistence of the bullying.[67]

Some studies showed a relationship between poor school performance and bullying.[68] There are conflicting research findings as to whether low achievement in school is linked to bullying others, with some research indicating there is a relationship and others showing no relationship. Some studies show bullied kids avoid and/or drop out of schools, while others show there is no link. Common sense would dictate that bullying would have a negative influence on a bullied child's school performance.

THE BULLY-VICTIM

Some children play both roles in the bullying performance—that of the bully and that of the victim.[69] Very often it is with the intent of revenge that the victim decides to become the bully. This is probably especially true when school officials do not intervene and stop the bullying. Verbal bullying, for example, is often not recognized by school officials and not stopped. The bully-victims display their own set of characteristics:[70]

- Hyperactive and restless
- Difficulty concentrating
- Immaturity
- Quick tempered
- Social and emotional problems
- Grades 6 to 10:[71]
  - Poor relationships with classmates
  - Lonely
  - Increased risk of smoking
  - Increased risk of fighting
  - Lower school grades
  - Depression
  - Less self-control
- Black and Latino sixth graders:[72]
  - Psychological distress
  - Most troubled
  - Avoided by their classmates
  - Disengaged from school

Less is known about the family of the bully-victim. The family may include dysfunctional parenting, abuse, inconsistent discipline and neglect, and emotionally cold parents. Sibling bullying was more common for the bully-victim than it was for either the bully or the victim.[73]

Students acknowledged that they started to bully when they had been bullied because they were mad and decided to fight back.[74] Others said that they had been bullied in one school, and then, when they moved to a different school, they started to hang out with bullies and became a bully too. Student comments support what the research has found that bullies hang out with other bullies.[75]

THE BYSTANDER OR WITNESS

Generally speaking, bystanders feel very uncomfortable when witnessing a classmate being bullied and, if they don't intervene to help, often feel ashamed and are afraid to attend school.[76] We tend to think of bullying as one student bullying another, engaged in some kind of power struggle. However, bullying is a group endeavor with children, including the bystander, playing any one of a variety of roles.[77] The bystander is not a passive witness, as most of us believe, and can take on any of the following five roles: (1) follower—who does not initiate the bullying but takes an active role; (2) supporter—who does not take an active role but supports the bully, (3) passive supporter—who likes the bullying but shows no support, (4) disengaged onlooker—who dislikes the bullying but fails to help the victim, (5) defender—who attempts to help the victim.

One study found that 80 percent of middle school students felt sympathy for the victim but did nothing to stop the bullying and/or support the victim.Fifth graders still empathize with the victim, but eighth graders do not, and feel no need to intervene![78] Students hesitated to try to prevent the bullying because they feared they may be the bully's next target, may make the bullying worse, or, finally, they didn't have the skills to intervene and stop the incident. Unfortunately, many bystanders actually support the bully and/or blame the victim. In fact, a British study found that the bystanders of bullying experience more mental stress than either the bully or the victim.[79]

Bystanders respect a code of silence and do not want to be known as someone who rats out their classmates. They recognize that it is difficult, scary, painful, and challenging to speak up. (Look at how few adults do it.) The following thinking also holds bystanders at bay from intervening to help the victim:[80]

- I am a friend of the bully.
- It's not my problem, and it isn't about anything I'm concerned about.
- The victim isn't my friend.
- The victim is a loser.
- The victim asked for it.
- The bully will toughen the victim up so he/she won't be so much of a wimp.
- I want to be included with the popular kids, and not with the weird kids.

Any one of these reasons alone might be enough for a bystander to hesitate to intervene, and, when taken together, it is more difficult for the bystander to help the victim. The success of the bully's tactics gives the bully a sense of privilege, and erodes both the bully's and bystander's empathy and compassion.[81]

CHARACTERISTICS OF SCHOOLS WITH HIGHER RATES OF BULLYING

In addition to characteristics of the child, the family, and the peer group, the school itself plays an influential role in the amount of school bullying that occurs, and across the country a uniform pattern of bullying appears in schools.[82] If children remained together throughout K–12, there was a steady decline of bullying from elementary through high school. Middle school may result in an increase in bullying because it is generally larger and more impersonal, kids have different teachers for each course, there is less supervision by teachers, social competition begins, and there may be a loss of a feeling of "community."

In schools with a high level of both student-student and student-teacher conflict, where teachers were ineffective in managing classroom behavior, and students defied teachers, bullying was more prevalent.[83] Students tend to hang out with classmates who shared similar behaviors in aggression. As long as these behaviors are considered normal, as they are in many schools, they will likely continue.[84]

Teachers' perceptions of the amount of bullying that occurs differ from that of their students. Teachers see less bullying than their students experience and witness.[85] Teachers identify several reasons why they are not aware of the same degree of bullying as are their students. Some view bullying as a rite of passage, and discount the seriousness of the behavior and the impact on the victim. Others don't recognize some misconduct as bullying. For example, many do not identify name calling, spreading rumors, or non-verbal intimidation as bullying. They also are less likely to view or consider relationship bullying, such as exclusion, as bullying. Another influence may be their tenure; the longer a teacher's tenure, the less sympathetic they are towards victims.[86]

Students are not likely to report a bully when some teachers are bullies and face no consequences.[87] Students indicate they won't report their victimization because they fear retaliation, that they won't be believed, and that school officials will fail to stop the behavior.

Students identify hallways, locker rooms, bathrooms, and school buses as the most insecure locations because of lack of adult supervision.[88] Many students avoid the bathroom all day if possible.[89] The school bus is a popular location for bullying and sexual harassment because the bus driver is sitting in the front of the bus focused on driving. The bus rides to and from school may be the worse times of the school day for students.[90] Elementary students tend to be bullied on the playground and in their classroom.[91] Some middle school children are bullied in hallways, cafeterias, bathrooms, and at recess; others indicated the bullying took place outside of the teacher's ability to see or hear.[92] School officials may inadvertently establish bullying when they fail to supervise locations where bullying is likely to occur.

It is fairly obvious what is meant by physical bullying—poking, punching, shoving, hitting, kicking, spitting, and damaging clothing or other property, to name a few. Verbal bullying includes name calling, abusive phone calls, texts, e-mails, rumors, taunts, and threats. It is a little more challenging to give examples of relationship bullying because it is sometimes subtle and, therefore, more difficult to hear or detect.

Behaviors associated with relationship bullying are those that ignore, exclude, or isolate a student, often a girl by other girls.[93] Sometimes the victim of relationship bullying may not be aware of what she has done that causes others to exclude her. For example, "don't hang out with her, she lives on the north side of town," or "his mother is an alcoholic so he will be too." Relationship bullying often includes non-verbal behavior such as eye rolling, crossing one's arms across the chest, turning away from the victim, or a sneer or a loud sigh. During the middle school years, when having strong peer friendships take on more importance, relationship bullying becomes more potent. Unfortunately, adults tend to dismiss this form of bullying. Exclusion from birthday parties and sleepovers and playground group giggling is not as obvious as hearing an obnoxious name, torn clothing, or a bruised cheek, and the psychic pain may not be obvious to an observer.

DISABLED STUDENTS AND BULLYING

Most studies on bullying of students with disabilities show that those children experience more physical abuse, name calling, verbal abuse, exclusion and mockery because of their disability.[94] However, other studies show that students with disabilities don't experience any more victimization than non-disabled students experience. Some research suggests that students with disabilities are more likely to bully than those without disabilities, which could also be a defense against their victimization. Students with attention deficit hyperactivity disorder (ADHD) are almost four times more likely than their classmates to be bullies, and ten times more likely to be the victims of bullies before the onset of ADHD symptoms.[95]

SCHOOL BASED ANTI-BULLYING PROGRAMS

Students have thought of several creative ways for schools to decrease bullying: Get students involved in extra-curricular activities; provide students, especially bullies, with positive attention; send them away; reward them; and provide consequences for their misconduct.[96] Few of these students' suggestions were evident in anti-bullying school programs. Perhaps that is why the current programs have shown mixed outcomes in decreasing bullying, and, in some cases, the programs actually increased bullying.[97]

The best results occurred when the anti-bullying initiatives were school-wide and included consequences for bullying behavior, training of all students and teachers, and conflict resolution strategies.[98] Some programs showed an increase in student knowledge, attitudes, and perceptions of bullying, yet student bullying behaviors did not change.[99] Other anti-bullying programs that tended to be more effective went beyond student and faculty curriculum and included parent education, playground supervision, discipline, school-parent communication, improved classroom management and classroom rules, and the use of training videos. Studies also found that the more aspects included in an anti-bullying program/strategy, the more successful the outcome.[100] Anti-bullying programs were often lax in teaching how to intervene with bullying.

Programs were also more effective in Europe than in the United States.[101] The Scandinavian countries, particularly Finland and Norway, have shown improved results when students take anti-bullying pledges three times a week, and when school officials annually review and revise their programs. Because Scandinavian countries are more homogenous than the United States, what is effective there may not necessarily be as effective here.[102]

Some anti-bullying student programs have successfully decreased the amount of bullying and increased the number of bystander students who would help the victim. A study that analyzed sixteen different anti-bullying programs found that, while some of the programs positively impacted students' and teachers' perceptions, attitude, and understanding of bullying behaviors, they had very little effect in reducing bullying.[103]

Programs that have been studied to determine their effectiveness in decreasing bullying (evidence-based programs) are essential in dealing with the misconduct.[104] Anti-bullying programs and policies tend to ignore the cultural and societal elements. Most states do not require evidence-based curriculum in teaching their students. For example, William Woodward, director of training and technical assistance at the Center for the Study and Prevention of Violence based at the University of Colorado, examined 178 Colorado school districts and found that only twenty-eight of them were using evidence-based curriculum.

Parents think a law exists against bullying, but the district doesn't have to take it seriously. Most bullying prevention laws do not come from a public health perspective, but rather are politically oriented.[104]

Using a public health perspective, two evidence-based programs showed promising results—HALT! and a Pennsylvania program called PA CARES. Research on the two programs found that students were less likely to bully and to be bullied and they were more likely to help a victim of bullying.[105] Students also saw that adults were more responsible in responding to bullying. These two programs were inclusive of not only students but teachers, parents, and lunchroom monitors, the entire school population.

STATE ANTI-BULLYING LAWS

Though forty-five states have various types of anti-bullying laws, as of January 2011, none of these laws has served as an impediment to bullying or cyberbullying.[106] Several courts, for example in Connecticut and Georgia, have found that their states' anti-bullying laws failed to provide the right to sue the district because the schools are protected by sovereign immunity (meaning the government/school cannot be sued).[107] The state laws vary greatly, with some using the words "hate crime," others requiring faculty training and counseling services for students, and others only requiring a policy. Other states list all of the "groups" the law covers; for example, Iowa identifies seventeen groups. Some states only require that districts have policies, with no guidelines that detail the elements of an effective policy. Additional states provide financial funding for anti-bullying efforts, while other states require tracking incidents and giving consequences to districts.[108] Unfortunately, the states' statutes have been largely ineffective. Woodward critiqued the laws as being too vague and that schools don't take them seriously but rather view them as just another requirement. For the most part, the state laws don't mandate any tracking of bullying incidents, and therefore no monitoring will occur.[109] In Massachusetts, attorney Abigail Williams said that the new Massachusetts anti-bullying law "has no teeth to it."

Bullying is starting at younger ages, even preschool, when it is often physical. Why do children feel they have the right to disrespect another child merely because the other child is different? In a year's time, almost one out of every four children between the ages of two and seventeen has been physically or emotionally abused. If a child was bullied when younger, he or she may be a victim all through school. The statistics in this chapter are alarming to say the least, and constitute a huge problem for children, teens, parents, and school districts. Although forty-five states have laws against bullying, how the laws are understood and enforced varies across state lines. Schools must train all staff and students on what constitutes bullying, and how teachers should intervene to stop it. Without the school's support, children are at risk.

5

THE DIFFERENCE BETWEEN SEXUAL HARASSMENT AND BULLYING AND WHY IT MATTERS

Too many administrators embrace and promote the bullying frame-
work and discourse because they believe they will not end up in fed-
eral court if they label behaviors "bullying." By doing this, they are
conflating harassment behaviors and definitions with "bullying," the
tsunami of bullying is winning out—disregarding and displacing the
legal rights of students under federal civil rights in education laws.

—Dr. Nan Stein[1]

Often missing from discussions on school shootings is the gendered aspect of the tragedies.[2] Girls were the intended targets in eleven of thirteen highly publicized shootings in the United States over a period of six years, including the incident of a six-year-old boy killing his six-year-old female classmate. Sexual harassment played a role in instigating the shootings; yet absent from the media coverage was any analysis of sexual aspects, including traditional masculinity and patriarchy, as factors in the shootings. Writer Jesse Klein stated:

> Violence against girls is easy to render invisible because the behavior that precedes actual incidents is often perceived as normal; even after fatalities have occurred, the gendered components of crimes do not seem to register. . . . "Normal" violence against girls—indeed, social acceptance

of male hostility towards girls—tends to aid in concealing even the most dramatic incidents.[3]

Violence towards girls in school, because it is normalized, is almost invisible. This played itself out when the perpetrators of the school shootings discussed their homicides, and commented on their violence towards girls as sexual harassment or jealousy or dating violence.[4] Psychologists point out that masculinity as a norm masks violence and violence towards females. Researchers and psychologists commented that Harris and Klebold, ridiculed and demeaned for not fitting the masculine stereotype, were only behaving in ways they were taught— to be violent. Many of the school shooters since Columbine mirrored the same features as Eric Harris and Dylan Klebold, the Columbine perpetrators.

People magazine published an article about Tyler Clementi, the Rutgers University freshman who committed suicide by jumping off the George Washington Bridge into the Hudson River. Tyler committed suicide after his roommate streamed a live sexual encounter between Tyler and a man in his dorm room.[5] *People* referred to the incident as cyberbullying, yet later in the same article referred to it as harassment, demonstrating the publication's confusion as to which word to use.

Another issue of *People* featured several students' stories under the label of bullying. These young people were harassed, not bullied:[6]

- Thirteen-year-old Seth Walsh was harassed for being gay.
- Thirteen-year-old Asher Brown was harassed for being gay and a Buddhist.
- Billy Lucas, age fifteen, was harassed for being gay.
- Seventeen-year-old Khoshnoor Paracha was harassed because she is Muslim and from Pakistan.
- Being biracial was the motivation for fifteen-year-old Moriah Kilgore's harassment.
- Fifteen-year-old twins, Alex and Philippe Haussman, were identified as overweight, and were bullied and harassed since kindergarten. They may have been bullied for their weight (which is not a federally protected class), but, in reading about their torment, they were accused of having sex with each other and the word "twincest"

was yelled at them, making their "bullying" not bullying at all, but sexual harassment.

- Sixteen-year-old Joey Kemmerling was harassed because of his sexual orientation.
- It appeared that MacKenzie Spanier, seventeen, was sexually harassed but more information would be needed than what was discussed in the article.
- Jamie Isaacs, age fourteen, was the only teen who appeared to have been bullied.

So, out of the seven young people featured in an article on bullying, only one seemed to have experienced bullying.

People, along with most media, incorrectly labeled the abuse these teens experienced as bullying rather than harassment based on the teens' protected class. Mislabeling the behavior as bullying rather than calling it harassment negates the role that sex and gender (and religion, race, sexual orientation, and national origin) play in the abusive behavior. Bullying is "status blind," harassment is not. In other words, students are bullied because they may be annoying to a classmate, wear their hair "wrong," not wear the "right" brand of shoes, or come from the wrong side of town. Their victimization is not based on their protected class (that is, characteristics of a group such as race, religion, or disability that are legally protected from discrimination and harassment). Harassment of someone because of their protected class is a violation of federal and state civil laws. There is no federal law against bullying, and, while many states have anti-bullying laws, currently none are actionable, meaning there is no opportunity to hold a school legally responsible for the behavior and sue under any anti-bullying law. Some states, anti-bullying laws specifically state that the schools are protected from liability for bullying in their states' schools.

When researching bullying, researchers very often include behaviors that constitute sexual harassment, particularly sexual harassment of GLBT students, in their examples of bullying behavior.[7] As discussed in chapter 4, when research includes *bullying* of GLBT students because of their real or perceived gender identity or sexual orientation, it skews the statistics regarding the frequency of bullying because GLBT *harassment* is included in the research findings. School officials are also more likely to label behaviors as bullying even though many of them fall under the umbrella of sexual harassment, including GLBT harassment. Why is that? Researchers are often psychologists whose research is approached from a psychological perspective. Some may be unaware of the distinction between bullying and illegal harassment. Or perhaps they may not be familiar with other perspectives of studying the behavior such as sociology, law, and anthropology. The same may be said of school officials; or perhaps school officials would prefer the use of the word *bullying* because it carries no legal ramifications, sounds less egregious, and provides a false sense of security that they are not liable for stopping the behavior.

Use of the word *bullying* as an overall term to encompass both sexual harassment and bullying creates confusion over the term, the behavior, the potential consequences, and which policy schools should use when responding to complaints. OCR has been very clear that, despite the label a school uses, they must conduct an investigation to determine whether the behavior is bullying or harassment.[8] Failure to investigate is at the district's own peril.

The misconduct must be investigated to determine if it is a civil rights violation for gender or sexual harassment (or race, color, national origin, or disability harassment) and if it created a hostile academic environment. If it is concluded that the misconduct is based on sex or gender, it must be treated as a civil rights violation, and the school must respond based on civil rights statutes set forth by OCR and Title IX. This requires that discipline, a probable first step, is often not adequate.[9] It requires schools to eliminate or minimize any hostile environment created by sexual and gender harassment, as well as to address the impact on students and the school culture. Additionally, school officials must ensure there is no retaliation and establish a process to make sure the harassment is not ongoing. Sexual harassment often requires a different response than bullying.[10]

In the fall of 2010, OCR sent a letter to all U.S. schools, praising them for their efforts to curtail bullying but reminding schools that not all student misconduct falls under their anti-bullying policy. When schools fail to assess the misbehavior and automatically label it bullying, they fail to consider whether harassment has occurred. When school employees tolerate, ignore, inadequately respond to, and even encourage harassment, sometimes by mislabeling it as bullying, they are violating civil rights statutes and OCR's regulations. However, even if the misconduct does not fall under a violation of civil rights law, school officials should still implement strong sanctions and training to prevent and protect students from the abuse.

Both print and television media proclaim the recent suicides of GLBT youth are a result of bullying. Schools conduct anti-bullying programs and use the bullying framework in which to label student misconduct. The term *bullying* is the default label for student misconduct whether it is sexual harassment, racial harassment, religious harassment, gender harassment, or sexual orientation harassment. What's the big deal, you may say—it is only a word. But is it? Bullying is not illegal—harassment is illegal. When school districts mislabel illegal harassment as bullying they are negating the civil rights violations of students. It appears as though school officials espouse the bullying terminology in their curriculum, discussions, and teacher training as a means of camouflaging student civil rights violations and therefore diminishing their likelihood of liability.[11] As harassment and bullying expert Dr. Nan Stein stated, "I consider it a placeholder word for what we should call 'racism,' 'sexism,' or 'homophobia.' Why do we use a word that minimizes criminal actions of an individual or the requirement of a school district under civil rights laws?"[12]

When consulting with a school official about the requirements of Title IX, I was shocked to discover that she didn't know what Title IX was. The school district did not have a Title IX coordinator identified in its policies, and they had done no sexual harassment training with students, faculty, staff, or administrators. While they did have a sexual harassment policy, numerous errors were noted when addressing civil rights law. Another of their policies merged bullying and sexual harassment into one policy that watered down the seriousness of harassment, and applied civil rights law to bullying which is incorrect. Additionally, all of the training to students and staff was on bullying. Because there was no sexual harassment (or harassment of other protected classes) training, the faculty, staff, and school administrators were not knowledgeable about Title IX or their state's civil rights laws. Consequently, they were unaware of what behaviors constituted sexual harassment, and faculty, staff, and school officials' legal and ethical requirements.

PHOEBE PRINCE

Perhaps one of the most famous bullying stories to gain notoriety around the world was about fifteen-year-old Phoebe Prince at South Hadley Middle School in Massachusetts, who had recently moved from Ireland. After experiencing months of harassment, coined bullying by the media, by numerous male and female classmates, she committed suicide.[13] There was no discussion of her victimization as sexual harassment or national origin harassment, which it clearly was.

Phoebe was repeatedly called a "ho," bitch," "slut," "Irish slut," "Irish whore," and other obscene names. She was told she "should get her ass kicked for trying to get with" another student's boyfriend. Because she had a relationship with a popular senior boy, she was raped, sent threatening text messages, and her books were knocked from her hands. She was harassed throughout the school hallways, library, and lunchroom and on social networking sites continuously throughout the day. Most South Hadley students were aware of her victimization as were some faculty and administrators, yet they failed to protect Phoebe from the onslaught of abuse. On the day of her suicide, she was harassed on her way home from school and had a soda can thrown at her as classmates yelled "You Irish slut, you Irish whore."

As a result of Phoebe's abuse, six South Hadley high school students, three of them juveniles, were charged with violating a range of laws from statutory rape, criminal harassment, civil rights violations resulting in bodily injury, and stalking. Her victimization appeared to be the result of a relationship with a popular football player that had ended weeks prior to her suicide. Three of the students, a male and two females, were charged with assault. The district attorney specifically said that school administrators' lack of understanding about harassment, and their failure to enforce appropriate policies, played a role in Phoebe's victimization.[14] South Hadley school officials urged Phoebe's mother, Anne O'Brien, to press charges against the students rather than against the district. However, her parents successfully filed a sexual harassment claim with the Massachusetts Commission Against Discrimination resulting in an out-of-court settlement with the school district.[15]

Following Phoebe's sexual harassment, rape, and tragic suicide, the Massachusetts *anti-bullying* law was passed but fails to hold school officials accountable for their [in]actions.[16] Massachusetts is missing a major point in their lawmaking if it is based on Phoebe's victimization and suicide. Phoebe was not bullied. She was sexually harassed, which means that school district officials were accountable for their actions under federal anti-discrimination laws, not an anti-bullying law.

Use of the term *bullying*, when labeling behaviors that may be sexual harassment, as in Phoebe's case, degenders the misconduct and diminishes the likelihood that students' civil rights are protected.[17] As a result, school officials are not held legally accountable for their responsibility in creating a safe and equitable school environment based on Title IX requirements. This labeling continues to decrease safety for students and thwarts the legal rights of students based on federal and state laws.[17]

MISLABELING THE MISCONDUCT

One study found that GLB students and students who were questioning (Q) their sexual orientation and gender identity experienced more sexual harassment and bullying than did straight students.[18] All students experienced a more negative effect on their health from sexual harassment than from bullying, with girls and GLBQ students experiencing poorer health (mental, physical, self-esteem, and trauma symptoms). This is of concern since the current educational focus is labeling both bullying and sexual harassment as bullying, which shifts attention away from the more negative health impact from harassment.

Use of the word *bullying* by schools and the media when describing behaviors that are sexual harassment (including harassment based on gender expression and sexual orientation) supports the status quo. The mislabeling avoids delving into the root cause of the misconduct— patriarchy (see chapter 9), which includes oppression, sexism, and homophobia. When harassing behaviors "are used to marginalize groups who have experienced systemic discrimination," it normalizes and "gives authority to the invisible structures of social power and leaves many students feeling hurt, excluded, and limited in their chances for educational success," reports researcher Elizabeth Meyer.[19]

Both the U.S. Department of Education and the U.S. Department of Justice have decided to work with state and local governments as well as non-profit organizations to tackle the problem of bullying and harassment. The Department of Justice intends to increase its research initiatives, including evaluating existing anti-bullying programs for their effectiveness. Russlyn Ali, the Department of Education's civil rights head, stated that, "To fix this problem, requires all hands on deck."[20]

Mislabeling sexual harassment as bullying negates the role that gender plays in the abusive behavior and fails to recognize students' civil rights. No federal law exists against bullying. Bullying carries no federal legal ramifications, sounds less egregious, and provides a false sense of security to school officials. Many educators and school officials are unaware of the behaviors that constitute sexual harassment, and how to differentiate between sexual harassment and bullying. As a result, they are remiss in meeting their legal and ethical requirements. An investigation must be conducted for all misconduct to determine if it is bullying or sexual harassment. If, after the investigation, it is concluded that the misconduct is sexual harassment, it must be responded to as a civil rights violation, as required by Title IX.

Table 5.1. **Comparison of Sexual Harassment and Bullying**

Sexual Harassment	Bullying
• Occurs because of sex or gender—females and non-conforming males are primary target	• "Status blind" —is not based on gender or GLBT identification
• Against federal Civil Rights Act Title IX—there is a right to sue	• No federal legislation—no right to sue
• Against states' civil rights laws—there is a right to sue	• Anti-bullying laws in some states—no right to sue
• 81 percent of students (AAUW)	• 30 percent of students (U.S. Department of Education)
• Federal agency oversight: U.S. Department of Education, Office for Civil Rights (OCR), Title IX	• No federal agency oversight
• Researched from various perspectives: civil rights, education, anthropology, sociology, legal, and feminist scholarship	• Researched from psychology perspective
• Consistent definition based on law, case law, and research	• Ambiguous, inconsistent definition based on researcher, school district, and state

6

CYBERHARASSMENT AND CYBERBULLYING

It's a new kind of crime.

—Minnesota Hennepin County Sheriff Rich Stanek[1]

Cyberspace is alive and kicking, and offers a myriad of avenues for youth to contact their friends, classmates, and family. Texting, e-mails, Facebook, chat rooms, blogs, and mobile phones provide exciting technological options for our youth to bully and harass their classmates. Even school officials are sometimes the brunt of cyberharassment and cyberbullying. The inequality of power is present in electronic communication, and the same types of inequalities that poison the off-line world are also present in the online world. When online bullying and harassment are present during school, it disrupts student learning.[2]

Cyberharassment looks very much like face-to-face harassment, for example: disrespectful and offensive comments made about another student's body and sex life; sexist, misogynist, and vulgar messages; risqué photos and pornography (sexting); and disparaging comments about GLBT youth, all of which may be sent to groups and individuals via texting, websites, blogs, and chat rooms. The drastic difference between cyberharassment and face-to-face harassment, however, is the anonymity, and therefore the willingness for the offender to take risks and act with abandon and viciousness. The target of cyberharassment is afraid about who is going to read and/or see the nasty sexual comments or pictures. Once the comments are released to a world-wide audience at the click of "send," it is next to impossible to delete them, and therefore there is no escape for the victim. Youth are not likely to complain to their parents because they don't want to lose their cell phones and access to social media.

Minnesota Senator Amy Klobuchar convened a panel to discuss adolescent cyberbullying and cyberharassment.[3] One of the panel members, Shayla Thiel Stern, an assistant professor at the University of Minnesota who researches youth communication, said that, just as in the school environment, students are upset that they are being ignored, isolated, and "defriended" by friends and classmates on Facebook and other social networking sites. Brian Hill, a computer forensic investigator, found that some teens are first physically assaulted, then cyberbullied. Then, after filing assault charges with police, the victim is retaliated against in the form of further online bullying. Nicole Jackson Colaco, a Facebook public policy manager and another panel member, said Facebook actively investigates complaints about cyberharassment and cyberbullying, and monitors the site for content that violates its policies, warning the violators and/or removing them from the website.

WHAT THE RESEARCH SAYS

A June 2008 report by the Pew Internet and American Life Project indicated that out of 94 percent of teens who go online, 63 percent do so every day.[4] Unlike most of us reading this book, the Internet has been part of a teen's everyday life since they became aware of technology. A more recent report by Pew found that, from February of 2008 to September of 2009, the percentage of teens texting daily has risen from 38 percent to 54 percent.[5] Boys average thirty texts a day and girls average eighty. Girls ages fourteen to seventeen text an average of one hundred messages a day, and young teen boys text only about twenty messages per day. The frequency of texting is coupled with the quantity of texting. For example, fifteen hundred texts a month (equal to a minimum of fifty texts a day) are sent by about half of all teens. Three thousand texts a month are sent by one in three teens. Fifteen percent of teens who text send more than two hundred a day or six thousand a month. Texting is *the* mode of communication, exceeding instant messaging, e-mail, or face-to-face communication. The exception is when attempting to reach parents—the good old telephone is favored, perhaps because it is the parent's preferred mode. About 22 percent of teens send one to ten texts a day.

SEXTING

Teenagers are sending nude or partially nude pictures of themselves via cyberspace called sexting. The Houston school district defines sexting as "using a cell phone or other personal communication device to send text or e-mail messages or possessing text or e-mail messages containing images reasonably interpreted as indecent or sexually suggestive while at school or at a school related function."[6] This new fad includes a broad spectrum of teens who don't necessarily understand that the pictures sent out into cyberspace can be found by anyone at any time—even years later when they are adults beginning their careers.

The increase in sexting has become a major issue challenging schools, and both schools and students are finding themselves in legal problems when it occurs. This is challenging schools, law enforcement, and the courts to establish effective policies and laws to reduce the possible destructive impact, including legal, emotional, and relational conse-quences, on those who engage in the behavior. Schools and teenagers are beginning to come face to face with the ugliness this behavior casts over teens.

According to a Pew Internet and American Life Project study, 4 per-cent of twelve- to seventeen-year-old teenagers admit to *sending* sexu-ally suggestive nude or almost nude pictures or videos of themselves via text messaging (sexting), while 15 percent of teens have *received* sexts from a person they know.[7] Older teens are more likely to *receive* sexts; and 17 percent of teens who pay all of their cell phone costs are more likely to *send* sexts compared to 3 percent of teens who pay for some or all of their cell phone costs. Those teens that spend an inordinate amount of time on their cell phone are more likely to receive sexts.

Another study found 9 percent of thirteen- to eighteen-year-olds sent sexts, 3 percent had forwarded sexts, and 17 percent received a sext. Yet another survey discovered roughly 20 percent of teens sent naked or scantily clad pictures or videos of themselves or others, and 48 percent received the same messages.

Pew's research found the sexts are most likely to be shared between (1) two romantic partners, (2) between partners but then sent to others as well, or (3) between teens that are not in a romantic relationship but one of them hopes to be.[9] The sexts are a type of "relationship currency" used as part of teens' sexual relationships and part of sexual activity. However, teens said the sexts are used as a joke or for fun as well. Some girls felt pressured to send sexual images because boys ask them to. One girl was afraid her boyfriend would ignore her if he didn't receive sexual pictures of her. In retrospect, she wished she wouldn't have sent the pictures, but at the time it didn't seem to be that big a deal.

The Minnesota Internet Crimes Against Children Task Force, Minnesota School Safety Center, and Cyberbullying Research Center found the following rate of sexting:[10]

- 10 percent—rate of teens that parents believe have sexted
- 20 percent—actual rate of teens who sexted
- 69 percent—teens who sexted to someone they dated or wanted to date
- 11 percent—teens who sexted to strangers
- 40 percent—girls who sexted as a joke
- 34 percent—girls who sexted to "feel sexy"
- 12 percent—girls who felt pressured to sext

CYBER LAWS

New and emerging technology, such as sexting, require a new look at current law, or perhaps new laws. Sexting is creating challenges for law enforcement and the courts, and it is compounded by different practices in different jurisdictions. Child pornography laws are used by some states; yet other states are contemplating reducing the charges of possessing and sending sexual pictures of minors to a misdemeanor instead of a felony.[11] Should minors who sext receive a lesser charge as some believe, or should the child pornography laws be strictly enforced? This question requires consideration from a number of perspectives—parental, legal, and social—and the answer will likely be affected by the particular perspective taken.

Seventeen Pennsylvania students were found with, or posed for, provocative images on their cell phones.[12] The district attorney told the students and their parents that, if the students agreed to attend a five-week sexual harassment, sexual violence, and gender roles program, and agreed to probation, they wouldn't be charged for child pornography. All but two girls agreed; the parents of these two girls, along with the American Civil Liberties Union, sued, contesting that the girls could not be forced to attend the school's program. The court agreed.

A fourteen-year-old girl posted nearly thirty sexually explicit pictures of herself on MySpace for her boyfriend to see.[13] She was charged with child pornography and distribution of child pornography. It is possible, though unlikely, if convicted she could spend seventeen years in jail and would need to register as a sex offender. Six Massachusetts teenagers between the ages of twelve and fourteen were accused of sexting pictures of a thirteen-year-old girl.[14] Their charge included both possessing and distributing images of a child in a sex act. Many other states including Connecticut, North Dakota, Ohio, Utah, Vermont, Virginia, and Wisconsin (as of this writing) are grappling with similar occurrences.

When eighteen-year-old Floridian Phillip Alpert became angry at his sixteen-year-old girlfriend of two and one-half years, he forwarded a naked picture of her to her family and friends.[15] While he agreed it was a stupid thing to do, law enforcement didn't see it as merely stupid. They arrested him and charged him with sending child pornography, and he is now a registered sex offender. His attorney is trying to get him removed from the sex offender registry, indicating that the law has not kept up with the technology and that sexting should not be treated as child pornography.

Around the country, teens have been charged with a myriad of violations including disorderly conduct, child pornography, distribution of pornography, illegal use of a minor in nudity-oriented materials, sexual abuse of children, and more. Jessica Logan was an eighteen-year-old senior in Sycamore High School in Cincinnati who sent nude photos of herself to her boyfriend. Once he received the photos, he sent them to hundreds of students at numerous schools, which served as a springboard for months of intense sexual harassment by other students at her home, at school, and when she went out in public.[16] Her mother, Cynthia, said her daughter was called "filthy" names, had things thrown at her, and everywhere she went people knew about the picture. Cynthia labels the treatment her daughter experienced as torture. Her grades plunged, she skipped school, and if she did attend school she would hide in the bathroom—using it as a refuge from the harassment. One awful day, Cynthia went home and found her daughter hanging in her closet in her bedroom.

When a student's in-school conduct leads to cyberspeech outside of school, there is additional confusion. Gregory Requa sued Kent School District, the district's superintendent, and the principal for violating his freedom of speech, his right to due process, and his liberty and property rights after he was suspended for forty days for posting an offensive video about one of his teachers on YouTube.[17] In addition, he was denied participation in a state-wide leadership competition, thereby losing an opportunity to compete for scholarship money. The school said the suspension was for the disruption generated in the classroom when students danced behind the teacher's back and disrespectfully mocked her while he secretly videotaped the incident. The school denied that the discipline tied into his YouTube posting. The court's ruling supported the school—while his YouTube video was protected speech, the punishment for his conduct in class was not protected, so his punishment stood.[18]

Little research about the impact of cyberbullying on children has been conducted. One recent study found cyberbullying victims experience higher levels of depression than other bullying victims.[19]

Few cyberbullying or cyberharassment lawsuits exist as of this writing; however, we'll be seeing more of them. One example of a litigated case involves honor student Justin Layshock, who created a sexually seedy imposter MySpace in his principal's name (fake site which appears to be created by, in this case, this principal).[20] His Pennsylvania school district disciplined him with a ten-day suspension, transferred him to an alternative education program, and rescinded his privilege to attend his graduation ceremony. His parents sued the school district for violation of Justin's First Amendment rights, using the *Tinker* standard, which protects student speech unless it substantially invades the rights of others (see chapter 10 for more information on the *Tinker* standard).[21] The U.S. District Court for Western Pennsylvania found in favor of Justin stating that "the mere fact that the Internet may be accessed at school does not authorize school officials to become censors of the world-wide web." The court specifically remarked that families, the church, community organizations, and even the court system must work in tandem with schools to share in the supervision of children. The court's remarks typify the thinking of "it takes a village." Other courts have found in favor of students' First Amendment rights as well, using the *Tinker* standard.[22] However, the *Tinker* standard does not address disruption of school activities, but rather applies a lewd or profane standard. When districts discipline students for speech that is generated from outside the school, they should assess the discipline based on the *Tinker* standard.[23]

To demonstrate the confusion and unfamiliarity with the law, two different panels of judges from the U.S. Court of Appeals for the Third Circuit gave conflicting views on two similar student speech cases involving cybermisconduct at home by students.[24] One panel of three judges ruled that a Pennsylvania school district violated a student's First Amendment rights when it punished him for creating an online mockery of his principal. The second panel of three judges found that a different school district did not violate a student's freedom of speech rights when it punished her for virtually the same infraction because her misconduct created a threat of "substantial disruption" to the school atmosphere. Both panels used the *Tinker* standard in their ruling, however, with opposite findings.

Some school districts are creating and implementing new electronic communication policies or expanding upon their earlier renditions by including cyberharassment and cyberbullying in their codes of conduct. New policies can be problematic because students' free speech must be protected as well as their off-campus electronic communication, including sexting.[25] One example of what can be implemented is found in the Houston School District's policy that warns that cell phones will be impounded, and law enforcement will be notified of any photos that may potentially violate criminal law.

Girls are the more likely to cyberbully and more likely to use indirect forms of cyberbullying, just as they do in face-to-face bullying.[26] Female students are increasingly likely to cyberbully and cyberharass using "prurient, lewd, and sexually explicit" messages.[27] Other cyberbullying and cyberharassment tactics include the following:[28]

- Flaming—sending angry and/or rude messages to a victim or group, often in chat rooms or other public arenas
- Harassment—sending offensive messages using e-mails, texts, or instant messaging
- Cyberstalking—sending threats of possible harm to a victim, usually when a sexual relationship has ended
- Denigration—sending brutal or hurtful comments about someone to a broad audience
- Masquerading—sending or posting nasty comments about a victim by a perpetrator who pretends to be someone else
- Outing and trickery—sending, posting, or forwarding private, delicate, or embarrassing information
- Exclusion—rejecting or banning someone from an online group

THE MINNESOTA INTERNET CRIMES AGAINST CHILDREN TASK FORCE, MINNESOTA SCHOOL

Law enforcement and lawyers indicate that cybercrime is complex and difficult.[29] With new technology comes new laws, and we are just beginning to see the very small tip of the iceberg. Impersonating someone else on Facebook is now a crime in California. Missouri and Massachusetts have made it a crime to engage in cyberbullying. Stalking and orders of protection statutes in Minnesota now include electronic media.

Most adults cannot fathom feeling devastated if we have been "unfriended" on Facebook, but just ask a teenager how that feels. The Internet—and the good and bad that goes along with immediate access to people—has always been part of young people's lives. Technology allows them to do texting, e-mails, instant messaging, Facebook, chat rooms, and blogs, all from their mobile phones. It offers great fun until it becomes cyberbullying and cyberharassing, and sexting. A cyberbully or cyberharasser needs to be disciplined, but what laws create obstacles in understanding a school's role and responsibility, and what are reasonable consequences? States and school districts are facing that big challenge now.

7

THE IMPACT OF
SEXUAL HARASSMENT

I will not be going to yet another high school reunion—my 50th—because the pain of being subjected to verbal taunts and written comments about my large breasts still haunt me.

—A retired sixty-seven-year-old woman, in a letter to Deena

In a nutshell, sexual harassment interferes with a student's right to an education. The ramifications may be severe and long lasting, sometimes resulting in suicide and school shootings. Sexual harassment negatively impacts a victim's health and takes a heavy behavioral and emotional toll as well. The AAUW 2001 research found 66 percent of girls and 28 percent of boys reported being upset as a result of being sexually harassed. Girls were far more likely to report being "very upset" (33 percent) than were the boys (11 percent). However, 23 percent of boys and 7 percent of girls said they weren't upset at all. Girls were significantly more likely to be targeted by sexual harassment, and to experience more frequent consequences.[1]

The AAUW's study found victims of harassment experienced the following effects:

- Loss of appetite
- Feeling sad, nervous, or angry

- Loss of interest in their usual activities
- Feeling isolated from friends and family
- Nightmares or disturbed sleep
- Feeling afraid, upset, or threatened
- Lowered self-esteem
- Poorer mental health
- Poorer physical health
- Tardiness

Sexual harassment negatively affected students' health and attitudes about school. Middle school students were affected more than high school students.[2] Middle school and high school girls were more severely affected than boys.[3] Sexual harassment lowered middle school girls' self-esteem more so than their male classmates, but by high school this gender difference, as well as the overall effect of harassment, was reduced. Both mental and physical health are affected less by harassment in high school than in middle school. Boys were less likely to be tardy in middle school or high school. Tardiness was a mechanism used by girls in middle school but not high school.

The 2001 AAUW study examined sexual harassment from the perspective of African American, Hispanic, and Caucasian students.[4] Physical harassment caused less behavior change in African American boys compared to their Caucasian and Hispanic male classmates. All three races were most likely to avoid the harasser. Hispanic boys tended to be more negatively affected than Caucasian or Black boys. Like the boys, Hispanic, African American, and Caucasian girls avoided the harasser. African American girls were significantly more likely to change their group of friends compared to their Hispanic and Caucasian female classmates. Caucasian and Hispanic girls found studying to be more difficult than did African American girls.

African American and Hispanic boys were less likely than Caucasian boys to experience self-consciousness, fear, and embarrassment.[5] African American boys didn't change their behavior in response to the harassment as much as their Caucasian and Hispanic male classmates. Additionally, Caucasian boys were more likely to question whether they would be able to have a happy boy-girl relationship. Both Caucasian and Hispanic boys were more emotionally impacted by sexual harassment than were their African American classmates.

Similar to their male classmates, African American girls were not emotionally impacted as much as their Hispanic and Caucasian sisters.[6] Girls from all three races were confused about their self-identity, and whether or not they would have a good girl/boy relationship. African American girls said the sexual harassment did not interfere with their ability to study, but they were significantly more likely to change friendships as a result of their victimization.

The 2011 AAUW study showed that Hispanic students were more likely to stay home when sexually harassed than were their white classmates.[7] African American students stopped their involvement in a school activity or sport, got into trouble at school, and found it hard to study more so than their white classmates. Both Hispanic and African American students changed the way they went to and from school and were more likely to change schools than were white students.

The 2001 AAUW study included numerous student comments.

One female student claimed that boys are "slapping our butts every day so that when we walk we keep our backs to the lockers. After a while you get used to it." This student's comment reflects a common theme that many girls have come to believe—that "this is the way boys are," "there is nothing I can do to stop it," "it's just something I have to get used to," and so on. What a sad commentary that girls have learned an infectious apathy, helplessness, and hopelessness because they don't believe they have control over their own bodies in school where it is supposed to be safe; and that boys can do with them as they will without any repercussions.

Distressingly, sexual harassment occurs in public places in the school such as hallways and classrooms, where faculty and staff witness the misconduct and often collude with the perpetrators by not intervening to stop the abuse.[8] Both girls and boys receive a loud and clear message, then, that sexual violence is an accepted school norm; this can be a catalyst for increased sexual violence within the school and the community.[9] When teachers do intervene, even in instances of sexual assault, the boys sometimes face few consequences from school officials. A female teacher shared that one of her female students told a male teacher about a male classmate grabbing her breast—which is a sexual assault. The male teacher's response was to merely tell the male student that he shouldn't have done it, and then told them both to go to class. The message was clear—the boy had the right to accost his female classmate, and she had no legitimate right to her own body.

Sadly, sexual harassment has far-reaching ramifications for children and teens. The quote in the beginning of the chapter by the retired sixty-seven-year-old woman was from a letter written in support of Deena, the teen who brought a formal charge of sexual harassment against her school district with her state's civil rights department. Another woman, age thirty-two, also wrote to Deena about being sexually harassed and assaulted on her bus in front of her seventh and eighth grade classmates. She said that she is still dealing with the psychic pain because, even though it was reported, no one did anything to halt the ongoing behavior that was a common occurrence in the bus and in the hallways.

What does this mean for the future of those students victimized by sexual harassment? Will it alter their career aspirations? Will victims tend to stay in traditionally female or male occupations to further avoid harassment? How will this impact their long-term economic potential? The impact is potentially long term and serious, including alcohol and drug abuse, depression, suicide, and poor grades resulting in an inability to be accepted into colleges, thereby impacting their career and income.

You may wonder why students say they engage in sexual harassment. The 2011 AAUW report found that 44 percent didn't think sexual harassment was "any big deal." Many students said they were trying to be funny; others were retaliating for a wrong done to them; a small number of students said they wanted to date the person or thought the person enjoyed the sexual attention.

There were certain student characteristics that put them at more risk to be sexually harassed than others. Boys who were not seen as athletic or "masculine" were more likely to be harassed, and boys who were "good looking" were the least likely to be sexually harassed. Girls were in a more awkward situation because both attractive girls and unattractive or unfeminine girls were targets of sexual harassment. As well, girls who were "too sexual" or "too masculine" were at an increased risk of experiencing sexual harassment. Girls whose bodies were more developed were also a more likely target. These at risk characteristics "reinforce the complexity of predicting who may be the victim of sexual harassment in middle and high schools, as unwanted sexual attention and the policing of gender norms are both part of sexual harassment."[10]

Both male and female students reported in the 2001 AAUW study feeling doubtful as to whether they would have a happy romantic relationship, and were confused about who they were. Unlike girls, boys sometimes said they enjoyed the girls' sexual attention. Girls also had a broader range of negative reactions and feelings than did the boys describing feeling "dirty, like a piece of trash," "grossed out," "angry and upset," "scared," and "like a second-class citizen."

The AAUW's 2001 study found the sexual harassment girls experienced impacted their behavior significantly more than what the boys reported, with both genders reporting the following behavior:

- Avoided the harasser (40%)
- Didn't speak as much in class (24%)
- Changed their seating (22%)
- Had difficulty paying attention (21%)
- Avoided certain areas within the school or on school grounds (18%)
- Had difficulty studying (16%)
- Lost their appetite (16%)
- Stayed home from school or cut class (16%)

Students responded to the sexual harassment in a variety of ways based on the AAUW's 2011 study. Forty-nine percent of both boys and girls ignored the misconduct, 31 percent of girls and 13 percent of boys told the harasser to stop, and 11 percent of girls and 22 percent of boys attempted to make a joke out of the misconduct.

As in 2001, girls who were sexually harassed in 2011 were impacted more so than their male classmates. A comparison of girls and boys responses to their sexual harassment included the following:

- Found it hard to study (37 versus 21%)
- Did not want to go to school (37 versus 25%)
- Had trouble sleeping (22 versus 14%)
- Stayed home (14 versus 9%)
- Got into trouble at school (11 versus 7%)
- Changed the way they went to school or home (10 versus 6%)
- Stopped involvement in an activity or sport (9 versus 5%)
- Switched schools (5 versus 2%)

For the first time, the AAUW's 2011 study examined whether income differences of students played a role in their victimization. Unfortunately, the study found that those students who came from homes making less than $60,000 a year were more likely to be sexually harassed, more likely to experience unwanted touch, and more likely to want to stay home from school. Also for the first time, the AAUW examined whether witnesses tried to help the student who was experiencing the sexual harassment. Of the 56 percent of students who witnessed sexual harassment, 24 percent of female students and 17 percent of male students tried to help the victim by telling the harasser to stop (the most common action), asking the victim if she or he was ok, or by reporting it.

The 2011 AAUW report examined whether students responded differently to *in person* sexual harassment differently than *online* harassment. Forty-six percent of students sexually harassed online *and* in person did not want to go to school compared to 19 percent who were harassed in person and 18 percent who experienced online harassment. Forty-three percent of students sexually harassed online *and* in person said it was hard to study compared to 17 percent of students sexually harassed online or in person.

Girls were more threatened by peer sexual harassment than boys.[11] Classmates they knew casually were viewed as the most threatening while close friends were less so. Seventy percent of victims of sexual harassment in the schools were harassed by classmates they knew casually.

Both teens and adults viewed the sexual harassment of teenagers as normal adolescent behavior, which challenges the impetus for teachers to intervene when it is observed. The belief that sexual harassment is typical of adolescents is evidence of how entrenched that idea is in the schools, adolescent relationships, and male dominance.[12] Because sexual harassment in the school setting is of normal, everyday life for many girls (and boys who don't fit the masculine stereotype), they have difficulty in even identifying offensive behavior as harassment. But girls who have attended school in both single sex and mixed gendered schools recognized the sexist behavior in mixed gendered schools.

Some victims of sexual harassment are diagnosed with post-traumatic stress disorder. This diagnosis brings with it a myriad of physical and emotional difficulties, including depression, sometimes to the point of feeling numb, suicidal thoughts, insomnia, anxiety, inability to concentrate and make decisions, nightmares, and ruminating about the harassing incident.[13] These symptoms may worsen when exposed to any situations that resemble the original harassment incident. The moodiness that results may interfere with their ability to maintain healthy relationships with their friends and family. Fear that the harassment will continue or escalate, or that they may be retaliated against for reporting the harasser, may increase their feelings of vulnerability.

Victims may feel shame or guilt, believing they are somehow to blame or deserved the behavior. As a result, they may be less likely to come forward to report the misconduct. Those students who experience shame or guilt due to their religious traditions may have difficulty in describing what happened to them, particularly in identifying where and how they were touched and repeating the words they heard.[14]

Girls may wear baggy clothes or sweat suits to school to hide their figure, indicating on some level a degree of self-blame for their own victimization. Middle school girls are usually self-conscious about their developing bodies, in particular if their sexual development is earlier than their peers. This precocious sexual development increases the likelihood of being targeted for the harassment. Their developing bodies coupled with sexual harassment may increase girls' self-consciousness and perpetuate a negative body image, potentially giving rise to eating disorders.[15]

As if the educational, emotional, and behavioral impact that sexual harassment has on its victims isn't enough, their physical health is compromised as well. Sexual harassment is a stressor, and the body responds accordingly by affecting the immune system. Headaches, stomachaches, and acne are but a few of the symptoms, and students may be more susceptible to colds and the flu, as well as more serious conditions.[16]

Sexual harassment of girls reinforces the second-class status of females. As discussed in chapter 1, harassment occurs in public places such as classrooms and in hallways, under the eyes of adults who either ignore what they see and hear or trivialize the girls' complaints. It doesn't take long before the girls begin to experience a sense of helplessness and hopelessness, and it becomes obvious that the school allows boys to treat them as sex objects.

The hostility and anger that many victims experience may increase the risk of using and/or escalating the use of alcohol, drugs, and/or cigarettes, as well as engaging in other acting out behavior. The cumulative effect of even the more subtle sexual harassment can be overwhelming and abysmal when one is in a culture that daily tells you that you are but a mere sex object and that it is okay to treat you as such.

Victims who reported their harassment to school officials, to OCR, or their state's civil rights office, or sued in court often experienced secondary victimization, which brings on its own set of responses. The 2001 AAUW reported that 20 percent of sex discrimination complaints to OCR were cases of retaliation against the victim for filing a complaint under Title IX. Those brave enough to speak up and file formal complaints were often ridiculed, assaulted, blamed, excluded, further harassed, and lost their friends. They felt betrayed and discredited, unsupported and negated by their peers and school staff. Consequently, they lost trust in people, began to doubt their own perceptions of the behavior, and questioned if they did the right thing in speaking out.

When one high school girl was brave enough to testify in front of her state's legislature about the sexual harassment occurring in her school, one of the legislators, a neighbor to the principal of the girl's high school, informed the principal about the girl's testimony. Instead of the school lauding the girl's moxie to speak out, and using her as a positive role model for civil mindedness and courage, the superintendent and the principal called her into the superintendent's office and ostracized her for lying. Neither asked her to discuss the behaviors she had documented and complained about numerous times to the principal. The school's defensiveness and irresponsibility fueled her desire to continue to speak out, and she was featured on numerous national television programs about the issue, much to the chagrin of the school district.

The difficulty for any child and her or his parents in bringing a formal charge or lawsuit against a school district about their victimization was captured in an article in *The American School Board*: "No matter . . . the simple truth is that filing a lawsuit against a school district can bring the wrath of the community, if not God himself, down on a family and a child." Rebecca Jones, the author, goes on to say that "filing a constitutional lawsuit against a school district guarantees that a child will be harassed."[17] Her article quotes professor emeritus Robert S. Alley, who said "I have no idea how many children can stand that kind of pressure and live with it and mature to be happy, balanced citizens."

The impact of sexual harassment on the victimized student has reverberations throughout the family. Retaliation against the student and/or the family sometimes comes from some unlikely places. Some families have been asked to leave their church for "going against" the school. One mother was physically attacked by her minister when she went to him for help through the stressful time of her son's harassment by his male classmates. Other parents have been told they are no longer welcome as members of parent-teacher associations, and others have had to move out of their communities. Some families have had bricks thrown through their home's windows with nasty and threatening notes attached, been stalked by angry teens who support the harasser(s), lost long-time friends, received threatening phone calls, had family members physically assaulted, experienced drive-by epithets, and had their home and car defaced. This is on top of the stress of supporting a daughter or son who is experiencing their own trauma, trying to get the school to stop the harassment, and dealing with the backlash from the community and the school's supporters rallying support for the school and the harassers. In addition, there may be a lack of support from family and friends, and, in some cases, families are dealing with the stress of a lawsuit or formal charges with OCR or the states' civil rights agency. The familial stress is further trauma on the victimized student.

How does this backlash from so many directions impact the child or teen victim's sense of well-being? The victim's distress will be compounded when she or he is living in a family that is stressed. For that matter, how does this noxious retaliation towards the victim and her or his family impact the well-being of other students within the school and the greater community? How safe would other students feel to speak up in support of the victim, or to report their own victimization? The sexual harassment incident(s), the lack of adequate prevention and intervention by the school, and the backlash by the community against the victim and her/his family perpetuates the sexual harassment by negating the experiences of the victim, minimizing the behavior of the harasser, and excusing the school's inadequate response.

The target of the harassment is not the only one that is subjected to negative consequences. Teachers' and administrators' silence in the face of the harasser's behavior is loud and clear. Students who are allowed to harass learn some disturbing lessons. They learn that they have done nothing wrong, their behavior is accepted and acceptable, and they have permission to victimize others. If there are no consequences, the offender's behavior may increase in severity and pervasiveness, creating more victims and reinforcing the misconduct. This reinforcement has the potential to desensitize the harasser to the victim's trauma and to increase the likelihood of it being viewed as normal behavior by the harasser, victim, witnesses, and other students.

On the other hand, the student harasser may experience consequences such as a drop in grades, suspension, expulsion, and restriction from extracurricular activities. The harasser's parents are forced to deal with their son or daughter's violation, and, if the severity of the harassment is criminal, parents will be forced to deal with police and the cost of hiring lawyers and other resultant financial obligations.

When sexual harassment occurs in public areas such as the hallway, classroom, and cafeteria, those students who are bystanders or witnesses to the harassment are also victimized in a closely similar way as the target. Even though they may not have been targeted, witnesses realize they are not safe either, and will alter their behavior to minimize their vulnerability. Like the target, witnesses may change their route to class, alter their style of dress, and avoid certain classmates or teachers. Witnessing the sexual harassment of their classmates affects bystanders' physical health, emotional health, and school-related behavior, for example, their grades. Third parties, the student bystanders, learn that it is acceptable to harass and demean others based on their sex, sexual orientation, and gender identity. When sexual harassment continues to occur in these public spaces it becomes part of the cultural norm for the school and therefore becomes accepted.

Sexual harassment interferes with a student's right to an education. It takes a toll on the victim's physical and emotional health, affects behavior, and may encourage drug/alcohol use. The ramifications may be severe and long lasting, sometimes resulting in suicide and school shootings. Girls are targeted by sexual harassment more often and with more frequent consequences. When students are harassed in public areas of the school, with faculty and staff as witnesses, both girls and boys receive a loud and clear message: Sexual violence is an accepted school norm. Sexual harassment of girls reinforces the second-class status of females who doubt their own perceptions of the behavior and question if they did the right thing in speaking out. Bystanders who witness the assault are affected, as is the victim's family who seeks justice for their child from the school and the legal system.

8

WHY DON'T SCHOOLS STOP SEXUAL HARASSMENT AND BULLYING?

School is supposed to be positive. You can't go there and have it negative and expect to come out, smile, and want to go back. I'm transferring schools and, if it happens again, I don't know what I am going to do.

—Raychel, high school student[1]

If we can't turn to our . . . principals and they're not going to do anything for us, what's the point. That's what they're there for. They're supposed to help us learn and if we can't learn in an environment where we're being called names and stuff, then they're not doing their jobs.

—High School Female[2]

During lunch, a male classmate approached eighth grader Kristie and yanked the snaps on the front of her blouse causing them to pop open exposing her bra. The boy was known for his pranks. Angry, embarrassed, and determined not to be his victim, Kristie took a handful of her mashed potatoes and smashed it into his face. The vice principal saw the exchange, said nothing to the boy, but made Kristie go into a small janitor's closet as punishment for her actions. The vice principal effectively gave the message that Kristie should not stand up for herself and the boy's misconduct was approved.

The Eden Prairie, Minnesota school district gave superintendent Jerry McCoy public praise in his [mis]handling of the country's first elementary school sexual harassment complaint. The praise was despite the fact that both OCR and the Minnesota Department of Human Rights found probable cause in the sexual harassment of first grader Cheltzie Hentz. The school board felt he had done such a stand-up job, despite the government's findings, that they awarded him a 3.9 out of a possible 4 on his performance. Board member Ken Foote stated, "In the six years I've been on the board, Jerry continues to amaze me."[3] Other board members had similar words of praise at the school board meeting, and they specifically mentioned McCoy's handling of the sexual harassment complaint against the district. The school board's comments and behavior would be effective in preventing any other parent from fighting a system that clearly did not support the district's students.

Sexual harassment and bullying may be widespread and public or hidden in uncommon school locations. It may be verbal comments and jokes or physical altercations, and may occur on a student's cell phone and computer. Sexual harassment may or may not rise to the level of a hostile environment depending upon the severity, pervasiveness, or persistence or offensiveness of the behavior, and whether it interferes with a student's ability to take part in, or benefit from, the various opportunities offered by the school such as sports, band, and debate. Schools have an ethical and often legal responsibility to intervene in connection with bullying and sexual harassment behavior even if sexual harassment does not rise to the level of a hostile environment based on the OCR's requirement and Title IX law.

In October 2010, OCR sent a *Dear Colleague* letter to all U.S. schools that spelled out school districts' responsibilities in addressing bullying and sexual harassment.[4] The letter was sent earlier than originally planned in response to the suicides of five teens following harassment based on their real or perceived sexual orientation. The letter outlines potential disciplinary measures schools can take such as separating the victim and perpetrator, and offering counseling and other services for both. The letter also stressed the need for competent investigations, and a requirement to prevent retaliation.

TEACHER-TO-STUDENT SEXUAL HARASSMENT

Research findings about school districts' responses to students' sexual harassment complaints against teachers are alarming.[5] Child protection agencies or police were seldom called when students complained to administrators about sexual harassment by teachers or other school staff. One of the most distressing outcomes was that, if any investigations were conducted, they were not done by an independent third party but by an individual within the school district. Those conducting the investigation were not trained in how to conduct a criminal investigation, which teacher-to-student sexual misconduct may constitute, and were often incompetent in conducting a sexual harassment investigation required by civil law. School investigators were not skilled in interviewing students, and witnesses were often not interviewed to corroborate allegations by either the victim or the alleged perpetrator. The teacher who was accused was often believed when he (with rare exception, the educator is male) claimed he was innocent of the allegation, or that a student misunderstood the incident(s), resulting in no further follow through by the school. The teacher was not disciplined and was allowed to continue to teach and perpetrate. Because the police were not notified, it was unknown if the sexual harassment also rose to the level of a crime, therefore resulting in no criminal repercussions as well. Tragically, the teacher was allowed to have ongoing access to children and youth.

High school girls were sometimes blamed for their own victimization by comments made about their tight shirts or short skirts. Additionally, girls were implicitly blamed if they had a well-developed figure, or if any girl was viewed as exhibiting a sexual demeanor—thereby excusing the teacher's misconduct.[6] Superintendents acknowledged that, while the teacher's harassment may be improper, it was understandable because of how the girl dressed and acted. School staff, other faculty, and even the victim's classmates touted similar perceptions and responses. Blaming the victim was even stronger if the girl had stayed after school in the teacher's classroom for whatever reason, including getting extra help with her studies. Support of the accused teacher continued even if the school was sued and a jury found that the teacher had sexually harassed or criminally sexually abused the student. The harassing teacher is usually well liked by students, parents, school administrators and staff, and the community. Consequently, it is much easier to blame a student than to believe that her allegations against a beloved teacher are true.

Superintendents did not know what behaviors encompass sexual harassment, or the impact teacher harassment has on students.[7] Surprisingly, superintendents did not view the following teacher-to-student behavior as particularly destructive to the student victim: sexual name calling and sexual comments, exposing genitals, obscene gestures, showing pornography, and inviting a student to his home. Researchers also discovered that:

- Female students were less likely to be believed than were their male classmates.
- Female students' allegations were taken less seriously than were male students' complaints.
- No assistance was provided to the student victim in roughly 60 percent of cases.
- Superintendents did not comprehend the impact of sexual harassment on students nor realize the necessity to intervene.
- Grievances against female teachers were seen as more severe than those against male teachers; therefore female faculty received more severe discipline.
- Students who alleged same-sex harassment were more likely to be seen as truthful; a teacher's homosexual behavior was seen as more grave than was heterosexual misconduct.
- 17 percent of educators charged with sexual harassment were allowed to continue to teach and were not formally reprimanded; some were transferred to another school building or assigned different responsibilities.
- Superintendents sought to rescind a teacher's license in only 1 percent of cases.

Many school districts seemed to be more concerned about protecting the district from poor publicity and the potential liability from the victim's family and/or the accused educator, than about the safety and well-being of the student victim.[8] There were repeated instances in numerous school districts where school officials turned a blind eye to student complaints and failed to act appropriately.[9]

Mobile Molesters and *Passing the Trash* are terms used in defining the harassing teacher who is "let go" from a school district, and begins teaching at another district that is often uninformed of the harasser's sexual misconduct.[10] However, 37 percent of accused educators were allowed to continue to teach within their school district even when the superintendent presumed the students were telling the truth. Title IX fails to hold school districts accountable when they allow teachers who are known sexual predators to teach at another school without informing the new district of the teachers' sexual offenses.[11] Title IX does not demand that school districts fix the problem because schools are not liable for the context of the harassment or the harassers that they cannot control. This allows school districts to evade liability for passing on sexual predators to another school.

It is difficult to terminate educators who sexually harass, according to school boards and superintendents.[12] Union contracts and some laws protect the teacher's privacy and job, thereby creating barriers to effective discipline. And, of course, sometimes even after a competent investigation, it is not always clear what the real facts are.

The Government Accountability Office (GAO) report outlined incidents where individuals with histories of sexual misconduct were hired by schools in the role of teachers, staff, and contractors, or were brought in as volunteers.[13] They studied fifteen cases, and discovered at least eleven involved sex offenders of children who had been hired as school employees or volunteers. The GAO found several elements that factored into perpetrators being hired by schools:

- School officials allowed teachers who were found to have harassed or abused students to resign without being punished, thereby allowing positive references going to the next school.
- Schools failed to conduct pre-employment criminal history checks or did inadequate history checks that, for example, included only state criminal history.
- School officials failed to follow up on questionable details on employment applications, for example, allowing applicants to self-report criminal background information, and failed to follow through when an applicant indicated he or she had been convicted of "a dangerous crime against children."

Two recent court rulings of teacher-to-student sexual harassment have added stricter responsibilities for school districts. All school employees who suspect questionable behavior between a student and a teacher must inform the appropriate school official of the teacher's behavior even if it merely hints at impropriety. Failure to do so could cause the school district to be held liable under Title IX , Section 1983, and other laws.

One of the court rulings resulting in the stricter mandates involved Alexandria Dyess, a student at Tehachapi High School in California, who sued her school district, school administrators, and numerous other teachers for failure to address the sexual harassment by her teacher Rick Cotta.[14] She sued under Title IX, and also filed claims for the violation of the Equal Protection Clause of the Fourteenth Amendment, conspiracy under Section 1983, (see chapter 10 for more on Section 1983), Section 1985, and other laws for failure to prevent sexual harassment. These conspiracy claims were in response to several teachers who witnessed Cotta sexually harass Dyess on different occasions, and yet did nothing to intervene nor report the behavior to school officials. Even after Dyess's father complained to school administrators, Cotta continued to harass Dyess. OCR investigated following Dyess's father's complaint and found that Cotta did sexually harass Dyess, and the school district failed to respond appropriately. Dyess then sued the school district. Her complaint argued that the school district conspired to deprive her of her constitutional equal protection rights.

SCHOOL'S RESPONSES TO STUDENT TO STUDENT SEXUAL HARASSMENT AND BULLYING

Few studies have examined the reasons teachers and administrators do not intervene on bullying and sexual harassment. Only one study was found addressing the issue specifically related to bullying. It found that teachers and other adults think they are doing a much better job at intervening than what the students perceive.[15] Seventy percent of teachers believed that they intervened "almost always" in bullying altercations, whereas only 25 percent of students agreed with the teachers' perceptions.

School officials often ignore or minimize sexual harassment because they don't recognize the conduct as sexual or harassing. Euphemisms such as "boys will be boys," "that's just the way football/hockey players are," or "they are just teasing," and even, "that's how they let a girl know they like her," are phrases used to excuse the behavior.

It is frustrating for parents when their child comes home and tells them about their victimization, that they informed a teacher—often several times—and still the harassment or bullying persists. Why don't teachers intervene? Teachers may at times be at a loss as to how to intervene or they may be embarrassed because of the sexual nature of the misconduct.[16] Teachers often indicate that they think kids should handle it themselves, and may not be aware of their legal and ethical responsibilities to intervene. Failure of adults to protect students when they are bullied or sexually harassed gives unspoken approval for the behavior to continue, and interferes with a student's ability to learn.

Surprisingly, sexual harassment occurs in the most prominent and congregated areas of the school—hallways and classrooms—where teachers are tasked with supervising student behavior.[17] When teachers don't intervene, it allows the misconduct to continue unabated. Years ago when I spoke on sexual harassment at a large conference, one of the male teachers angrily claimed, "If I intervened every time I observed or heard sexual harassment, I would never get any teaching done." I asked him if there was that amount of sexual harassment occurring in his classroom, how did he think it was impacting student learning? He had no answer. His comment reflected his ignorance about his ethical and legal responsibility to stop the misconduct. It also showed his failure to grasp how this serious misconduct negatively affects students' (both victims and witnesses) emotional well-being, and their ability to learn.

A high school English teacher, who had recently re-entered mainstream education after teaching five years at an adolescent juvenile detention facility, said she was horrified at the daily sexual misconduct she observed at the high school where she now taught. Her comments were very telling in that the sexual harassment occurring within the high school mirrored the same behaviors that had brought her male students for their court-ordered stays at the detention facility where she had previously worked. Her new school failed to hold male students accountable for their sexual harassment by not intervening, and thereby giving tacit approval for it to continue. However, male adolescents ended up in court and the juvenile detention facility when they engaged in the same misconduct toward girls in public, non-school settings. How have school officials reached this point of allowing students to sexually harass their peers—sometimes criminally—within the school environment? What sort of infectious malaise has infected the school's climate?

Students routinely claim that their teachers are apathetic and unresponsive when teachers either observe sexual harassment in classrooms and hallways or are informed of harassment by students.[18] The question is why would faculty not intercede in such instances of aggressive, discriminatory, and painful behavior from one student, usually male, to another, usually female or to a male student who doesn't fit the masculine norm? Very little research has examined this question. One study of high school teachers explored what they termed *gendered harassment* (referred to as sexual harassment in this book), which included verbal, physical, or psychological harassment that is used to challenge heterosexual gender norms and includes [hetero]sexual harassment, homophobic harassment, and harassment of students who don't fit the stereotype of maculinity and famnity.[19]

The teachers in the study identified four elements that impacted teachers' views and responses to sexual harassment[20]: (1) school culture, including the structure of the district's administration and how administrators responded to reports of sexual harassment; (2) teachers' workload and curriculum demands; (3) teacher education and training; and, finally, (4) the districts' written policies. These four formal elements were coupled with the district's social or informal social norms such as the perceptions of administration, interpersonal relationships, and the values of the community and therefore the school.

Teachers' comments about the informal school climate focused on teachers' conduct and comments in the teachers' lounge and at staff meetings.[21] By their very speech, those teachers expressed their biases through sexist, racist, and homophobic comments, which were supportive of a masculine and oppressive culture. When one teacher informed the school administrator about another teacher's sexual harassment of students, the administrator said he knew about the sexual harassment, but no apparent discipline was dispersed and the teacher continued to teach.

So, what did this all really mean? First, if teachers lack awareness and understanding of their district's policies and grievance procedures, and are not clear about Title IX and their state's civil rights law, their motivation to intervene to stop harassment is reduced.[22] The study found that teachers believed that they could not stop sexual harassment due to the barriers within the school culture, and also their own hesitancy in challenging sexist, homophobic, and other social inequitable comments. Sexism, misogyny, heterosexism, and homophobia have been normalized in society, and therefore within the school environment, making the issues invisible or unacknowledged.

Most of the teachers said they were committed to address the harassment they witnessed in their schools but they didn't trust that their administrators (and many colleagues) would support them.[23] One common complaint was that administrators failed to deliver the discipline required to communicate the importance of a student's misconduct—they just weren't firm enough. Additionally, teachers were frustrated about administrators not being available to discipline students. Administration was responsive to other types of school violence, particularly physical violence, or racial harassment, but they were weak and ineffective when it came to sexual harassment, verbal harassment, or psychological abuse. Teachers perceived their administrators' inaction as a clear sign that they didn't view sexual harassment as important enough to bother them! It stands to reason, then, that, when there is an absence of administrative discipline, student misconduct will increase.

Teachers in the study spoke about other administration issues such as leadership style, values, priorities, and policy implementation. One teacher talked about his administrator, who was a jock, who would sit the boys down like they were in a football huddle.[24] Another stated that administrators did not want to get involved in issues dealing with GLBT students. Therein lies one of the problems, administrators' (and teachers') own mentality about sexual harassment, and in particular harassment against GLBT students. Teachers were clear that, because bullying is easier to deal with, it is usually at the top of issues that get attention. Gendered behaviors such as sexual assault and homosexuality are more sensitive and controversial, and administrators keep their distance from these issues. These teachers' examples showed poor administrative leadership, which had amazing power in dictating the climate of the school. Administrators minimized the seriousness of sexual harassment and did not devote the attention required, both ethically and legally, to intervene and prevent the misconduct, which is a violation of Title IX.

School policies were not always actively communicated to teachers, especially when outlining how policies should be enforced.[25] In addition, teachers saw administrators as unsupportive of school policies, adding to teachers feeling isolated when intervening with non-physical bullying and gendered harassment. Since many teachers did not study the policies, they were unaware of their role in curtailing harassment. Schools often held a zero-tolerance policy for physical violence, but not for bullying and sexual harassment, which added to teachers' confusion.

Teachers' relationships with their administrators and coworkers played a role in dealing with sexual harassment, according to the study.[26] Some teachers struggled to defend specific discipline with some students, when other teachers did not. The teachers didn't feel collegiality with many of their peers due to the inconsistencies with discipline. Students observed the inconsistencies, which led to more student misconduct.

And, finally, the study showed that the relationships teachers had with students and with parents influenced their responses to sexual harassment. They spoke of positive relationships with their students, and some problematic relationships with parents. One teacher was subjected to homophobic taunts and name calling by parents. Parents increasingly were not supportive of teachers disciplining their children in the classroom, sometimes swearing at the teacher, and demonstrating the very behavior for which their child had been disciplined. When parents used homophobic and other rude and disrespectful language and behavior towards educators, and when school officials did not support school or classroom rules, it demonstrated the antithesis of efforts to eliminate sexual harassment.

Relationships with students' parents sometimes added to the difficulty of intervening in student misconduct. Parents' behaviors did not evolve in a vacuum, but rather were reflective of the community where the school was located.[27] The teachers in the study were from three different schools and each had a distinct climate based on the community in which their school resided. One teacher said the perception of her school district was that it was close to perfect because their academics, sports, and cultural events were priorities—but the school was certainly not perfect. A second district bowed to male students by giving them power in the activities in which they belonged, such as sports. The third school was located in a poverty-stricken neighborhood, inundated with violence, racism, and socioeconomically deprived families. In examining the three neighborhoods, it was easy to see how the community values, resources, and beliefs greatly infiltrated each school's climate.

The study found that another factor in how teachers sense and intervene in sexual harassment incidents is the amount of energy they have to do so.[28] Teachers were feeling drained and swamped with increased demands on their teaching, without the support or resources required to be competent teachers. It makes sense; we need only open the newspaper and turn on the TV to learn how, yet again, financially strapped school districts are being forced to lay off teachers, increase class size, and ask families to provide more supplies. When class sizes continue to expand, it becomes more difficult for teachers to hone in on misconduct.

Training educators about sexual harassment and GLBT issues was lacking, which creates a third element of concern. Teachers spoke to a lack of skill and knowledge regarding how to intervene in harassment incidents.[29] Furthermore, they were limited in seeking the training by an outside vendor because they were encouraged to use their few training days to acquire additional knowledge and skill about the topic they taught. These teachers had received no sexual harassment education while attending college, and their school districts failed to provide sexual harassment training as well. Fortunately, a few of the teachers took the initiative to learn about harassment, GLBT students' needs, and similar topics. GLBT harassment was difficult to effectively intervene on because the school climate supported the harassment by allowing anti-gay jokes and comments made by teachers and administrators.

Sexually obnoxious language, such as "slut," "fuck," "cunt," "gay," and so on, have become so normalized within some school cultures that teachers said the sheer magnitude of the language and behavior has a paralyzing affect in attempting to intervene.[30] When teachers intervene in connection with boys' sexual harassment of girls and the boys responded with "It's only a joke," teachers often did not challenge the boys' retort, thereby disregarding the girls' complaints and both supporting and reinforcing the boys' sense of entitlement and control.[31] High school sophomore Olivia told of hearing a boy yell "Fuck you, cunt," to a girl in the hallway when Olivia was sitting in class. She said everyone heard it including the teacher, who merely closed the classroom door rather than confronting the student.

Remember Deena, the girl whose name was on the "25 Most Fuckable Girls" list? When her mother called the school counselor to ask what the district intended to do about the list, the counselor told her there wasn't much that could be done and that the school didn't want to make "a big deal out of it." Here were twenty-five girls who had been sexually tormented by the list circulating throughout the school, but the school didn't want to make "a big deal out of it." Despite Deena's mother speaking to school administrators, there was no follow-up with students about sexual harassment and the school district's policy. It's understandable why Deena decided she could no longer ignore the school's culture and filed a formal complaint with the state's civil rights department.

Perhaps the force that brings the most to bear on a teacher's response is who the teacher is in his or her core—their own identity, experiences, history, and more.[32] Had teachers and school officials been marginalized as children or adults, had they been bullied, and/or had they struggled with their gender identity or sexual orientation, then one would think that those experiences would be a catalyst to act on behalf of students. The study showed that it did make a difference, and a teacher's own childhood victimization was often a strong indicator of teacher advocacy for students. However, teachers said they sometimes struggled when they observed a student harassed because it reminded them of their own vulnerability. Female and gay teachers and teachers of color were particularly vocal about their vulnerabilities and their own biases.

Teachers' responses to sexual harassment were based on their personal values and beliefs about sexuality, power, violence, children, and their role as a teacher, as well as the complexities of how all of those beliefs intertwine. They acknowledged that it was easier to intervene in connection with severe cases such as physical attacks and unwanted touch.[33] They indicated that, if the harassment was repeated or involved grabbing, students were sent to the office, but they weren't sure what happened then. One of the confusing points for teachers was whether to intervene when the harassment was subtle—almost invisible—which it often is, and they had no guidance from their district's policy. Another challenge was that they didn't know how to respond to jokes and teasing between friends.

Teachers were also perplexed as to what their role should be when they heard and saw any harassment with a dating couple, including nasty name calling.[34] They questioned whether they had the authority to step in. They tended to blame both students for the violence even when it was the male who was aggressive. Teachers failed to perceive and address the potential of violence to the male student's girlfriend outside of school, which is alarming when one out of ten youth are victims of dating violence.

One study found that teachers focused on the victim's behavior rather than on the harasser. Did she cry? Did he get angry? If she cried, they intervened immediately.[35] Because teachers felt harassment was often so subtle, they said they relied on female students to report it. This placed the responsibility on the female students to end the sexual harassment, and to take on the role of the fragile and vulnerable victim in order for staff to intervene. Another study found that educators were willing to intervene in connection with male-to-female sexual harassment if the female student was a *quiet girl*.[36]

Female teachers tended to mentor their female students on how to identify sexual harassment *but* pointed out how the female students' own behavior contributed to their victimization![37] The teachers thought they could help the girls prevent their own harassment if they told them to change their style of dress, their sexual behavior, and not allow the boys to touch them without their consent. Female teachers saw this role as empowering their female students, but it blamed the girls for their own harassment.

Male teachers, similar to female teachers, tried to show the boys that they had a male-to-male connection with them. However, they were inclined to attribute male students' misconduct to immaturity rather than see the seriousness of sexual harassment. Unfortunately, the teachers' viewpoint and message to their male students was that their sexual harassment was normal and just part of adolescent sexual development.

Though teachers would repeatedly warn students about calling their friends "gay" or "fag," it was not followed by any discipline when the name calling persisted.[38] GLBT students, particularly boys, played the role of both target and harasser; an effeminate boy would call his harassers names as a tool to defend himself. One teacher told of a male student refusing to sit next to one of his classmates because he was gay. The teacher's response was: "He's not hitting on you. If he starts hitting on you, you don't want him hitting on you and that's sexual harassment, we'll take care of that." The teacher did not understand the sexual harassment of the gay student, and instead talked to the harasser as though he could be a potential victim of the gay student he harassed. Other discussions with teachers showed they blamed GLBT students for their own victimization.

Students view teachers' inactions as a way of condoning sexual harassment and bullying. No wonder so few students seek out assistance from their teachers, staff, or administrators. Teachers view male-to-female sexual harassment as normal adolescent sexuality and immaturity rather than seeing the domination, coercion, or violence inherent in the behavior. Teachers are often blind to bullying unless it is seen as severe or happens in public. They are unaware of gender harassment due to its normalization and subtleness and because, unlike sexual harassment, it is often outside of staff vision and hearing. When teachers emphasize that attention should be given to the sexual harassment of *quiet* and *crying* girls, it emphasizes traditional feminine stereotypes. Teachers are also less likely to view female-to-male sexual misconduct as sexual harassment.

Teachers said any steps taken to reduce GLBT harassment were ineffective and diminished GLBT students' sense of equal importance to straight students, according to one study.[39] Teacher interviews reinforced patriarchal, sexist, and heterosexist norms that were supported by school cultures, including inadequate policies. Schools' lack of commitment in creating a detailed plan to address heterosexual and GLBT harassment by, for example, conducting training and having comprehensive policies left teachers with their own ideas of gender and homosexuality which, unfortunately, also included blaming the victims.[40] It is critical that educators and administrators receive comprehensive education to prod them to confront their own sexist and heterosexist belief systems.

One male teacher taught a building-trades course to high school juniors and seniors. One of the teacher's friends asked if the students could make a large outhouse that he could take to his cabin. Since building structures for community members was a somewhat common practice as a learning project for students, the teacher complied with his friend's request. When the outhouse was finished, the teacher invited other teachers to see the completed outhouse. Two of the female teachers were aghast at what they saw. The teacher had asked all of his students from three different classes—all boys—to bring in pornographic pictures to use as wallpaper in the outhouse. The entire interior of the outhouse, including the ceiling, was covered with pictures of female genitalia. Only one teacher negatively responded—a female teacher who taught a human sexuality course was livid. This is an example of what has been referred to as a *hidden curriculum*.[41]

This teacher's hidden curriculum was rife with misogyny, violence towards women, patriarchy, sexism, and heterosexism. The teacher had assumed that all the boys would be comfortable contributing pornography for a class project. What if some boys did not want to do so? How would the teacher's assignment pressure those boys to abide by traditional male behavior to be accepted by their male classmates and get a good grade from the teacher? What message did the teacher convey about women's worth and about masculinity? The only consequence to the teacher was—"Get that outhouse off the school's property and don't do something like this again." No discussions took place between the teacher and the students about the inappropriateness of the class project.

Now graduated, a young woman from Virginia still has a strong gut reaction when she has to drive by the homes of the girls who tormented her in high school.[42] They shouted obscenities, attempted to beat her up, and threw toilet paper and eggs at her house. Finally, she received a death threat. The school's response? Rather than make the perpetrator(s) accountable, they appointed a security guard as an escort for her when she moved from class to class.

OCR was consulted about an allegation of sexual harassment at the Amoret, Missouri school district. When OCR investigated the allegations of sexual harassment by two third graders it discovered that school officials were ignorant about Title IX's investigation requirements.[43]

POLICIES

Handbooks do very little to help students understand sexual harassment, nor do they help faculty and school administrators know how to respond when it occurs. Legal experts reported that schools consistently fail to adopt policies, requiring sexual harassment training for students and all school employees.[44] A vast majority of school anti-harassment policies are not in compliance with OCR.[45]

- Policies that are in place are lacking key ingredients such as what behaviors constitute sexual harassment, and how employees should respond when they observe or are made aware of incidents.
- Policies should address sexual harassment between students, between students and employees, and between employees (a school is also a workplace so schools are covered under Title VII).
- Often missing from policies are specific issues addressing teacher-student relationships and the boundaries required in these relationships.
- Policies often do not include retaliation by including a definition and providing examples of behaviors that constitute retaliation.
- Policies often use the legal definition of sexual harassment, which most adults struggle to grasp, let alone students; it should be written in easy-to-understand language.
- Policies must be written in age-appropriate language and include specific examples of sexual (and other protected class) harassment and examples of bullying for the bullying policy.
- Schools should review and revise, where appropriate and necessary, their Title IX sexual harassment and bullying policies, but often they do not do so.

Some schools combine their bullying and harassment policies, and attempt to apply sexual harassment legal standards to bullying. Or conversely, because bullying does not carry any civil rights protections, the joint bullying/sexual harassment policy is watered down with very little attention paid to the legal mandates of Title IX and sexual harassment.

Zero tolerance policies are intolerable! While the intent of implementing these policies in school is worthy, they are ineffective.[46] What exactly does *zero tolerance* mean? A teenager in Minnesota was expelled from school for having a box cutter in his car that was parked in the parking lot. He worked for a grocery store and used the box cutter at work. It wasn't brought into the school, but the school's zero tolerance policy outlawed any weapons, even in the student parking lot. His parents appealed, and, after much haggling, the school allowed him back in school. In another incident, a kindergarten boy told his female classmate that he liked her blouse and she looked nice. He was made to stand in the corner and could not attend the class outing because he was accused of violating the school's zero tolerance sexual harassment policy. A first grader pretended a breaded chicken finger was a gun, resulting in a three-day suspension for violating the district's zero tolerance policy. Even within a zero tolerance framework, these three districts applied very different standards and viewpoints as to what was meant by their zero tolerance policy. Zero tolerance does not take into consideration the need for a teachable moment—that a breach of a policy is an opportunity to teach a child or teen about sexual harassment, bullying, respect, and rules.

The previous examples demonstrated that *zero tolerance* has become an all-or-nothing effort by sanctioning students for the most mild, and sometimes innocent, violations. Fortunately, the American Bar Association agreed, and in 2001 issued a statement stating that zero tolerance policies are not a "solution for all the problems that schools confront," and are inappropriate.

Schools do not always enforce the districts' anti-discrimination policies when additional allegations of harassment (which is discrimination) are discovered during an investigation, increasing the schools risk of liability. When schools are investigating allegations of harassment, bullying, or any other inappropriate behavior, and during the course of that investigation they become aware of sexual harassment (or harassment of any other protected class), they must investigate the sexual harassment allegation to comply with Title IX. Westfield Public Schools in Massachusetts, while investigating a claim of disability discrimination, discovered what appeared to be sexual harassment of that same student, but failed to investigate. The district did not interview any witnesses to the alleged sexual harassment, and they didn't collect any other evidence required when investigating. They ignored the sexual harassment complaint. Because no investigation of the sexual harassment occurred, the school took no steps to end it and eliminate the hostile school environment, or to implement prevention strategies to minimize recurrence and to remedy the effects of the misconduct.

This chapter has discussed how schools have responded to allegations of teacher-to-student harassment and student-to-student harassment and bullying. The question is so often raised by students, parents, and the community—why don't schools intervene in connection with bullying and harassment and make it stop? Very little research has explored the question. The studies discussed here are only a beginning. More research needs to be conducted to determine why. Until the question is answered, it is difficult to make whatever necessary changes are required to change teachers' and administrators' lack of intervention.

THE CAUSES AND CONTRIBUTING FACTORS OF SEXUAL HARASSMENT

Society treats women as second class—that's why this happens. It's a symptom of a bigger problem.

—High School Female[1]

Let's face it. If a woman becomes a construction worker, she's bold and brave. But if a man stays home to cook and clean, he's a wimp.

—Heather, age fourteen, ninth grade[2]

The causes and contributing factors of bullying and sexual harassment are systemic, including sexism; sex role stereotyping; role modeling by parents, teachers, and other adults; and our sexualized and misogynist culture that daily bombards us on billboards, toothpaste ads, movies, song lyrics, and clothing. Schools support sexism, resulting in belief systems reflected in adages such as "boys will be boys" or "it is emerging adolescent sexuality." Bullying is part of our continuingly uncivil, angry, and disrespectful social mores that we read about in newspapers and on the Internet or hear about on the news.

Don McPherson, a former National Football League quarterback as well as the former executive director of Sports Leadership Institute at Adelphi University, began challenging patriarchy when he realized his silence was perpetrating violence towards women. Don said, "We make our sons better by degrading our daughters," and we don't raise boys to be men, but rather to "not be women," because to be female is to be inferior.[3] Don's insight and quote depicts the essence of what this chapter discusses—the nexus of the causes and contributing factors of bullying and sexual harassment in our schools.[4]

Sexual harassment and bullying in schools will probably never be completely eliminated, and reducing incidents of both types of misconduct will continue to be a challenge. As mentioned earlier, the schools are a reflection and representation of society, and the issues underlying bullying and sexual harassment occur in society at large. What complicates an effective approach in addressing bullying and sexual harassment that schools and society allow and sanction is that the causes and contributing factors are much broader than the school environment alone. Contributing factors, such as the media, for example, play a dual role of both contributing to and being symptomatic of *patriarchy*, the damaging unacknowledged social system that sanctions bullying and sexual harassment in our schools, and has at its core the issues of power and control.

THE ROOT CAUSE: PATRIARCHY

Patriarchy is the foundation for both bullying and sexual harassment. Patriarchy is interwoven into our population and institutions in ways that appear natural and ordinary—it is the norm.[5] We don't see it because it is invisible and we live in it. Sociologist and writer Allan Johnson says, "It finds its way into everyone who grows up breathing and swimming in it, and once inside us it remains, however unaware of it we may be."[6]

Johnson describes patriarchy as a social system that is *male-dominated*, *male-identified*, and *male-centered*. Patriarchy is a type of *society*. It is not a euphemism for a "man" and is not about "male bashing," but rather it refers to a system in which both men and women participate.

The first element of patriarchy, according to Johnson, is that it is *male-dominated*. This refers to power positions within, for example, the military, political, economic, legal, educational, and religious institutions and organizations usually reserved for men, with a token woman or two as exceptions to the rule. Male dominance is about the differences in power based on gender in which men, *collectively*, have power over women. For example, men:

- Earn larger salaries and are wealthier than women (only 5 percent of top wage earners are women[7])
- Mold our culture by, for example, determining the content of media (discussed in more detail later in the chapter)
- Pass our laws (the U.S. ranks 90th out of 186 countries worldwide in representation of women in government; 83 percent of the U.S. Congress is comprised of men;for the first time since the 1970s, the number of women in Congress is declining[8])
- Run our corporations (only 3 percent of CEOs for Fortune 500 companies are women; 15 percent of their boards are comprised of women[9])
- Comprise the majority of partners in law firms (although women are now more than half of law school students, only 18 percent of them become equity partners of law firms)[10]
- Oversee college and university boards (29 percent of board members are women)[11]

Male-identified recognizes that masculinity is the norm, and is preferable. Though it is much less prevalent now than in the past, one of the most obvious examples of this was the widespread use of the male pronoun "he" as the default gender pronoun when referring to people, lawyers, doctors, and even animals. We refer to female committee chairs as "chairman," yet see the inappropriateness of labeling a male chair as a "chairwoman." The concept of *male-identified* exceeds merely our vocabulary, however, and includes what society views as preferential, such as being tough, logical, rational, and strong and in control of one's emotions. This gets translated into the type of work that is most valued—politics, business, sports, law, and medicine. Traditionally, female work, such as day care providers, teaching, housekeeping, social work, nursing, and waiting tables, has not been valued as much as male work because female attributes, such as sharing, caring, compassion, and cooperation, are not valued as much in our society. Females are valued and rewarded for beauty and as sex objects. In a patriarchal society such as ours, powerful women are "unsexed." As sociologist Johnson states, "Power looks sexy on men, but not on women."[12] Some women, such as Margaret Thatcher and Indira Gandhi, reached positions of power; however, their country's societies still sustained patriarchy, especially through male-identification.

The third element of patriarchy is *male-centered*, which means that society's attention is focused primarily on men, their interests, and what they do.

- Research studies show, for example, that men dominate conversations by determining the topic, interrupting more, and talking more (despite the myth that women talk more than men).[13]
- Women's suggestions in meetings are often minimized or ignored unless a man makes the same comment.
- Pick up the newspaper—count the number of bylines by women compared to men, and the number of pictures of women compared to men; how many stories in the sports section feature women's athletic teams, especially on the front page?
- Look at the typical movie selections, and the number that center on violence (movies that are not the norm, for example, geared towards a female audience—are usually referred to as "chick flicks").
- When there is a crisis somewhere in the country or the world, the news stories are from a man's viewpoint and feature pictures of men.
- Women play a secondary role in movies and news stories.
- The male experience and world viewpoint is the *human* experience and world viewpoint within the patriarchal culture.

At the heart of patriarchy is the oppression of women. Oppression is a system in which certain characteristics or groups of people are the norm or privileged while others are disadvantaged. Examples of women's oppression include women's exclusion from politics, religion, and, historically, from attending a university. Oppression is obvious in the economic, political, religious, medical, and legal institutions where sexism is pervasive with unequal pay and lack of women in senior level positions in the corporate C-suite (chief executive officer, chief financial officer, chief operating officer). Yes, there have been great inroads in all of these industries and institutions, but a real substantial change has yet to occur. Extreme oppression to women is evident in misogynist behavior such as pervasive sexual violence in the form of sexual assault, rape, domestic violence, sexual harassment, and pornography.

Despite the fact that dominance and oppression comprise the foundation of patriarchy, not all men in our patriarchal culture feel dominant any more than all women feel oppressed or experience oppression equally. The dominance and oppression in a patriarchal system refers to relations between groups of people—in this case, males and females.[14] (How dominance and oppression interplay in a specific male-female relationship is another matter.) There is no female who is immune, for example, to society's devaluing of the female body as a sex object that is exploited in advertising and pornography, and the ongoing threat of sexual violence.[15]

In addition to the oppression of women, patriarchy has as its foundation heterosexuality and homophobia.[16] It is the driving force to what is meant by being a *real* man. It demands rigorous standards that few men can live up to, but from which all men benefit. Patriarchy is a belief that women don't count in important matters, and anything feminine is "less than." Patriarchy, then, also discounts males that display feminine qualities.

Patriarchy is a form of masculinity that refers to stereotypical masculine traits of logic, rationality, and strength.[17] For example, patriarchy keeps men in line when males or females express disgust with gay males or any males who don't behave as a "real man," when they express any qualities usually associated with femininity, such as compassion or caring, or if they cry. Patriarchy is our popular culture.

Males take for granted, largely unconsciously, a right of entitlement, a male privilege that is assumed, awarded, and not questioned by society. Men have learned that it is okay to make catcalls and sexual comments, and to yell obscenities, while females are expected to view the behavior as a compliment to be enjoyed because she is recognized as a sex object. One high school boy, Anthony, captured his entitlement when he said, "It's a man thing! When a girl has on something revealing, you have to say something about it or at least look at it. If the girl doesn't tell us we're sexually harassing her, we're going to continue to do it."[18] Anthony clearly places the responsibility for his ogling and comments on the girl. Patriarchy allows him to believe that he has that right, an entitlement, to look and say whatever he chooses unless she tells him otherwise. When males and females subscribe to these unhealthy sexist myths about male-female interactions, it justifies and excuses the harasser's misconduct and teaches victims to blame themselves. This perpetuates sexual harassment. Patriarchy refers to the way society's dominant group—men—establish and retain their dominance in society.[19]

Activist and author Paul Kivel's work with violent men has taught him that from very young ages boys get the message to "act like a man."[20] What does that mean? It's about patriarchy. It means that men are socialized to be in control and in power, to be strong and aggressive, not to back down and appear weak, to take charge, to be rich, and to be sexual. And, of course, males clearly get the message that acting like a man means you do not cry. But, as Kivel points out, boys experience all the usual feelings of being human yet, with the exception of anger, are told to hide those feelings. Boys love, feel vulnerable, are curious, and feel excitement and joy. They also feel sad, humiliated, lonely, confused, and experience grief and pain, but to act like a man means keeping those feelings inside. Kivel refers to this phenomenon as the "act like a man box" in which boys must fit inside 24/7 or risk being labeled with names that imply he is weak, gay, or like a girl. The name calling may lead to the threat of violence. If boy "A" approaches boy "B" and calls him a "girl" or a "queer," boy "B" will have to punch "A" in the face to prove he most definitely is within the "act like a man box."

For boys, the fear of being labeled gay begins young. The fear causes boys to police their own and their friends' behavior so they stay in the "act like a man box."[21] Bullying, ridiculing, and classmate intimidation work as a type of discipline for boys to act in accordance with masculinity. This type of violence also functions as a form of male bonding to create male privilege.[22] On the other extreme, the violence towards boys who do not meet the tradition of masculinity may evolve into murder, an extravagant and outrageous display of violence to ensure gender conformity.

Oppression and Misogyny

Bob Herbert, a *New York Times* columnist, wrote a powerful article on the normalization of misogyny or female hating. He said, "We've become so used to the disrespectful, degrading, contemptuous and even violent treatment of women that we hardly notice it. Staggering amounts of violence are unleashed against women and girls every day. Fashionable ads in mainstream publications play off that violence, exploiting themes of death and dismemberment, female submissiveness and child pornography."[23]

Our popular culture is blatantly misogynist in, among other things, touting sexual aggression in anything from the lyrics of rap music to the TV show *America's Next Top Model*, where models are made to appear beaten and bruised to compete in a "beautiful corpses" photo shoot.[24]

Misogyny often leads to sexual or gender violence as a reflection of gender inequality in U.S. culture.[25] A tapestry of gender violence originates in the imbalance of power between the genders in a gendered hierarchy of socially accepted views of what constitutes masculine and feminine behavior.[26] This book addresses violence related to masculinity and femininity; however, it cannot be divorced from the complexity of the relationship among gender, race, and class. When society complies with stereotypical gendered behavior, it sustains a culture of power and privilege—the core of gendered violence.[27]

- According to the Center for Disease Control and Prevention (CDC), two of the key risk factors for perpetrating sexual violence include being male and being exposed to social norms that support sexual violence.[28]
- Violence is built into the foundation of masculinity in the United States, according to research.[29]
- The power and privilege that come from patriarchy are the driving force behind gendered violence that targets females and non-gender conforming males.[30]
- One in five high school girls has been assaulted or sexually abused by her boyfriend, according to the U.S. Bar Association.[31]

- "If she does something to provoke you, then you have to put her in her place," said a high school boy. Girls also believe that violence is normal and even justifiable in dating relationships.[32]

VIOLENCE AND GENDER VIOLENCE: ELEMENTS OF PATRIARCHY

As Americans, we tend to hold a nebulous viewpoint on violence. We cheer vehemently when hockey players end up fighting on the ice, and we've become complacent to rape and murder because they are not uncommon. Violence is used to precipitate laughter in children's cartoons, and in some forms of comedy. Boys and men, particularly young men, are the most likely victims and perpetrators of violence.

Females are often exploited, abused, and harmed. Both girls and women are sold into sex trafficking, raped, and murdered—crimes motivated by gender and sexuality.[33] Most violence between males and females is sexual in nature, such as harassment, assault, and rape. Sexual and gender-based harassment in schools is rife, and boys either engage in it or comply with it.[34] Numerous research studies have shown that males who are violent towards females tend to endorse traditional and patriarchal views of male power, stereotypical gender roles, male supremacy, and misogyny.

CONTRIBUTING FACTORS

We can make ourselves look better, from being not very good looking to great looking with the help of make-up and perms. Then, after we look great, we usually don't have to pay for the date.

—Jessie, age eleven, grade six[35]

I would rather be a woman because the best thing about a woman is her looks. It's her long, shiny, gorgeous hair. Her lovely eyes. The worst thing about a woman is when you grow old you lose your beauty.

—Diana, age nine, fourth grade[36]

Sexualization of Girls

The American Psychological Association's (APA) research report entitled *The Sexualization of Girls* exposed how sexual images and messages influence girls' self-image as nothing more than objects of desire.[37] Girls, then, evaluate themselves under these unhealthy gender norms. Alarmingly, the report describes how parents, teachers, and other adults unknowingly buy into the sexualization when they favor girls who are physically attractive and, therefore, unconsciously perpetuate the sexualization. Over time, the sexualized standard for girls has become the frame for understanding girls' sexuality. Once we become aware of the standard in our everyday environment, it is an Aha! moment and we can see it everywhere. At the same time, it is invisible because it has become the unchallenged and widespread norm. Consider the following examples from the APA report and studies discussed in the books *The Lolita Effect* and *So Sexy So Soon*, which demonstrate that sexualized childhood begins in early childhood:

- Five-year-olds can now buy their "first make-up kit."
- Girls as young as seven are dissatisfied with their body, which is leading to depression, eating disorders, and low self-esteem.
- High heels are available for three-year-old girls and padded bikinis for seven-year-olds.
- *Toddlers and Tiaras* television show features nearly one hundred girls (though recently a two-week-old baby boy competed) who compete for the title of "Ultimate Grand Supreme" and $1000. Dresses can cost $3000, and one family spent $70,000 on such things as fake hair, photos, and fake tans.[38]
- In the pageants, girls as young as five wear fake teeth, make-up, and hair extensions, and they are encouraged to flirt with the audience by batting their false eyelashes. The pageants make little girls into sexualized "women." Compare the irony when, in the 2005

Victoria's Secret fashion show, adult women were made up to resemble sexy young girls.

- 43 percent of six- to nine-year-old girls are using lipstick or lip
  gloss; 38 percent use hairstyling products; and 12 percent use
  other cosmetics. According to a *Newsweek* examination of common
  beauty product purchases, by the time a ten-year old girl is fifty,
  she will have spent nearly $300,000 on her hair and face.[39]
- Halloween costumes for girls include halter tops, bare midriffs, and
  miniskirts. Skimpy costumes are aimed at six- and seven-year-old
  girls. A firefighter costume included fishnet stockings, and Little
  Bo Peep's costume was complete with a corset and a short skirt.
- Girls' fashions are sexy, risqué, and mature in contrast to boys'
  baggy jeans and oversized T-shirts that keep their bodies covered.
- *Cosmopolitan*, a magazine for young women, and *Maxim,* a magazine for men, both exploit women's half-naked bodies.
- Dolls aimed at preschoolers, including Bratz dolls, Barbie, and
  others more risqué, are sometimes half-dressed representations of
  women in music videos and soft-porn magazines; children and pre-
  teens' fashions are indistinguishable from those of adult women.
- Fashions for children perpetuate their sexualization and victimization. For example, toddler boys' T-shirt slogans read "Pimp squad,"
  "I'm a boob man," and "chick magnet," while a little girl's T-shirt
  reads "scratch and sniff." These fashions, toys, and other products
  illustrate the normalization of sexualizing children as cute and sexy
- Little girls can buy play makeup and pedicure sets, and invite their
  friends to spa treatment birthday parties that include makeup, nail
  polish, and hair styling, while they are taught to pose and strut like
  a model.
- Between 2003 and 2004, there was a three-fold increase in girls
  under eighteen getting breast implants.[40]
- Approximately two million children, primarily girls, are victims
  of prostitution and sex trafficking.[41] Nine-year-old girls are now
  becoming involved in prostitution.[42] One in three girls and one in
  seven boys are sexually abused during childhood.[43]
- Abercrombie and Fitch marketed thong underwear for ten-year-
  old girls with slogans that read "wink wink" or "eye candy." One
  of the most disgusting marketing ploys involved Wal-Mart selling

tween and teen panties that read, "Who needs a credit card . . . ?" on the crotch. Not to be outdone by Wal-Mart, a toy manufacturer, Tesco, sold a pink "Peekaboo Pole Dancing" kit including a small garter and toy money.[44] A British chain, BHS, sexualized tweens when it launched a line of "Little Miss Naughty" underwear, including push-up bras and lacy panties.[45]

- Preschool teachers have observed toddlers humping each other; youth and teens are performing oral sex on school buses; teens sponsor "rainbow" parties in which the girls wear different colors of lipstick and perform oral sex on boys. The boys' goal is to get a rainbow of colors on their penis. Teen sex in the United States begins at age eleven.[46]

- Teen girls see their role as a sexual service provider to boys, using oral sex to sexually pleasure the boys, with little or any pleasure or emotional fulfillment in return.[47]

- A 2005 *Boston Globe* news story declared "Bombarded by sexualized cultural forces, girls are growing up faster than ever."[48]

Child and adolescent psychiatrist Dr. Karen Brooks described the role adult consumers play in the sexualization of girls:

> By gazing at these images, adult consumers are forced to engage in cultural pedophilia, that is, to view under-age girls and boys as sexualized objects whether we want to or not. Our consumption of these images is often passive and uncritical; we're not even aware we're doing it. But instead of remaining in the realm of visual fiction, these images creep into our everyday language, behavior and dress codes of our children who, desperate to grow up, see them as blueprints for their identity."[49]

Boys

The sexualization of girls also harms boys. The APA report and the books *So Sexy So Soon* and *The Lolita Effect* provide the following examples of the harm to boys:[50]

- Society's messages define masculinity narrowly by telling boys that machismo and insensitivity is manly.
- Boys are taught to use violence as a form of problem solving.

- Boys are deluged with messages that teach them to define femininity based on false appearances of women as shown in advertisements and movies.
- Sexualization tells boys to want and expect sex from girls.
- Boys and girls learn that sex is often coupled with violence.
- Boys' toys such as toy guns, Transformers, Mighty Morphin Power Rangers, and boys' heroes including Batman and Spiderman, along with video games, cartoons, and even toys in children's fast food meals, support and normalize violence.
- The violent messages create obstacles for boys to develop into caring people capable of healthy and connected intimate relationships.
- Boys also receive harmful messages about themselves, girls, and relationships.
- Boys might lack empathy with females.
- Boys learn that it is best to repress their feelings.
- Boys learn to rely only on themselves and not others.
- Men who treat woman badly are often portrayed as heroes in the media.
- To create healthier boys, they need permission and encouragement to redefine masculinity to include warmth, nurturing, and compassion.

School Culture

The school, alongside the family, is an environment in which children learn about gender and gender relations that are built on socially approved inequalities.[51] When girls hear sexist and derogatory comments aimed at a boy with female characteristics, it both strengthens masculinity and devalues femininity. The comments challenge a boy's masculinity by explicitly or implicitly attacking a feminine characteristic of the targeted boy. The comments devalue girls when the female characteristic is used to discredit boys.[52] Girls at school are within a social culture of violence towards girls—just because they are girls. Therefore, attending school in an environment in which abusive behavior flourishes and goes unabated reinforces girls' vulnerable position in society, as well as in their school environment. This context should not be ignored in viewing the bullying and harassing behavior in schools.

Schools implicitly support patriarchy. They do so by allowing male entitlement, bullying, and sexual harassment, enforcing traditional masculinity regarding GLBT students. When sexism and sexist systems are not challenged, as in the school environment, then day-to-day practices are invisible and accepted, thereby reproducing inequality and patriarchy.

Most schools approach bullying programs from a psychological perspective, by focusing on the personal and interpersonal dynamic rather than on system(s).[53] They may examine the family system, or the peer group, or the media, but often don't examine the school system's role in bullying and sexual harassment as forms of violence. Violence is embedded within the fabric of the school's culture and power relationships, and is, therefore, sometimes subtle.[54]

Students should be active agents of reform of the system rather than merely passive recipients of it.[55] Schools are structured around the power of adults over children/teens, where the needs of the organization are dependent on controlling the students; therefore the organization's and the teachers' needs are more important than a student's.

Sexism is such an intimate element of the school's culture that it is not recognized. Take, for example, the research done on gender bias in the classroom. Teachers do not purposely treat girls and boys differently. They usually are not aware that they do so unless they can view a recording of themselves using specific gender bias criteria in their interactions with students. Numerous studies suggest a disparity exists between boys' and girls' treatment in the classroom, such as the following:[56]

- Boys receive more attention.
- Boys are called on more frequently.
- Boys are encouraged to come up with the right answer if the first answer is incorrect, in ways that girls are not.
- Boys learn that girls aren't as important as boys.
- More money may be spent on boys' sports than on girls' sports.
- Boys hockey gets the better ice time than girls hockey.
- Teachers segregate the sexes for games and exercises.
- History books leave out women's contributions.
- Girls are expected to speak quietly and raise their hands.
- Boys yell out their answers.

- Girls are taught to defer to boys.
- Girls are not as likely to be directed towards math and science as their male peers.
- Girls are praised for neatness and appearance over innovation and intelligence.

These differences in behavior are invisible, and well-meaning teachers are unaware of their sexist behavior.

When we think of the school climate, what words come to mind? Safety? Dignity? Equality? Respect? Inclusion? Does the image of the school as a warm and nurturing environment percolate into your mind? Are the behaviors that are allowed to flourish within the school environment acceptable in the workplace? The school is often not a safe haven for students. When we are at work, we have a choice—we can always quit if we don't like our employer. Children, however, are stuck. The law requires that they attend school; but many of the behaviors they experience as a victim and a witness would be illegal or considered grounds for termination in the workplace. Why do we allow this pervasive hostile environment to encompass our children's daily lives at school?

How may schools inadvertently support a school culture that allows bullying and harassment by not examining the misconduct from a systems perspective? Let's face it: words like equality, inclusion, and even dignity are not words characteristically used to define the school system.[57] One quality of a system is to maintain balance through obvious and hidden rules and norms.[58] A system will even seek to maintain a hostile environment if it has become what people within the system are acclimated to. Therefore, to effectively address bullying and harassment, individuals within the system must be actively committed and involved since they are part of the system.

School systems are gendered and sexual. Different schools allow different sexual behaviors to occur in their hallways and at school events. Some schools do not intervene when students are "making out" in the hallways, and some allow more sexual behavior at their school dances. On the other hand, other schools have canceled dances because of the sexualized behavior such as lap dances; "sandwich" dances, where a girl dances between two boys who are pressing against her; or "freaking," in which a boy and girl simulate sex by grinding against each other. A Minnesota school district distributed a memo to students and parents outlining the following unacceptable behavior for an upcoming dance:

- Inappropriate dancing will not be tolerated.
- No dancing that is simulating sexual activity.
- No dancing where either partner is not standing upright.
- Any clothing that is overly revealing will not be allowed . . . may include very short dresses or skirts, or tops that are cut too low (No rules were specific to boys' clothing).

How come students would think that type of sexual behavior would be acceptable in school? What brought them to this point?

The Media

Research shows that media shapes our society rather than merely reflect it.[59] The images and messages about sex and sexuality that children are exposed to at earlier ages are harmful, and many children are confused and frightened.[60] Exposure to sexual lyrics, pictures, fashion, and role models caused girls to think of and treat their own bodies as sex objects, according to one study.[61] This narrow sex object definition of femininity and sexuality encourages girls to focus heavily on appearance and sex appeal. At a young age, girls learn that their value is determined by how attractive and "hot" they are.[62] All they have to do is walk past a Victoria's Secret store in a mall, and bigger-than-life posters of pouty, semi-nude, soft-porn underwear models scream a sexualized value of women.

The *Handbook of Children, Culture, and Violence* discussed the effects of violent television programs and the increase in children's aggression.[63] One study showed that, if an individual is already angry, aggressive media stimulates that person to act on their anger using aggression.[64] Another study discovered that, if a child had been exposed to violence, say at home or in the streets or via the media, the child would be more likely to use aggression as a mode of problem solving.

The American child spends less time in school than time spent watching television. It is estimated that, by the time a child is eighteen years-old, she or he will have seen 16,000 TV murders and 200,000 episodes of TV violence.[65]

- Violence is more prevalent in children's television programming than in any other category.[66]
- Exposure to media violence increases aggression in children, causes them to become desensitized to violence, and creates fear.[67]
- Slasher films associate violence and sex; girls are victimized and it is linked to their sexuality; males are linked with sadism.[68]
- More than 80 percent of TV shows aimed at teenagers contain sexual content.[69] Because comprehensive sex education is generally not taught in our schools, children use media to learn about sex, and often do not ask their parents questions.
- Eleven- to eighteen-year-old girls and boys who frequently watched TV and were exposed to R- and X-rated movies were more likely to accept sexual harassment.[70]
- The average teenager watches a minimum of two thousand sexual acts per year on TV.[71]
- Girls who have watched sexual movies are more likely to engage in sex.[72]

Popular magazines such as *Cosmopolitan* tell girls how to be beautiful, sexy, and to appeal to boys, while *Maxim*, *Playboy*, and *Sports Illustrated Swimsuit Edition* condition boys to expect girls to be sexy and want sex. The Internet allows easy accessibility to pornography. Twelve percent of websites are pornographic, and 25 percent of search engine requests are for pornography.[73] Many radio DJs devalue and degrade women with an audience that views the degradation as entertainment and humor.

Less is known about the effects of violent music and music videos, although a few studies found that it taught children aggressive behaviors:[74]

- Teens who listen to heavy metal or gangsta rap, where lyrics are particularly violent against women, learn that violence against women is acceptable.
- These teens were also much less likely to trust people compared to teens who listen to other categories of music.

- Additionally, they were more likely to have been suspended or expelled from school for misconduct, as well as to have been arrested.
- Lyrics such as "that's the way you like to fuck . . . rough sex make it hurt" and "I tell the hos all the time, bitch get in my car" link sexual violence to females.
- 93 percent of music videos have references to sex.[75]

Video

Video games contain violence specifically geared towards children, and have been shown to increase aggression in children. The average child, predominantly boys, plays ninety minutes of video games every day. The games cater to gender stereotypical roles and victimize women and specifically Black women.

One of the most widely sold video games is *Grand Theft Auto*, played by millions of teen boys (and men). A description of the game reads, "You can pick up a hooker, take her out in the woods, have sex with her many times, then let her out of the car. Then you can shoot her, pull over, beat her with a bat, then you can get into the car and run over her."[76] The game is renowned around the world and has sold well over 65 million copies in the United States.[77] Another popular video game that hypersexualizes women within the tapestry of violence is *Manhunt*, which features a sex club with a torture chamber, and depicts women as strippers, streetwalkers, and sluts.[78]

Mainstream movies do little to demonstrate healthy or male sexuality. Consider the following:[79]

- Females are shown in sexual attire more often than males (24 percent compared to 4 percent of men), and are also portrayed as younger, than their male counterparts.
- In crowd scenes, only 17 percent are women.
- Only 17 percent of narrators are women.
- Only 29 percent of speaking characters are female (and 80 percent are White).
- Only 7 percent of directors, 13 percent of writers, and 20 percent of producers are female.

Children as Victims and Perpetrators

The 2009 Children's Defense Fund study found that, on a daily basis, 2,175 children are *confirmed* as abused or neglected. Think how many more were victimized and it wasn't reported.[80] Additionally, 4,435 children are arrested, and 18,493 suspended from school. Hispanic and Black children comprise the majority of both perpetrators and victims. Nine children are murdered and an additional twenty are victimized by guns. Street violence, gang violence, and drive-by shootings are commonplace for some children. America's homicide rate for fifteen- to twenty-four-year-old males is the highest in the industrial world.[81] Children are victimized by child abuse, sibling abuse, and witnessing domestic abuse. These children often become adult perpetrators, repeating the cycle in which they grew up. The U.S. Department of Health and Human Services estimated that approximately one million children are abused by their parents and guardians every year and even more are neglected.

As a country, we don't do enough to protect and honor our children. Children are more at risk for violence than any other age group. What does that say about us as adults and as a society? Some groups of children are more at risk than others. Females are at more risk for sexual offenses; however, for most other types of offenses, males are more at risk. Black children are more at risk for homicide, abuse, neglect, assault, and robbery. They also watch more TV and therefore see more violence.[82]

Children are more and more likely to be the perpetrators of violence:[83] Twenty to 25 percent of crime is committed by twelve- to seventeen-year-olds. Children, including those under the age of twelve and primarily boys, sexually assault other children. According to the Federal Bureau of Investigation, 4,600 juveniles, the majority male, were arrested for rape and 18,000 children, again primarily male, were responsible for other sexual violations. This accounted for approximately 20 percent of arrests in sexual offenses and rape. A very strong link exists between those who were offenders and those who are victimized, often by family members and specifically their fathers.[84]

Empathy

Educators, psychologists, and neuroscientists increasingly see empathy as pivotal in reducing bullying and other forms of violence.[85] Empathy ensures a trusting society and spurs most of us to think of others over our own self-interests, at least some of the time. Absent empathy, we would be a community of sociopaths with no moral conscious to guide us. Over the past decade, research has suggested that empathy may be *the* essence to all human social interaction and morality.

Empathy appears to be an inherent element of being human and is evident soon after birth.[86] A baby will cry when it hears another baby cry, and, without being asked, a one-year-old will attempt to help an adult who is trying to reach something.

History shows that in ancient cultures, such as Sparta, middle class boys as young as seven were sent to camp to become warriors.[87] Their teachers used atrocious and vicious techniques to harden them into killers. In contrast, boys in Athens were nurtured by their mothers and nurses and educated in the arts and culture to be molded into future leaders. These lessons are from not only ancient times; children raised in abusive and neglectful homes are at an increased risk of being abusive and aggressive themselves, sometimes becoming psychopaths or sociopaths. They've learned that they cannot trust others, they feel vulnerable, and as a result they are unable to empathize with others. Many bullies do not demonstrate empathy after they have bullied, they seem unaffected by how their perpetration negatively impacted their victim.[88]

DISNEY—SHAME ON YOU!

> *I would rather be a woman because you get to have babies. You get to wear makeup. You could even marry a prince.*
>
> —Christen, age eight, third grade[89]

Sexualization of childhood, especially girls, is a public health issue controlled by large transnational mega-corporations such as *Disney*. Disney is willing to exploit children too young to understand, in their drive for profit.[90] All the Disney princesses, including Cinderella, Snow White, Ariel, and Jasmine, have bodies representing a *Sports Illustrated* swimsuit edition model—long shapely legs, large breasts, and beautifully proportioned. Even little Minnie Mouse is becoming sexualized.

Minnie Mouse, one of the icons of Disneyland, needed a boost in sales. After years of children growing up with Minnie Mouse as a cute little girl mouse, Disney decided she needed a make-over. The new Minnie, no longer the innocent little girl, now has become glamorous with long legs. She had been an icon associated with the innocence of toddlerhood, but the new Minnie seems to have succumbed to the popular culture of sexuality.[91]

Despite complaints, Disney's *Pirates of the Caribbean* continues to engage children and adults in observing the sex trafficking of girls and women.[92] As forty thousand of Disney's daily guests float through the popular attraction, they are exposed to the scene of a pirate selling kidnapped women complete with a banner that reads, "Auction: Take a wench as a bride!" As cheerful, lively music plays in the background, the guests witness a disturbing scene of a women being sold into sexual slavery. The scene includes a woman with her breasts partially exposed, loud catcalls and yells from the encircling drunken pirates, and several women roped together, including a crying teenager. Disney's *Pirates* dismisses a grievous gendered crime, sex trafficking, by attempting to normalize it with humor.

According to Disney executives, the film *The Princess and the Frog*, one of the last princess movies, was just that, one of the last. Why? Because not enough boys want to see princess movies.[93] On the one hand, it is nice to know that no more movies will be made of distressed damsels who will be kissed by a prince and live in a castle. On the other hand, with females more than half the population, fewer than half the movies are made with them in mind. So, like adult women, little girls will now have to watch "boy" movies with male heroes, even though boys won't watch "chick flicks" with girl heroes. Disney decided that little girls were not a big enough audience to cater too. In fact, they changed the name of the fairy tale *Rapunzel* to *Tangled* when they made their very last princess movie, hoping that the more gender-neutral title would have more appeal to boys, according to the *Los Angeles Times*. I wonder what would happen if Disney quit making movies that appeal to boys? Or, a novel idea—make movies that appeal to both genders and where both genders are heroes.

Parents and members of society need to be aware of how pervasive the hidden sexual messages are to even our youngest. Modeling positive gender roles at home, minimizing exposure to videos, and selecting movies with healthy depictions of females and males are critical. Parents must be ever vigilant to teach their daughters and sons about healthy male-female relationships. With the media and general entertainment such as movies, games, toys, and theme parks undermining healthy sexuality and healthy sexual relationships, parental oversight and control has never been more important.

The school's culture, where children spend much of their childhood, is a collection of society's ideologies, politics, biases, and values. These prejudices divide youth along gender (and race, class, and religion) lines and create a toxic school environment. Couple these issues with poor school leadership and inadequate prevention and intervention strategies, and the misconduct continues to fester and infect our children. Sexual harassment and bullying are an adoptive response to the patriarchal system of our schools. Where is the outrage? Where are the objections?

ADDITIONAL LAWS

To make laws that man cannot, and will not obey, serves to bring all laws into contempt.

—Elizabeth Cady Stanton[1]

This book focuses on Title IX of the Education Amendments of 1972 which prohibits discrimination based on sex. The U.S. Department of Education, Office of Civil Rights (OCR), however, enforces a number of other laws such as Title VI of the Civil Rights Act of 1964, which prohibits discrimination based on race, color, and national origin, and Section 504 of the Rehabilitation Act of 1973 and Title II of the Americans with Disabilities Act of 1990, which prohibit discrimination based on disability. Just as sex discrimination may be protected under state and municipal laws as well as federal laws, the same is true of discrimination of other protected classes. It is a given, however, that, even if student misconduct and bullying are not a violation of civil rights laws, schools still have an obligation to investigate and protect students from any harm, as well as implement prevention strategies to minimize the continued misconduct.

Many parents contact me asking about their children's rights when they believe their daughter or son is being harassed. The contact generally

comes after attempts to work with school officials to stop the harassment or bullying have failed, and their child's victimization continues.
Often parents are unaware of steps they can take (see chapter 12) to hold
schools accountable for not stopping the sexual harassment as required
by Title IX. Sometimes, the behavior they describe constitutes what we
behaviorally think of as sexual harassment, but it has not risen to the level
of *illegal* harassment. In other words, it is not yet severe, pervasive, persistent, and offensive enough to violate the law. Sometimes parents call
because they want to file a charge with "someone" and they don't know
what agencies can help them. And, occasionally, parents call because they
want to file a lawsuit and don't know where to begin.

I believe, whenever possible, it is better to work with the school to
make the behavior stop. That is really what most parents and children
want. If that is ineffective, then I recommend they contact their state's
human rights department or the OCR and file a formal complaint of sex
discrimination. That is not the same thing as filing a lawsuit; in fact, it
will hopefully prevent filing a lawsuit. Lawsuits are expensive, lengthy,
and messy and often re-victimize the student victim.

For those parents and other youth advocates who are filing a lawsuit
and working with attorneys, this chapter, along with chapter 1, is for
you. When attorneys file a lawsuit, often numerous laws are included
within the lawsuit, many are discussed in this chapter. Because I am not
an attorney, but because I do expert witness consulting and am familiar
with the laws, the information is provided in non-legalese language to
make it easier to understand and to help you when working with an
attorney. To ensure my accuracy in the chapter, it was reviewed by an
attorney knowledgeable in these laws. When legal terms are used, their
definition is usually included here or in the glossary.

CIVIL RIGHTS ACT TITLE VII

Title VII of the 1964 Civil Rights Act prohibits employer discrimination
and harassment against individuals based on their race, color, religion,
national origin, and sex.[2] The Equal Employment Opportunity Commission (EEOC), a federal agency whose task is to oversee enforcement
of the Civil Rights Act, Title VII, defines sexual harassment as follows:[3]

Unwelcome sexual advances, requests for sexual favors, and other verbal or physical conduct of a sexual nature constitutes sexual harassment when (1) submission to such conduct is made either explicitly or implicitly a term or condition of an individual's employment, (2) submission to or rejection of such conduct by an individual is used as the basis for employment decisions affecting such individuals, or (3) such conduct has the purpose or effect of unreasonably interfering with an individual's work performance or creating an intimidating, hostile, or offensive work environment.

The first two examples of the EEOC's definition have historically been referred to as *quid pro quo* harassment—a Latin term meaning "this for that"—and always involves a person in positional power over the target of the harassment. The third example is commonly called the *hostile environment* segment of the law. In a hostile environment incident of harassment, the harasser may be a co-worker, vendor, client, patient, student, physician, or one's supervisor.

Title IX lawsuits may rely on Title VII case law, if pertinent, when deciding a case. For example, to determine whether same-sex harassment was unlawful in the Title IX lawsuit of *Theno v. Tonganoxie Unified School District*,[4] the court used *Price Waterhouse v. Hopkins*,[5] a Title VII lawsuit that determined that gender stereotyping was illegal under Title VII, even though sexual orientation sexual harassment is not recognized under Title VII. In *Price Waterhouse v. Hopkins*, the court acknowledged that the victim was harassed because she failed to live up to her peers' idea of femininity.

TITLE 42 OF THE U.S. CODE, SECTION 1983

When students sue their school districts under Title IX, they may also sue using 42 U.S.C. Section 1983, known as Section 1983.[6] Section 1983 allows students the opportunity to sue not only the school district but also to sue specific individuals such as teachers and school administrators for punitive damages for equal protection violations of the Fourteenth Amendment (which guarantees the rights to life, liberty, and property for all citizens). Section 1983 carries a higher standard than Title IX in that it requires the student, as a plaintiff, to demonstrate that it was a "custom or policy" of the district to deny the student the right to be free of harassment. In contrast, Title IX only requires evidence that the harassment took place and the district knew of the harassment, and was deliberately indifferent to the complaint.[7]

Section 1983 bars anyone acting "under color of state law" (which means a local, state, or national government official such as school officials and school boards) from denying citizens (students) their constitutional rights and privileges (such as the civil right of non-discrimination/harassment). Essentially it protects students against a violation of their rights under the U.S. Constitution. Section 1983 in the following ways:

- It provides students (citizens) who were deprived of these rights (civil rights), the right to redress (both monetary and non-monetary compensation; to seek relief from the court).
- It allows the student/plaintiff to seek injunctive relief (a court order that requires a school to do, or refrain from doing, a specific activity, for example to begin training students in sexual harassment).
- The right to pursue compensatory damages (money awarded to the student for pain and suffering and medical treatment), punitive damages (money awarded to the student that is intended to punish the school and deter other schools from engaging in similar misconduct; the school's misconduct must be malicious or show reckless disregard for the student's rights), costs of litigation, and reasonable attorney's fees are allowed.

For a school district to be in violation of Section 1983, it would have to show that the "harm" (physical or emotional) done to the student was due to an action by the school board or its agent, such as a teacher or administrator. School officials will often declare that they have "qualified immunity" (protection of school officials from being sued for damages unless they violated clearly established law that a reasonable school official should have known) from liability because the school official may not have understood that, for example, sexual harassment of the student was illegal. The student/plaintiff must be able to show that any "reasonable" school official would have known that sexual harassment violated the law in order to overcome qualified immunity.[8]

Additionally, under Section 1983, school districts can be held liable for their failure to receive, investigate, and act on complaints of conduct violating a student's constitutional rights, such as sexual harassment, and for failing to train its employees in the prevention of and intervention in the misconduct.[9] Students may sue school districts under both Title IX and Section 1983. While both Title IX and Section 1983 allow students to sue schools for discrimination, only Section 1983 allows students to sue specific individuals within the school. Some courts have ruled that Section 1983 requires a less strict standard regarding "actual knowledge" and "deliberate indifference" by school officials.

If a student sues under Title IX, the student must demonstrate that a school official, who has authority to correct a harasser's conduct, responded with deliberate indifference. In contrast, if a student sues under Section 1983 alleging a violation of the Equal Protection Clause, the student must demonstrate that the harassment was the result of a school custom, policy, or practice.[10] An example includes the case of a gay student who successfully sued his school district for sex and sexual orientation discrimination using Section 1983 to enforce the Equal Protection Clause. The district failed to protect this student from harassment to the same degree it protected other students from harassment.

When the Fourteenth Amendment was written, it did not provide protections to citizens from government/public organizations, so Section 1983 was enacted to provide those protections. Section 1983 can only, then, be used to sue public institutions and public officials.

There is also a constitutional right of "familial association" (the right of a family member to the companionship of another family member), which is a right protected under the Fourteenth Amendment's guarantee of liberty. The government, in this case a public school, cannot interfere with family relationships. Schools must be knowledgeable of this right, and know how to deal with complaints of sexual harassment of a student when it may interfere with the familial relationship. If the school fails to respond to complaints of this right, they may risk liability for violating due process rights by demonstrating deliberate indifference and therefore liability under Section 1983.[11]

When Bill Dickenson sexually abused John Doe, the family sued Dickenson, a resource officer who ran the after-school program at their son John's elementary school, for a violation of John's rights under Section 1983. Jane Doe's fear was that the psychological damage from her son's molestation would impair John's chances of ever being normal. She was in such deep pain as a result of her son's victimization that it interfered with the normal mother-son relationship.

Dickenson disagreed, arguing that the damage done to the mother-son relationship was not permanent, and therefore it was not a valid claim. It was unknown how long John's psychological damage would last; therefore, the court disagreed with Dickenson, saying that the damage could end up being permanent. Even if the damage ended up being temporary and partial, it was still a valid claim, according to the court, because it was more about the severity of harm to Jane Doe for the loss of her relationship with her son, and the damage it caused.[12]

To successfully claim that a school violated a student's constitutional right to be free of bodily and emotional harm under the protections against due process violations under Section 1983, the student must show that (1) there was a continuing and widespread persistent pattern of the misconduct (sexual/gender harassment); (2) the school's policymaking officials (such as the school board or the superintendent) were deliberately indifferent to, or tacitly authorized, the misconduct once they were informed it occurred; and (3) that the student was injured by acts "pursuant to the school's custom" (that were the school's custom).[13]

To receive a monetary award, a student/plaintiff must show that an administrator, teacher, or employee violated a constitutionally protected right (such as a violation of civil rights/sexual harassment or equal protection) while engaged in following school policy or practice, or usual school customs.[14] If Section 1983 is violated, punishment may be more severe. Punitive damages are intended to punish intentional misconduct or inaction that exceeds negligence. Monetary damages are used to set an example to other schools in hopes of discouraging them from allowing sexual harassment.

HAZING

Hazing refers to a group's intentional abusive misconduct towards someone who is hoping or expecting to join the group (or to maintain full status in a group) that humiliates, degrades, or risks emotional and/ or physical harm, regardless of the person's willingness to participate.[15] It is often sexual, and used as an initiation tool into a group, sports team, gang, or clique.

Criminal sexual assault and sexual harassment share some commonalities with hazing. The following examples support the overlap in the misconduct. The first is a New Mexico incident in which students were charged with criminal sexual penetration and conspiracy to commit criminal sexual penetration with a broomstick.[16] Another case occurred at a football camp when older players inserted a bicycle air pump into a student's rectum and activated it several times. The school is being sued under Title IX.

Sexual assault is frequently the hazing activity of choice as demonstrated in the two examples. When males haze other males, the victim is often anally penetrated by various objects as well as by penises. The rape denotes dominance and supports hegemonic masculinity. The male victim is forced into the role of a passive, submissive, and weak male, forcing him to feel powerless to the alpha males.[17] Female groups also may use sexual misconduct as a form of hazing, such as forcing girls to kiss strangers. Both male and female students may be involved in hazing, but male students are at higher risk.

QUALIFIED IMMUNITY

The Supreme Court concluded that school board members and employees should be allowed a safety net, of sorts (qualified immunity), from being sued for behavior they engaged in while performing their role, if it was in good faith and "within the bounds of reason."[18] The Court believed that to err is human, and that it is better to risk an error and potential injury than to not decide at all. The Court assumed that school officials would not behave with disregard, and would be aware at all times of their role in student supervision. However, the school board, for example, is not immune from acts that are in violation of Section 1983 where the board should have known about the rights of the student, and acted in violation of the student's rights.

In other words, qualified immunity under Section 1983 protects government officials (school employees) from liability/civil damages unless they were plainly incompetent, or knowingly violated the law. To determine if an official is entitled to qualified immunity, the court (1) must identify the specific right (such as civil rights/harassment) that was violated, (2) determine whether the right was clearly established, and (3) determine whether a reasonable school official could have believed that his or her conduct was lawful.[19]

Additional laws may be applied to sexual harassment including laws relating to the following: sexual abuse; stalking (which can also be applied to stalking online); hate crimes; sexual assault; child pornography (see cyberbullying/harassment chapter); indecent exposure; and various tort laws dealing with, for example, negligence in hiring, negligent supervision, and intentional infliction of emotional harm.

FAMILY EDUCATIONAL RIGHTS AND PRIVACY ACT (FERPA)

Parents often want the school to provide information about other students involved in the incident. Most often the school is unable to provide information due to restrictions by both federal and some state laws. FERPA is a federal law that protects the privacy of students' education records in schools that receive federal funding.[20] All public schools, and many private schools, receive federal funding. FERPA requires that schools have written consent from a student's parents before discussing any student's personal information contained in the student's educational records with few exceptions. One exception is in the case of an emergency to protect the health or safety of students or others. FERPA does, however, allow school officials to disclose student information if a school official has personal knowledge or has observed behavior independent of what is in a written record. Another exception is if a student transfers to another school; the previous school district may disclose the student's records without student or parental consent, including information about discipline.

School districts are generally prohibited from releasing information revealing any discipline taken against students who sexually harassed other students except if the discipline directly affects another student, such as mandating that the harasser not have contact with the target.

Included in FERPA is an exception to conform to the Clery Act Amendments that requires that schools inform both the victim and the perpetrator of the outcome of any school disciplinary hearing concerning a non-forcible sexual offense. In this case, the school cannot require the victim to not discuss the outcome with others.

FIRST AMENDMENT—FREEDOM OF SPEECH/ INTERNET ISSUES

The First Amendment to the U.S. Constitution guarantees freedom of speech. There are court-created exceptions, however. In 1969, in *Tinker v. Des Moines Independent Community School District*,[21] the court determined that freedom of speech is not a protected right of a student whose behavior is significantly disruptive both in and out of class or "involves substantial disorder or invasion of the rights of others" (the Tinker standard). The *Tinker* standard arose when five students were suspended for expressing their political views by wearing black armbands to protest the Vietnam war and the death of young soldiers and to express their desire for a truce.

In *Fraser v. Bethel School District*,[22] in 1986, the U.S. Supreme Court found that "Schools . . . may determine that the essential lessons of civil, mature conduct cannot be conveyed in a school that tolerates lewd, indecent, or offensive speech and conduct" (the Fraser standard) The *Tinker* and *Fraser* standards established that school officials have the right to (1) intervene and stop offensive speech by students, and (2) discipline students for speech that erodes the school's mission of education.

During the *Tinker* era, Facebook, YouTube, and text messaging may not have been even a glimmer in a computer geek's eye, but the *Tinker* standard of disruption applies to our ever-evolving world of technology, such as a student using a school computer to send offensive speech via the Internet. The challenge for school districts is how, or if, to discipline students for "speech" sent from a student's home computer or smartphone. In one incident, a student posted from his home computer a song about having sex with one of his teachers, and was suspended for ten days. Did the school have the right to expand its disciplinary sanctions beyond the school in this case? When another student created a web site of fake obituaries of his classmates from his home computer, a Washington federal court ruled that the school could not interfere with the student's speech. However, the Pennsylvania Supreme Court decided in favor of a school district that expelled a student for creating a sexually offensive website from home. And, finally, an at-home student designed a website with content that the court found interfered with the educational process of teachers, students, and parents. Clearly, each of these examples was a case-by-case decision, yet these examples show that the courts are just beginning to get their arms around the interpretation of the law in forming new and evolving social networking case law.

In the 1990s, Brian Seamons, a junior at Cache Valley School district in Smithfield, Utah, was a quarterback for his football team.[23] Following football practice, Brian's teammates assaulted him when they grabbed him, stripped him naked, bound his hands above his head, and bound his feet to a towel rack. One of Brian's team members wrapped athletic tape around his genitals, between his legs, and up and around his neck. His teammates then paraded a procession of other students into the locker room to view him lying naked and immobile, including his homecoming date.

When Brian told his parents about the assault he endured, they reported it to school administrators and to the football coach, Douglas Snow. During the follow-up meeting Coach Snow called between the captains, Brian, and himself, one of the captains berated Brian for betraying the team by reporting the misconduct to administrators. A heated debated followed. Coach Snow told Brian that he needed to apologize to the team, and forgive and forget before he would be allowed to play football. Brian refused to apologize

None of Brian's teammates was disciplined for their sexual harassment and hazing of Brian. In fact, during the investigation it was discovered that hazing was routine behavior that had been ongoing on for years. Coach Snow stated publicly that disciplining the players for hazing was inappropriate.

Brian's parents sued the school district for Brian's sexual harassment under Title IX, stating that the district had created a hostile educational environment that encouraged school officials to impose masculine stereotypes on their son. The lawsuit stated that the harassment was shrugged off by the coach and the principal by saying, in essence, "boys will be boys" and that Brian should take the hazing "like a man." The court dismissed the Title IX case indicating that Brian's experience was not sex discrimination/harassment. It would be interesting to see if the same finding would occur today—eighteen years later.

Brian shared his story on the Phil Donahue TV show, angering school officials and the community. He and his parents claimed that school officials discouraged them from speaking to the news media about the misconduct, and that the coach kicked him off the football team for his refusal to apologize to the team for reporting the incident.

In March 2001, years after the incident, a federal court determined that the Utah school district interfered with Brian's right to free speech after he complained of the misconduct, and returned a verdict in Brian's favor in the amount of $250,000 as damages for a violation of his freedom of speech.

In another case, a U.S. district judge allowed a 16-year-old Minnesota high school student, Elliott Chambers, to wear a shirt to school that read "Straight Pride."[24] The lawsuit sought to prevent the school from enforcing policies that prevent positive viewpoints toward heterosexuality. It began when school officials told the Woodbury High School student he could not wear the shirt to school. The school's handbook specifically prohibited student attire which created a danger or a disruption to the educational process. The policy had been used to prevent students from wearing clothing supporting alcohol, weapons, or sexually demeaning messages. While the judge said the intent behind the "straight pride" message was one of intolerance for homosexuality, he ruled that there was insufficient evidence that it would cause a substantial disruption of school activities.

Conflicting court decisions create confusion for school officials on how to intervene when a student's T-shirts may be anti-gay, for example, because it may be the student's right to express him or herself. The U.S. Courts of Appeals for the Ninth and Seventh Circuits were contrary in their findings in two different cases involving students wearing anti-gay comments on their T-shirts. The Ninth Circuit found in favor of the district that banned wearing a T-shirt denouncing homosexuality, and the Seventh Circuit found for a student wearing a similar T-shirt, citing First Amendment protection. The Ninth Circuit relied on the *Tinker* standard that allows schools to limit student speech when it "substantially and materially disrupts the school's educational mission, or substantially impinges on other students' right to learn." The Court's opinion considered the greater mental and academic health risks of GLBT students, and the injury the T-shirt's message conveyed, thereby deciding that the student's freedom of speech was not protected in this instance. The U.S. Court of Appeals for the Fifth Circuit found in favor of a Texas school's policy that bans all clothing with messages except school-supported clothing for sports teams, clubs, and the like.[25]

CYBERHARASSMENT AND CYBERBULLYING

If your child has been a victim of cyberbullying or cyberharassment, there are additional steps you can take. As parents, you can sue the bully and the bully's parents for financial damages, as well as for specific actions such as, for example, to delete and remove the cyberbullying text and images.[26] In some instances, cyberbullying/harassment may constitute an intentional wrongdoing called a tort.

Some areas of the United States dictate that parents may be liable, and therefore financially responsible, for behavior by their minor child when it results in intentional injury (same as above). In addition, parents are responsible for providing reasonable supervision of their child and may be found negligent for failure to do so. How this plays out is, if the school contacts parents of the cyberharasser/cyberbully, and the misconduct continues, parents may be held financially liable. Contacting parents of the cyberharasser/cyberbully is often one of the strongest catalysts to stop the behavior. The following additional legal actions may be brought as well:

- Intentional infliction of emotional distress, though often a tough claim to establish, requires outrageous, intolerable, and extreme distress.

- Invasion of privacy/public disclosure of a private fact may include a student divulging private information about another student that would be extremely harmful to a reasonable person.
- Defamation includes publishing false information about a student that is damaging to the student's reputation.
- Invasion of personal privacy/false light includes publicly portraying a student in a false light.

Is there a time when law enforcement should be contacted if your child has been victimized by cyberharassment or cyberbullying? Yes. There are times when "speech" by way of the cyber highway may be in violation of criminal laws and can result in an arrest and prosecution including the following examples:

- Threats to the student, student's family or friends, or their property
- Coercion (forcing a student to do something she or he doesn't want to do)
- Obscene and harassing phone calls, including texting
- Sexting
- Hate or bias crimes
- Stalking
- Pictures of a student in a place that is considered private (locker room, bathroom)

This chapter detailed additional laws that may be associated with Title IX. School officials don't want their districts or themselves to be sued. The student has the right to expect the harassment and bullying to stop and policies and training to be put in place to change the school culture. They also have the right to pursue compensatory damages to cover expenses and pay for their pain and suffering and medical expenses. The laws are in place to ensure that students' civil rights and Fourteenth Amendment rights are not violated by the school district. Hopefully, schools will respond based on their ethical and legal responsibilities, and students will be safe at school.

11

PARTNERING WITH SCHOOLS TO KEEP KIDS SAFE

Never doubt that a small group of thoughtful, committed citizens can change the world. Indeed, it is the only thing that ever has.

—Margaret Mead[1]

Schools are busy places with increasingly more government and local mandates requiring time, attention, and funding. It is often a challenge for schools to accomplish their mission without partnering with stakeholders including parents, state and national organizations such as the states' departments of education and OCR, law enforcement, and the community at large, to name a few. When school administrators, faculty, staff, and students work with these stakeholders, it enhances the successful implementation of numerous district programs, including your district's anti-harassment and anti-bullying strategy.

As parents, youth advocates, and interested community members, an opportunity exists for you to partner with and ignite your school district to design, develop, and implement a comprehensive anti-harassment and anti-bullying strategy. Ideally, your district has already established many of the steps discussed in this chapter. If not, this is your opportunity to assist them in doing so.

Effectively diminishing sexual harassment and bullying (as well as harassment due to race, religion, disability, and so forth) requires a broad holistic approach—an approach that examines and, where needed, changes the school culture. System change is a challenge, requires a multitude of human and financial resources, takes time, and necessitates a firm and clear commitment from the top or it is doomed for failure. A system-wide strategy is the most effective tactic to use to improve the success of negating the increasing problems of sexual harassment and bullying within schools. This is a strategy that takes into consideration students, their families, religious traditions, the community (including Little League, summer programming, community education, civic organizations, and early childhood family education), children's organizations, and sports organizations working with the school.

A SYSTEMS APPROACH TO SCHOOL CHANGE

A system-wide culture change requires a strategic, painstaking, and diligent effort. Merely creating and disseminating a policy and facilitating training will not change a culture. It requires a group of committed and loyal stakeholders to ask pivotal questions about the change initiative. Stakeholders include parents, students, teachers, administrators, and other school staff, including psychologists, social workers, bus drivers, nurses, and school board members, as well as pertinent community agencies, community members, and various ethnic groups. They need to come together to ask pivotal questions about the change initiative:[2]

1. Do we have a shared mindset and, if so, is it the "right" one?
2. To what extent does the district have the required knowledge, skills, and abilities to create a respectful, discrimination-free learning environment for our students?
3. What needs to be designed, developed, and implemented to ensure that there are the right processes, incentives, rewards, and measurements of our outcomes to demonstrate success?
4. Do we have the ability to do this and, if not, what's needed?

5. Does the commitment exist within the district (financial, human resources, time, and so forth) to reach the desired and measureable outcome/goal?

6. Who else needs to be involved in this change strategy?

7. What is required to accomplish our goal?

8. How will we measure our success?

9. How will our success be maintained?

10. What needs to occur to ensure that the change is approached as an integrated, comprehensive effort rather than as fragmented programs or just training?

11. Does the district have the leadership required for this effort?

This last question is key. A major change effort requires strong leadership.[3]

- Does your district have what it takes in the school board, superintendent, and other leadership positions for a successful change management initiative addressing harassment and bullying?
- Will district leaders both own the process and champion it as well?
- Are leaders willing to allocate the essential resources, such as human and financial, to promote a successful outcome?
- Are faculty, staff, students, parents, and community groups willing to invest what is required to reach the goal of changing the school culture to one of respect, integrity, safety, and non-harassment and non-discrimination?
- Do the stakeholders believe in the mission of the change initiative and understand its importance?
- Is there passion for its success to the degree that they will partner for a positive outcome?

When the initial discussions of a change initiative begin, the answers to the above questions are often answered in the affirmative. Stakeholders are energized, excited, and express their commitment, and then—there it sits. People get busy with their own personal and professional lives and lack the time, resources, and knowledge of how to begin or complete the process, which results in a weak or absent follow-through.

While there are several ways to address the change management process, a frequently used strategic planning model includes the following steps:

Step 1: Define the current school culture—based on an assessment of the district's environment

Step 2: Define the desired school culture—based on what you desire the school learning environment to be

Step 3: Identify the specific gaps between the current culture and the desired culture

Step 4: Identify the driving forces (pushing for success, such as a Title IX-compliant, respectful learning environment) and restraining forces (barriers, such as financial resources) that will impact a successful outcome

Step 5: Design and develop an action plan with measureable goals and objectives, to address the gaps between the district's current and desired cultures, including how to increase the driving forces and diminish the restraining forces

Step 6: Implement the plan

Step 7: Monitor the plan's effectiveness

Step 8: Make necessary changes along the way

Step 9: Evaluate/measure the plan's effectiveness

Even with strong leadership and commitment from stakeholders, change initiatives may fail for any number of reasons. By examining obstacles to change, the district can minimize or prevent the impact of the predictable and unpredictable reasons for failure. Many reasons exist as to why changes don't produce the desired outcome:[4]

1. The change is not tied to a strategy
2. It is more of a quick fix or a program rather than a long-term strategy
3. No long-term perspective is considered
4. Political realities are not planned for and might undermine the change
5. Grandiose expectations sabotage simple successes
6. Inflexible change designs create roadblocks
7. Lack of leadership knowledge and skill around change

8. Lack of measurable, tangible results
9. Fear of the unknown
10. Inability to mobilize commitment to sustain change

According to OCR, school officials must think broader than just the discipline of perpetrators of harassment. They need to examine and implement the necessary steps required to eliminate the hostile environment, which creates civil rights violations when students are sexually harassed. The OCR's *Dear Colleague* letter stated that "the unique effects of discriminatory harassment may demand a different response than would other types of bullying."[5] Considering OCR's requirement and the roadblocks to successful change listed above, the following, though not exhaustive, are recommendations for the district's anti-harassment and anti-bullying strategy. Some of these actions may involve confidential information protected by laws that prevent your active involvement. Most all of the steps will require administrative leadership, and, of course, the school district will have the final say as to what they are willing to implement and the degree of your involvement:

1. Establish a task force of stakeholders to begin the anti-harassment and anti-bullying strategy by asking those eleven difficult questions listed earlier in the chapter (pp. 160–61), and to strategically plan the district's initiative. The task force should be demographically diverse and include members from the following groups: students, parents, school staff such as counselors, representatives from student organizations including GLBT students, nurses, bus drivers, cafeteria workers, teachers, administrators, counselors, and community members. Make sure that students play an active role in the task force and are not overwhelmed and monopolized by the adults.

2. Assess the district's learning environment, including the frequency of sexual harassment and bullying incidents and misconduct involving GLBT students. What kinds of behaviors were reported and/or observed? What was the outcome of each incident? Does the behavior tend to occur in the same locations? How did school employees respond who witnessed the misconduct? Could it have been handled differently/better? Is there consistency in follow-up

and discipline? When was the last time the policies were reviewed and revised? By whom? What is the frequency and method of teacher and student training on harassment and on bullying, if any?

Survey students to determine the amount of sexual harassment and bullying occurring. Assess the degree of gender bias in the classroom, in sports, and in how money is allocated for programs and events. In addition to surveying the students, survey parents, faculty, and staff, and use other assessment tools such as focus groups and one-on-one interviews. Ask, for example, if the school district encourages students, faculty, and staff to confront and report harassment and bullying? If they do or don't, how is that evident? Review the extent of sexual harassment via open discussions and/or interviews with student groups and individual students.

Whatever assessment tools are used to kick off your strategy—surveys, interviews, focus groups, review of documents—use the same tools for subsequent assessments. After your change initiative has been completely implemented, and in place for a minimum of one year, reassess. Then, continue to assess the school's culture every one to two years. Compare the results of your initial assessment with the subsequent assessments to evaluate whether your strategy, including your policies, programs, and other activities, are making a significant difference. Is there a decrease in incidents, for example? Use the assessment results to identify key needs and plan accordingly to meet those needs.

3. Yearly, assess the district's bullying, discrimination/harassment, code of conduct, violence, and cyberharassment/bullying policies and grievance procedures for accuracy and clarity. This needs to be done to ensure the district is current with ever-changing case law. Use appropriate suggestions from your state's and other states' departments of education, other school districts, recommendations in professional magazines and journals, and OCR. Ask who was involved in writing the policy, and who is responsible for keeping the policy current? Is it written in age-appropriate language with student input? Get input from various groups about the effectiveness of the policy—faculty, staff, students, the district's attorney, minority students, and staff, to name a few. More is written about policy development later in this chapter.

4. Evaluate the strengths and weaknesses of the district from the assessment. Compare your district with other districts, review best practices from the professional literature, and follow OCR's recommendations. Write a formal report that outlines the results of the assessment and evaluation and then communicate it to all stakeholders.

5. Training on harassment and on bullying must occur yearly for the school board, administrators, faculty, staff, and volunteers; a process must be established to train all new school board members, administrators, faculty, staff, and volunteers. Training is not merely a review of the district's policies at the beginning of the school year, which is what a great many districts identify as training. Training must include the following:

    a. Definition of harassment and of bullying, clearly delineating between the two

    b. Title IX and state laws addressing sexual harassment (federal and state laws for harassment of other protected classes, as well)

    c. Legal and ethical requirements for addressing sexual harassment when it is observed or school employees are informed of the misconduct

    d. Any state laws addressing bullying

    e. Examples of behaviors that constitute sexual harassment and bullying

    f. Causes and contributing factors of sexual harassment and bullying

    g. Discussion of the district's pertinent policies

    h. The role of administrators faculty, staff, and volunteers in the prevention and intervention of harassment and bullying

    i. How to identify sexual harassment and bullying

    j. Tools for school employees to use to immediately and effectively intervene in the two types of misconduct

    k. Retaliation and examples of retaliatory behavior

    l. The how, what, who, and where of documentation

    m. How school personnel will assume responsibility to continually monitor the school climate and student behaviors

    n. Specific administrator training dealing with their legal and ethical role in prevention and intervention under both Title IX and Title VII

    o. Teachers must know how to recognize bullying and sexual harassment, how to intervene, how to support victims, and how to recognize symptoms of possible abuse by a staff member

    p. Educators must make use of the "teachable moment" as an opportunity to intervene and teach about the misconduct

    q. Law regarding mandatory reporting

    r. Gender bias in the classroom, and issues of sexism and power

    s. Healthy boundaries between adults and students, including how to spot warning signs that adult faculty or staff might be violating appropriate professional boundaries with students, such as seeking out specific students to meet with during study hall or after school, increase in physical contact and flirting, singling out students for personal attention, and social networking with students for non-educational reasons. These behaviors are sometimes referred to as "grooming" behavior, which is when the adult abuser begins to set the student up for sexual abuse

6. Schools must have guidelines and procedures for collaboration with law enforcement and other appropriate community agencies such as social services/child protection.

7. Create an avenue to monitor student behavior on busses and, if using cameras, assign responsibility for discussions with bus drivers and a review of camera footage to monitor student behavior.

8. Establish a process whereby the district really digs into how it creates and sustains deeply rooted patriarchy linking violence to masculinity; then create a plan to counter it.[6]

9. Schools should offer counseling to both the target and the harasser.

10. Evaluate the physical layout of the schools and their grounds; assure that all areas are safeguarded with increased supervision to protect students, particularly in areas that are more secluded or isolated. Students perceived narrow hallways as riskier for bullying and harassment because of close quarters.[7] The denseness makes it difficult for teachers to see student behavior and for students to ward off problems in the hallway.[8]

11. OCR requires that school districts identify a Title IX Coordinator. Even though OCR and Title IX apply only to sexual harassment and not bullying, the suggested role of the Title IX coordinator could easily include addressing bullying, as I suggest here. The suggested roles and responsibilities for the coordinator include: (1) investigating all complaints of harassment and bullying; (2) reviewing the district's harassment and bullying policies for effectiveness in the district's prevention and intervention efforts; offering suggestions to administration for improvement; (3) providing a central location for all documentation of both informal and formal sexual harassment complaints; analyzing complaints and their outcomes for appropriate practices; (4) partnering with administration so students, faculty, staff, and administrators are trained and are familiar with their role and responsibility in preventing and intervening in incidents of harassment and bullying; (5) establishing ongoing communication with parents about the district's harassment and bullying policies and the desire to partner with them; (6) providing the district's policies and behavior expectations to third parties that interact with students—vendors, job training locations, and contractors; (6) monitoring the effectiveness of the grievance procedure; (7) gathering statistics regarding the frequency of harassment and bullying—who was involved in the incidents, the process of resolving each incident, and the outcome.[9]

12. It is absolutely essential that whoever conducts investigations within the district is trained to do so or the district risks penalties from OCR. A school district is required to have conducted a prompt, fair, and unbiased investigation based on the district's policies. A poorly done investigation not only prevents an effective resolution to the complaint, but it can increase the potential liability for the district, increase the harassment and bullying in the school, and set the stage for retaliation. It's recommended that two people, ideally one male and one female, are competent in conducting investigations. There should be both a formal and informal avenue of redress for students (and faculty). If police are conducting a criminal investigation, the school is required to conduct its own investigation. If police find there is no criminal misconduct, that doesn't change the school's liability for pos-

sible civil action. Investigations of misconduct by school officials should be conducted by an independent outside investigator, not by the school investigator.

13. Inform the victim's and the perpetrator's parents of repeated and severe incidents of harassment and bullying; engage parental help in curtailing the misconduct.

14. Monitor the perpetrator's behavior, including follow-up discussions with the victims, witnesses, and perpetrators of sexual harassment and bullying.

15. Write clear classroom rules regarding respectful behavior and inclusion. Include students in creating rules, including teacher and student responsibilities for diminishing harassment and bullying.

16. Provide age-appropriate education to students on the following topics:

   a. Sexual harassment (and harassment of other protected classes)—including the definition, examples of the behavior, state and federal laws, school's harassment policy, causes and contributing factors, retaliation, what to do when the student is harassed or sees others harassed, the grievance/reporting procedure, and the impact of harassment on the target and witnesses.

   b. Bullying—including the definition, examples of bullying behavior, causes and contributing factors, what to do when the student is bullied or sees others bullied, the school's bullying policy, the grievance/reporting procedure, causes and contributing factors, the impact of bullying on the target and witnesses.

   c. Merely offering a bullying or sexual harassment education program is not enough; the programs used need to be evidence-based, meaning that research has shown the student education program you select caused a change in student behavior. Facilitate a discussion and learning activities around sexism, heterosexism, masculinity and violence, homosexuality, gender nonconformity, and society's and the school's norms and practices through which harassment and bullying operate. These issues need to be integrated into, for example, social studies, health, economics, history, civil rights, literature, and English curricula to demonstrate the complexity and perspectives of the misconduct.

d. Classes on analysis of media and pop culture, and the role of both in sexism, masculinity, and patriarchy.

e. History courses need to be inclusive of the history and contributions of women, GLBT persons, and racial minorities.

f. Use a variety of teaching methodologies including role-playing, media, artistic expression, and others.

17. When planning, create ways in which younger students would be safer by separating them from older students in hallways and on the bus.

18. Identify how the district, as a system and a microcosm of society, supports and promotes the reality of sexual harassment and bullying, patriarchy, and violence. Conduct a district-wide comprehensive workshop to address these issues, looking at the role the school plays in the behavior. For example, how much time, energy, and funding goes to sports rather than the arts; what is the behavior of student fans to the opposing school's fans during sporting events, for example, basketball; how much are male athletes lauded for their athletic prowess compared to student leaders in orchestra, theatre, and debate? Are the following topics integrated within your district's curriculum: sex role stereotypes, the role of the media in promoting violence, sex, and stereotypes; healthy sexuality including discussions on masculinity and femininity; dating violence and sexual assault; healthy relationships; sexism in our culture and language; boundaries; women's contributions to history and culture; GLBT's role in U.S. culture; conflict resolution; communication skills and assertiveness, and decision making to name a few?

19. Continue the discussions of the relationship among gender bias, sexual harassment, other forms of harassment, and bullying and degradation of anyone due to race, religion, or disability throughout the year rather than in only a class or one assembly.

20. Utilize the peer education concept by enlisting older students to teach younger students about bullying and sexual harassment. Younger students hear the message from their older peers in ways they do not hear it from adults—in their own language. The

older student is gaining a clearer understanding of the issue in the process of teaching, while at the same time gaining the skill of speaking in front of a group. Older students are better able to understand and relate to another student's experiences. Ask for student volunteers as well as seeking out student leaders from various groups representative of the student body—debaters, actors, musicians, and athletes, for example. Use the student teaching opportunity for students who may not be considered a "leader" but would be good role models and would enjoy and learn from the challenge. Special education students have done a great job in educating their peers and teachers on some of these issues with the result of changing some of their own behaviors.

21. Keep parents and community members abreast of the district's anti-harassment and anti-bullying efforts by writing articles, or encouraging students to write articles, for the local newspaper, student newspaper, newsletter to parents, and the District's website. Discuss the issue at parent-teacher conferences; if your district has a parent-teacher organization, make it part of their agenda. If the district uses Twitter and Facebook, post tweets and let the district's Facebook friends know the school's philosophy, policy, and anti-harassment and anti-bullying activities.

22. Preview all student skits prior to the presentation in class, general assemblies, or pep fests; partner with students to ensure the skits are free of discrimination and do not make fun of a particular type or group of student or faculty (for example, gay students, a female with large breasts, gender slurs, overweight students, and so on)

23. Offer support groups to students involved in non-traditional classes and courses of study where incidents of sexual harassment might occur more frequently. Propose separate discussion groups for female students and for male students to discuss sexism, patriarchy, oppression, bias, and sexual harassment, and then bring both genders together to discuss these issues. For example, South High School in Minneapolis has a Women's Resource Center where female students gather to discuss issues pertinent to them as teen women. Another high school offers similar programs for male students to talk about how it feels to be male, to discuss girlfriends, and how to be assertive rather than aggressive.

24. Promote and encourage teachers and students to plan, develop, design, and implement activities, programs, projects, plays, music, artwork, poster contests, writing contests, district-wide speak out, an awareness week, and so forth that deal with sexual harassment and sex and violence, and promote diversity, healthy sexuality, healthy relationships, inclusion, and healthy masculinity and femininity.

25. Offer recognition and/or awards for students and staff who serve as positive role models by treating others with dignity, respect, and equality.

26. Include educational materials about GLBT, women, sexuality, discrimination, patriarchy, and sex roles in school libraries and recommended websites.

27. Provide gender-neutral bathrooms.

28. Require exit interviews when students drop a specific course, change schools, or drop out of school to determine if sexual harassment and bullying played a role in their decision.

29. Publicly identify sexual harassment as a serious issue. Currently, schools are touting bullying and identifying it as a serious issue (which it is, but not to the exclusion of harassment). The same emphasis needs to occur relative to sexual harassment (including GLBT harassment). Do not treat it as teasing, emerging adolescent sexuality, "boys will be boys," or flirtation that went too far, or blame the victim by saying she wore her skirts short and her shirts tight. This treatment of sexual harassment gives tacit approval for it to continue, diminishes the trust that students have in the administration and the system, increases the likelihood of continued victimization, and increases the likelihood of a lawsuit or a formal complaint to OCR or your state's human rights department. When serious incidents of harassment occur, the superintendent or other school official must issue a public statement condemning the behavior. Lack of official response is often misconstrued as approval or lack of concern.

30. For students:

   a. Create a space for students to gather, discuss, rant and rave, express, meditate, cry, or share, where it is safe for them to be free to express themselves without groveling to the status quo.

b. Create opportunities for boys to learn alternatives to patriarchy; where they are free from constraints that prevent them from expressing compassion, nurturance, and tenderness rather than acting tough and in control.

c. Create leadership opportunities, clubs, courses, and service learning activities where the students are change agents rather than passive robots of school power and control.

d. Establish gay-straight alliance groups, which have been shown to create a more positive school environment for GLBT youth, including less victimization, less absenteeism, and less name calling.[10] For some of you reading this book, and for some students, your personal values and/or religious traditions may conflict with suggestions for inclusion of GLBT students. However, it is critical that all students are treated with respect, dignity, and humanity. All students today are soon to be adult citizens of an increasingly small world, a world that requires that all people are treated with honor and esteem.

e. Establish the Day of Silence[11] or No Name Calling Week.[12]

f. Use students as experts; establish a strategy whereby students are researchers.[13] After students are trained in the task, they keep tabs of common types of harassment and bullying that occur away from the eyes and ears of educators, yet still penetrate into the school climate, and provide the information (confidentially) to school officials for follow through.

31. Identify several school officials to receive student complaints. Students will not likely come forward to complain about incidents of harassment and bullying if there are too few school officials identified to receive complaints.

32. Create a plan for adults to monitor the social interactions among students. Research suggests that harassment and bullying incidents decrease with adult monitoring.[14] Students wanted more adult supervision, and, when it wasn't there, they perceived the school as not interested in their well-being. Forty-five percent of

students from twenty-five different schools indicated they were not happy in school because not enough adults were supervising.[15] Some students believed that some of their classmates needed schools to take on the role of a second parent by helping teens learn respect through formal classes.[16]

33. *All* students should be involved in critical decision making and discussions about the school climate, according to many students. Students seem to understand that students at different levels of the hierarchy have different experiences that need to be recognized and included in policy making.

34. Remember, it is the adults in the school that are responsible for the school climate. The responsibility does not rest with the students because they are not developmentally prepared for such responsibility. While it is great to teach kids how to stick up for themselves and their bullied and harassed classmates, the majority of adults do not speak up when they are victimized by harassment and bullying in the workplace, so we cannot expect kids to do so. It is not up to student-bystanders to stop harassment and bullying; it is up to the adults in the school. That said, students need to be responsible for their own behavior, and, if they feel safe in doing so, help a bullied or harassed classmate.

CYBERHARASSMENT AND CYBERBULLYING

Schools must respond to complaints of cybermisconduct. If school officials are not able to discipline the perpetrator due to student protections under freedom of speech, the district must follow through with other action. School officials are responsible for gathering evidence of cyberbullying/harassment, even though it might be difficult to do so. Just as locker searches are the norm, the same can be said about student Internet use searches. If a student is suspected of violating the district policy, a search of the student's computer and Internet activity should be conducted. Care needs to be taken to ensure the search is not a violation of wiretapping laws.[17] School officials are allowed by law to enforce restrictions on student speech if their speech is sponsored by the school or to ensure a proper school learning environment. The Iowa Department of Education offers the following actions school officials should undertake.[18] How many of these does your school district adhere to?

- Meet with the perpetrator and his or her parents regarding the allegation.
- Monitor the perpetrator's behavior and inform the perpetrator's parents that the school will be doing so.
- Inform the target's family of the right to notify law enforcement; law enforcement *may*, depending on the allegation/complaint, be able to take action the school district can't take.
- Notify law enforcement if the cyberbullying/harassment involved a threat. Inform both the perpetrator's and target's parents that law enforcement has been contacted.
- Comply with law enforcement.
- Do *not* discourage the victim's family from contacting OCR, or an attorney regarding a civil action for intentional infliction of emotional distress or invasion of privacy or other potential violations of law or statutes.
- As with any complaint, an investigation should be done, including confiscating the specific electronic device used in the misconduct, documenting the investigation, and keeping both families informed of the investigative process and outcome (not to include any disciplinary measures, however).
- Conduct necessary training for students and all staff.
- Ensure the computer filtering software is adequate and monitor it.
- Ensure school policies, handbooks, and rules are current.

PROCESS OF POLICY AND PROCEDURE DEVELOPMENT[19]

Many states require that school districts have a sexual harassment policy and a bullying policy; however, Title IX does not require that school districts have either. Title IX requires that schools have a discrimination policy and a grievance procedure. Because of the complexity of sexual harassment, I strongly recommend that districts have a separate Title

IX policy, which includes the grievance procedure required by Title IX. Separating bullying and harassment into two separate policies may enable students experiencing sexual and other forms of harassment to report the misconduct. The separation also clarifies the distinction between the two types of misconduct for school officials, students, and parents and emphasizes civil rights laws against sexual harassment, which have no bearing on bullying. Having separate policies shows that the district understands the distinction between harassment and bullying and that it will not tolerate or condone sexual harassment as a violation of Title IX.

The process for developing effective sexual harassment and bullying policies is an opportunity for the school district administration, faculty, staff, and students, in partnership with parents and other stakeholders, to come together towards a common goal—ensuring a safe and equitable learning environment for students (and employees). This can be problematic because of the limited amount of time stakeholders can devote to working on the strategy. Input from your state's department of education and school attorneys, and information from any of the resource websites at the back of this book, will be helpful. The sexual harassment and bullying policies require coordination with other district policies and procedures, particularly codes of conduct, safe schools, violence, and others.

Your district probably has a sexual harassment policy and a bullying policy. They may also have separate policies for other forms of discrimination based on race and disability, for example. Schools will be held accountable by the courts and OCR to follow their policy's mandates. As a result, some attorneys advise the "less is better" philosophy for district policies. The attorney's intent is to diminish liability if the policy is not adhered to. My perspective is a bit different. In my experience as a consultant and expert witness for Title IX lawsuits, when policies include more information than is generally advised by some attorneys, the policy serves as a resource for students, staff, faculty, the victim, the accused, administrators, parents, the Title IX Coordinator, and human resources. As a result, the policy may *prevent* the district from ending up in court. Some schools may have all the policies in one overall policy. There is no specific rule as to the requirement, and different schools do it differently. Since many of the components for an effective sexual harassment policy and an effective bullying policy are the same or similar, I'm combining them here:

- Write a strong philosophy statement clearly spelling out the district's commitment to create a safe and positive learning environment by minimizing bullying and harassment based on race, color, national origin, sex, sexual orientation, ethnicity, gender identity, and religion.
- Indicate who the policies cover—students, administrators, faculty, staff, vendors, visitors, substitute teachers, student job training mentors, and volunteers.
- List the laws pertinent to the policies including:

  - Civil Rights Title VII, which prohibits discrimination in the workplace
  - Civil Rights Title IX, which prohibits sex discrimination in schools
  - Civil Rights Title VI, which prohibits discrimination based on race, color or national origin
  - Section 504 of the Rehabilitation Act of 1973 and Title II of the Americans with Disabilities Act, which prohibits disability discrimination
  - Any state and municipal laws should be listed and defined as well. If your state has an anti-bullying law, include it in the bullying policy.

- Write student policies in age-appropriate language, avoiding all legalese that even most adults don't understand; work with school officials, the student council, parents, community members, and the district's attorney to ensure the district has a comprehensive set of policies. Policies should be included in student handbooks, on the school's website, on communication boards, and in the school's libraries and locker rooms. They should be sent home to all households on a yearly basis. Students should receive a copy of the policy every school year.
- Include a statement about false claims, including the seriousness of such claims, the impact on the target of a false claim, and the discipline to the student who falsely accuses another student or any school employee of misconduct that did not occur.

- Make clear that the school takes harassment and bullying very seriously, and that neither will be tolerated.
- Include a statement that encourages any target of harassment or bullying to write up their complaint. According to Title IX, this cannot be required for sexual harassment complaints; however it is in the best interests of the student and the district to do so to assure that whomever is taking the complaint heard it and documented it correctly.
- Encourage victims to report complaints as soon after the incident(s) as possible, and preferably within ninety days. The sooner sexual harassment is reported, the sooner school officials can respond to remedy the situation as required by Title IX.
- Address the district's obligation to contact law enforcement and/or child protection for criminal misconduct including sexual assault and physical assault. Require strong discipline for those administrators, faculty, and staff who are aware of potential criminal activity and fail to inform the appropriate school official, child protection, and law enforcement.
- Write a statement that the victim, the perpetrator, and their parents will be informed of the findings of the investigation and steps taken to remedy the situation.
- Acknowledge that sexual harassment, including GLBT harassment, and bullying are forms of school violence.
- Define sexual harassment, including gender-based harassment, sexual orientation, sex stereotype, and gender identity harassment. Define bullying and differentiate bullying from illegal sexual harassment. List examples of sexual harassment and of bullying in each of the policies. The policies need to address student-to-student sexual harassment and bullying, sexual harassment of teachers and staff by students, and teacher or staff sexual harassment and bullying of students.
- Include cyberharassment and cyberbullying issues, even though electronic media/social media/electronic communication policies should carry more extensive information.
- Appoint and identify the district's Title IX Coordinator—a requirement of the U.S. Department of Education, Office of Civil Rights. This person must be committed to the issue, be well trained in

bullying, harassment, sexism, sexual orientation, gender identity, power, and accompanying issues, and not merely have this responsibility tacked on to their already existing heavy workload. Publicize the coordinator's name, office location, and phone number in the district policy and on posters in each building. Either this coordinator or another person within the district should be identified as the individual tasked with preventing harassment and monitoring the district's Title IX compliance.

- Develop a detailed complaint/grievance procedure. If the school district fails to have an adequate grievance procedure, it may be in violation of Title IX. The procedure needs to include how the district will respond to complaints of discrimination, including information about the investigation and the approximate timeframe for the steps of the investigation. Students must be informed about how to file complaints. The procedure must be publicized in announcements, handbooks, and other bulletins. OCR requires "prompt and equitable resolution" to complaints, and requires timeframes for filing the complaint and for conducting the investigation. Additionally, part of the grievance procedure includes informing the target and the perpetrator of the findings of the investigation, the resolution, and the rationale for how the decision was made as to whether sexual harassment occurred. The investigation must be conducted even if the complaint appears to be from an angry parent. The grievance procedure must include:

  - a time frame for the various stages of the investigation
  - the title of the district employee conducting the investigation
  - a statement requiring that the investigator must be trained in the skill of investigating (including how to interview children and teens)
  - a statement as to whether students may have an attorney or student-advocate with them when interviewed
  - who determines the outcome of the investigation and whether it was a violation of the victim's civil rights
  - how the determination will be made
  - discussion about using informal versus formal complaint resolutions
  - who determines the discipline and the rationale for that discipline

- Differentiate between formal and informal complaint resolutions. Informal complaint resolution usually does not require a full-blown investigation as required by a formal resolution. The policy must indicate who decides whether a formal or informal resolution is required and based on what evidence.

- List the support services available to victims, harassers, and bullies, such as counseling and social services/child abuse services

- Identify several different people to whom student complaints may be brought. Though several people can be identified to receive complaints, have one clear avenue for who is responsible for complaints—that is usually the Title IX Coordinator (or Human Rights Officer, or whatever title the district uses that oversees Title IX). Ideally, students should be able to go to any trusted adult within the system, or outside the system, to complain about an incident. If the student goes to an employee other than the principal, assistant principal, or superintendent about a teacher or staff sexual harassment incident, that employee must contact the administrator about the complaint and comply with the district's policy for contacting law enforcement, as well as following your state's mandatory reporting law.

- Discipline any school faculty, staff, or administrator who is aware of student-to-student sexual harassment occurring and fails to document and inform the appropriate school official, law enforcement, and child protection.

- Contact parents of both the victim and the perpetrator for serious and/or repeated misconduct. If the sexual harassment or bullying appears criminal in nature and/or is by an employee of the school, school officials must immediately contact law enforcement and social services (and in some states the Department of Education). The accused employee needs to be removed from the school pending the outcome of an investigation.

- Provide information about the length of time the investigative report and other pertinent records concerning a complaint will be kept and in what location. Keeping documentation for at least a year or more is important to determine if there is persistent and pervasive harassment. The documentation will also be required as evidence for any formal complaint lodged with OCR, the state's civil rights department, or if litigation occurs. The statue of limitations for filing a complaint with OCR is one year. Check with your state if a complaint is filed with the state's civil rights agency; state limitations vary from six months to one year.

- Create a yearly process to continually review, monitor, and evaluate the effectiveness of prevention efforts, the policy, and training given to students and staff. Case law is continually evolving, which will alter the information included in training and in the policy. Identify the district employee responsible for the review of the policies and educational programs.
- Issue a statement about the requirement of school officials to investigate a sexual harassment complaint even if law enforcement is conducting its criminal investigation.
- Provide a list of examples of disciplinary actions that may occur.
- Include a statement about an appeal process.
- Discuss confidentiality, and that only those with a "need to know" will be informed of the complaint and the resolution.
- Include a statement about district technology and its relationship to harassment and bullying, and refer students to the district's electronic communication, cyberharassment, and cyberbullying policies, and note that technical monitoring of the District's Internet use will be ongoing.
- Discuss that retaliation will not be tolerated and it is a violation of civil rights; any complaints of retaliation will require an investigation. Provide examples of retaliatory behavior.
- Include a statement requiring the use of qualitative and quantitative indicators to review and assess all records of sexual harassment and bullying on an annual basis. Appraise, among other things, the types of behaviors, frequency and severity, location, ages of perpetrators and victims, and effectiveness of support systems offered by the district. Check for any patterns that emerge. Discuss the remedy of the incidents—was there a better way each incident could have been handled? In other words, use this review process as the teachable moment for school officials.
- Annually assess the effectiveness of both the sexual harassment and bullying policies and procedures and the degree to which both policies are enforced.

- Summarize and write two formal reports; one report will address the anti-harassment efforts, and the second report will address anti-bullying efforts with both reports discussing the number of incidents, outcomes of incidents, policy effectiveness, and evaluations by students, staff, parents, the school board, and the community at large.
- Develop a strategy addressing sexual harassment and bullying training of all students, administrators, faculty, paraprofessionals, aides, nurses, social workers, psychologists, counselors, new employees, police liaison officers, bus drivers, substitute teachers, maintenance/engineering, coaches, volunteers, cafeteria staff, office staff, and computer staff. Identify who is in charge of training and identify the qualifications of the individual(s) who will train, the frequency of training, and even what constitutes training. A brief review of both policies at the beginning of the school year is not training! Establish a process for training new employees and new students in sexual harassment and bullying, the district's policy and philosophy, to whom to report complaints, and so forth.
- Demonstrate how the harassment and the bullying policies interface with the student's code of conduct and school violence/safety, employee harassment, and other policies.
- Require a formal written investigative report following an investigation of every complaint of sexual harassment and bullying.
- Require an annual report that outlines the district's strategy in addressing sexual harassment and bullying. This report should go to the school board and be published on the website and in the local newspaper.
- Discuss services to victims of sexual harassment and bullying, including referrals to community agencies and psychologists, special programs, home schooling, and needed time off. Support systems should be extended to help victims handle any academic problems that might arise after their harassment or bullying incident(s).
- Require gender-inclusive language as the norm for administrators and faculty when teaching; require students and faculty to use gender-inclusive language in their classes and in their writing.
- Require that school staff members are knowledgeable about possible symptoms of sexual harassment/abuse and speak up when they see signs suggesting it. Identify what the discipline will be

for school staff who suspect or are aware of misconduct and fail to report it.

- Require that coaches take a strong stance against sexual harassment and bullying. They should not allow sexist or misogynist comments, sexual expletives, crude jokes, or jokes made at another's expense. Coaches must not engage in that language themselves.
- Meticulously screen new faculty, administrators, and staff. Criminal background checks must be done on all applicants. Require references from former employers and associates, and check their teaching credentials as a part of the hiring process. Be leery of gaps and frequent changes in an applicant's job history.
- Take all complaints seriously with direct and consistent consequences to the harasser. Students repeatedly say they do not trust school officials to intervene on sexual harassment. They back their statements up with alarming examples of denial, cover-ups, "boys will be boys" comments, and punishing the victim. Most have lost faith in the school taking their complaints seriously, especially if they are against a teacher. Others complain of a double standard with athletes, who are sometimes expected to behave "that" way, and therefore little or no consequences befall them. Ensure that sanctions imposed upon offenders are adequate to demonstrate the district's commitment to remedy and prevent sexual harassment and assault. Be sure that harassers do not receive less stringent sanctions for later offenses than earlier offenses. Remember that consequences should include using the experience as a "teachable moment," and not just be punitive in nature.
- Ensure there is a mechanism in place for coordinating a broad range of programs on harassment, sexism, and other related topics. Allocate funding for sexual harassment prevention, including purchasing and developing materials for use with students and staff.
- Label the behaviors that constitute sexual harassment as sexual harassment, not "inappropriate behavior" or "bullying" or "miscommunication." Procedures that would dismiss a finding of sexual harassment because of miscommunication, inappropriate behavior, or bullying do not comply with Title IX. Treat complaints of behavior that fall under the umbrella of sexual harassment as sexual harassment, a form of sex discrimination prohibited by law. Re-

member that staff and students might be civilly as well as criminally liable for psychological and physical injuries resulting from peer harassment.

- Promote activities in which students of both sexes, as well as different racial and cultural groups, can participate together and learn about each other.

- Establish a procedure whereby building areas, such as lockers and bathroom walls, and equipment, such as tables and library carrels, are periodically inspected for graffiti of sexually offensive and demeaning comment. Immediately remove the graffiti.

- Encourage teachers and administrators to examine their own biases. Issues related to sex and sexuality have the potential of provoking strong personal feelings. A teacher's own beliefs about the roles of males and females, feelings about teens, and biases based on style of dress, background, school performance, culture, and the teacher's own behavior in the past or present all serve to impact the teacher's response to incidents.

- Monitor hallway behavior between classes, since most sexual harassment occurs in the hallways and classrooms, and intervene when sexually offensive language or behavior is heard or seen.

- Include students in the evaluation of their teachers. Evaluate teachers on, among other things, their ability to be non-sexist, use of gender-neutral language, depiction of males and females in non-stereotypical roles, their use of humor, assumptions of heterosexual and non-heterosexual models when referring to human behavior, use of non-sexist curricula, and whether they give more attention to male students than female students.

- Ensure that educational materials, brochures, and the like are available in languages other than English for students and their parents who use English as a second language.

- Schools must include due process within their policies that includes a notice to an individual of the allegations against him or her and the opportunity for a fair hearing before an impartial person or panel.

As parents, youth advocates, and interested community members, this is the opportunity to partner with your school district to design, develop, and implement a comprehensive anti-harassment and anti-bullying strategy. It is a proactive move, rather than reactive. Changes like these require cooperation of all, starting at the top of the school's administration and school board. It is often a challenge for schools to accomplish their mission without partnering with stakeholders including parents, state and national organizations such as the states' departments of education and OCR, law enforcement, and the community at large, to name a few. Working together will enhance the successful implementation of numerous district programs, including your district's anti-harassment and anti-bullying strategy, on-going training, inclusive education, and identifying the problem and finding solutions—and developing and implementing effective policies.

⑫

HOLDING SCHOOLS ACCOUNTABLE

If we can't turn to our . . . principals and they're not going to do anything for us, what's the point? That's what they're there for. They're supposed to help us learn and if we can't learn in an environment where we're being called names and stuff, then they're not doing their jobs.

—High School Female[1]

When a child tells you about her or his sexual harassment or bullying victimization at school, as a parent or trusted adult, it is a challenge to determine what role you should play. Should you be a coach or mentor helping the child take care of the situation, an advocate by contacting the teacher or other school official, or a whistleblower by contacting the OCR, police, or a lawyer? When parents contact me as a bullying and harassment consultant, usually they have already tried, unsuccessfully, to get the school to stop the sexual harassment or bullying. Many don't have any idea of what additional steps are open to them to hold the schools accountable, and some are eager to contact an attorney to file a lawsuit.

The following guidelines will help determine the steps to take to hold schools accountable by stopping the sexual harassment or bullying. Also, refer to the OCR's *Revised Guidance on Sexual Harassment* available online (see the list of web resources beginning on p. 251) for additional help. If the incident is a sexual assault, rape, or physical assault, immediately contact law enforcement as well as the superintendent and school board. For all incidents, one of the first steps is for you and/or the student (depending on age) to document the incident(s) in detail including the following:

- What happened? Be as specific and detailed as possible using the exact words that were said by the offender(s) to the target of the behavior, even if the words are embarrassing and explicit. If there was touch involved, specifically document where the touch occurred using correct anatomical descriptions. The touch may be on the shoulder or face or on a more intimate body part. For example, if the victim's genitals were touched, be specific in labeling the genitals, such as penis, scrotum, or vulva. Do not use a euphemism such as "private parts." Describe the touch—a grab, a punch, a tap, a tickle, or an object (which needs to be specifically named) inserted into the victim's vagina, rectum, or mouth. Document each offender(s)' body language, facial expression, and tone of voice. Be sure to document this information for each offender separately. Indicate how long the entire incident lasted. In what positions were the offenders and the victim, for example, standing, sitting on the floor, or sitting in chairs? Did the victim respond back to the offender(s) and, if so, what did she or he say or do? Use verbatim quotes, and be as detailed and specific as possible. Did the offender(s) respond back to the target and, if so, how? How did the incident conclude? If there is more than one incident, document each incident in the same way and in chronological order.
- Where did it happen? Again, be as specific as possible indicating the exact location. If it occurred in a classroom, provide the name or number of the classroom, the actual location within the classroom, for example, "the southeast corner in front of the lab table." If it was in a hallway—which hallway and where in the hallway.
- When did it happen? Document the day and the time. If you cannot remember the exact day, you may remember it was, for example, on a Friday because a pep fest occurred, or it was the day of the first snowfall, or it was sometime the week of the prom.

Estimate as precisely as you can. The same is true for the time of day, even if the exact time is unknown, you may remember that it was in the morning after third period, for example.

- Who were the witnesses/bystanders? Name each witness and what the victim believed each witnessed. Not all witnesses see the entire incident, so, if the victim is aware of witnesses that were there for only part of it, what part of the misconduct did they observe or hear? Identify anyone the victim spoke to about the incident after it occurred—someone who could attest to the fact that, for example, they saw the victim crying in the bathroom following the occurrence, or saw a change in the victim's emotional demeanor. Identify those the victim may have called or texted after the incident and what the victim told them.

- How has the misconduct impacted the victim? There are several categories to document related to impact: school, emotional, behavioral, and health.

  ○ School: Has there been a decline in grades on assignments or courses? Has she expressed a desire to change schools or drop a class? Has she talked about losing her friends and feeling isolated at school? Does she not want to go to school or attend a specific class resulting in increased absenteeism and truancy? Has she lost interest in school activities in which she's been involved?

  ○ Emotional: Has he seemed more angry, irritable, and anxious? Has he expressed confusion, shame, or fear? Does he appear depressed? Is there self-mutilation? Does he appear to have a lowered self-esteem and confidence?

  ○ Behavioral: Does he seem more quiet at home or, conversely, more agitated in his behavior? Is he staying out past curfew or, conversely, not going out with his friends as frequently as he used to? Is he hanging out in his room more often?

  ○ Health: Have her eating habits changed—eating more or less? Has there been a change in her weight? Does she generally complain of not feeling well—headaches, stomachaches, more colds, an increase in acne, trouble sleeping? Has she begun or increased use of alcohol or drugs? Have you taken the child to a doctor, counselor, or therapist because of the symptoms you've noticed?

- Access and review your district's harassment and/or bullying policies. Often these can be found on the district's website or in the student handbook. The policy should include a grievance procedure for reporting the behavior. Follow that procedure and document every step taken that shows you adhered to the policy's mandate.
- If your child was subjected to any form of sexual harassment or bullying from a teacher or other school staff, report the behavior to the school board chair, the superintendent, and the principal immediately. Provide these school officials with a copy of your documentation. If the teacher touched your child sexually, contact the police department and child protection as well. Be sure to document the incident(s) that occurred, who you spoke to at the school, and what was said and/or done.

  If you meet with and/or call school officials to inform them of the incident(s), be sure you document to whom you spoke; the day, time, and length of the conversation (indicate the start and end times); what you said; what the school official said; the demeanor/tone of the school official; and what the official stated would occur as a result of the complaint. Be sure to get a timeframe of the school's proposed follow-up with your child, and when they will be getting back to you. Document the outcome of the conversation. If you called the school official and failed to get a return call, document that phone call and each additional phone call you made until the two of you were able to connect. More will be discussed about meeting with the school official later in this chapter.
- If your child was sexually harassed or bullied by a classmate in the classroom, inform the teacher; if the misconduct occurred outside the classroom, contact the principal or superintendent. Make sure you document the incident(s), and document who you contacted at the school and their response. Ask the teacher/principal what they intend to do in response to your complaint, when they intend to do it, and to inform you when their follow-through is completed, and document what they tell you.
- If the school official decided an investigation will occur in response to your complaint, it should be prompt, thorough, and impartial. Not all complaints require a formal investigation; some minor

misconduct may be successfully handled with an informal follow-through. If your sexual harassment complaint includes behaviors of a probable crime such as rape, criminal sexual assault, or battery, the police must be informed. The police will conduct a criminal investigation; school districts must, however, also conduct their own investigation. A criminal investigation and a school's investigation of sexual harassment, a civil offense, require different standards. When conducting a sexual harassment investigation, the standard used is a "preponderance of evidence," which generally means that more likely than not the alleged harassment occurred. If a criminal complaint involves two students, one as the offender, and one as the victim, the school may be required to contact child protection services.

- An investigation of the child's allegation should determine whether the sexual harassment or bullying occurred. If so, did the sexual harassment rise to the level of illegal harassment or was the behavior just a violation of the school's policy (and based on what evidence)? The investigation should determine the scope and severity of the behavior, identify the perpetrators, evaluate the harm to the victims, and determine the appropriate corrective action. If an investigation is required, ask the school official the following questions:

  ○ Who will do the investigation? Ideally, it would be important that your child is at least somewhat comfortable with the individual conducting the investigation. That may not be possible if, for example, the victim has never met the investigator. If the perpetrator was a boy/man, your child may be more comfortable with a female investigator.

  ○ What specific training has the investigator received in investigating such complaints and interviewing children? It's been my experience that most individuals charged with conducting investigations within schools have not been trained in how to do so, including how to interview children and teens. When there is an incompetent investigator, you cannot trust the process or the outcome of the investigation. It is key that the investigator is skilled and competent and has been thoroughly trained in how to conduct investigations. Their training should have involved more than a half day of training, for example, because conducting investigations is a complex skill to learn. Sometimes a school district will call its attorney to do the investigation. That doesn't mean the attorney has been trained in investigative techniques or in how to interview children. Ask the same questions about the attorney's competence as you would a non-attorney. Request an investigator who is skilled and has been trained.

- How many investigations has their investigator completed? This is *somewhat* important as it *should* denote competence. However, if the investigator has never been trained in the correct investigative techniques, then they may have completed, say, fifty investigations but they were all incorrectly done due to never being taught how to conduct an investigation.
- When will the investigation begin? Ideally, it should start within forty-eight hours, but there is no hard and fast rule. The sooner the investigation begins the better, so memories don't start to fade, and witnesses and others can't meet to corroborate and/or fabricate their stories. The sooner it begins, the sooner there is an opinion and a remedy can be implemented.
- What is their investigative process? There are certain elements and steps contained in a good investigation including: interviewing the victim, witnesses, and the harasser/bully. In addition, it may require speaking with the offender's and victim's parents, teachers, or even a coach, and reviewing student records and other evidence, policies, and laws.
- When do they hope to complete the investigation? It is sometimes hard to speculate; however, it usually shouldn't take more than a few days. One parent waited three months for the completion of the investigation. There is no excuse for that kind of timeframe, and, if the investigation is in response to a sexual harassment complaint, waiting too long may be a violation of Title IX.
- Who will make the decision as to whether the behavior was sexual harassment and/or against the district's policy? What qualifications does this person have to make the decision? If the decision maker has never been through harassment training, how can she or he have enough knowledge to make the decision?

○ How will the decision be made—based on what criteria? To determine if sexual harassment occurred, a number of factors need to be considered in making the decision:

- Was the behavior welcome?
- Was it severe, persistent, pervasive, and offensive enough to interfere with the victim's ability to learn or take part in school activities?
- Was the standard for the decision that of a "reasonable person/ girl/victim"? In other words, "would any other 'victim' in the same or similar situation feel that she or he has been sexually harassed?"
- Was it sexual and/or gender-based misconduct?

○ Who will determine the consequences to the perpetrator and how will that decision be made? For example, a verbal warning, suspension, expulsion, or a transfer to another classroom are a few of the possible consequences.

○ What remedy will be implemented with the victim? For example, will he or she be transferred to another classroom, home schooled with the district's support, transferred to another school, receive a psychological assessment, and so on? Your child should not be re-victimized or penalized by the remedy. For example, unless your child wants to transfer to a different classroom or school, it is the offender who should be transfered.

○ What steps will the school take to prevent retaliation and the re-occurrence of harassment and bullying for all students as a result of this incident(s)? For example, the school should provide training for the perpetrators, the larger student population, faculty and staff including bus drivers, the school board, and any family members of students. Additionally, the school policy and grievance procedure may require review and revision.

- A school is required to take prompt and effective steps to end the harassment, prevent harassment from reoccurring, prevent retaliation, and take measures to curtail the harassing behavior from the school environment. These steps should occur whether the investigation demonstrated that misconduct was harassment or bullying, according to OCR.[2, 3] Schools should monitor the behavior of the perpetrator and ask the victim and her or his family if the behavior has indeed stopped and whether there is retaliation. As parents, the school should inform you of the steps to take if there are continuing problems.

- Unfortunately, schools do not always follow through in the way we would like, or the interventions the school implemented were ineffective and the bullying or harassment continues. If that happens, a stronger stance with the school may be required. Again, inform the teacher or principal of the misconduct. This time you may want to make an appointment for a face-to-face meeting rather than to speak over the phone, if that was what you did previously. Bring a copy of your documentation and the school's harassment and/ or bullying policy with you to the meeting. Give a copy of your documentation to the teacher or principal, always keeping a copy for yourself. Inform the teacher or principal that it is unacceptable that the harassment or bullying has continued, and it is against the school's policy. Point out the portion of the policy that states the misconduct is unacceptable. Tell the teacher or principal that you expect steps will be taken so the harassment or bullying stops immediately, and ask how they are going to do so. Stress that sexual harassment is a violation of Title IX and therefore must be stopped or the district is at risk of liability.

- Do not agree to a school mediation between your child and the perpetrator. It is too easy to re-victimize the victim because, unless they have been trained in mediation, adults don't have the skill. Often, the victim is made to accept some of the blame, either explicitly or implicitly, for her or his own victimization.

- Document your meeting—what you said, how the teacher or principal responded, and how the meeting concluded. If the behavior continues after this meeting, and you have discussed it with the teacher but not the principal or superintendent, now is the time to meet with the principal or superintendent, bringing your documentation, discussing the complaint process outlined in the policy, and the expectation that the behavior will stop immediately. Document the details of the meeting. If the sexual misconduct was severe, you may need to meet with the principal and the school superintendent before you meet with the teacher. As mentioned earlier, if the misconduct was by a teacher, speak immediately to the superintendent and school board chair, police, and child protection services.

- If your efforts to this point seem to be falling on deaf ears, and the sexual harassment or bullying is continuing, and if you have yet to meet with the superintendent, do so now. If you have met with the superintendent and the behavior continues, now is the time to meet with the school board chair. Depending on the severity of the harassment or the bullying, you may want to meet with the superintendent or the school board chair earlier in the process.

If the behavior is, in your opinion, sexual harassment, including harassment of GLBT students, and/or same-sex harassment, and if you still are not able to impel the school district to intervene and make it stop, you have yet more options. You may contact the OCR (see "Resources" beginning on p. 259 for regional office locations and phone numbers), your state's human rights office (states may label their state human rights/civil rights office differently; see "Resources" beginning on p. 263 for phone numbers and websites), or an attorney. If the behavior is bullying, at this time there is no federal agency or federal bullying law for you to use to file a lawsuit. Check with your state's anti-bullying law to see if you have any redress, and try contacting your state's department of education for assistance. If the bullying has escalated to physical assault, contact law enforcement.

Once OCR or your state's office of civil rights has received your complaint, they will evaluate it to determine if the agency should conduct an investigation to determine if there is a violation of Title IX or state law. If OCR or your state decides to conduct an investigation, it may take months before it occurs. After the completion of the investigation, you will more than likely wait several more months to be informed of their findings. This is a long, stressful, and frustrating process. The process is free, however, in contrast to skipping this formal complaint option and hiring an attorney. Remember too that filing a formal complaint with OCR or the state is not filing a lawsuit; rather it is an attempt to pressure the school district to implement the required sexual harassment prevention and intervention strategies to be in compliance with federal or state laws.

Some families have chosen to contact their newspapers and television stations to share their story publicly with positive results. Often schools will respond to complaints when they receive poor media attention. Be prepared for the school's denial, however. They will claim (and may see it as the truth) that they took all steps possible to stop the misconduct. Contacting the media, while it may be effective, may have negative consequences to the victim and the victim's family (as discussed in chapter 7).

Be prepared for a backlash towards the victim at any point in this process. Your family may potentially be victimized as well if OCR or your state's human rights department is involved and begins an investigation, or if you begin legal action against the school, and if the media covers the story. If you contact an attorney and the attorney feels you have probable cause for a lawsuit, there is a risk of retaliation from some within the community.

After a state's human rights department found probable cause for sexual harassment against a teenage girl in her school, the city newspaper's *letters to the editor* became the battle ground about the harassment and the finding of probable cause. While some former students and adults wrote letters in support of the teenager and the courage she had in filing a complaint with the state, numerous other adults wrote in support of the school, minimized what this girl experienced by labeling the behavior as merely "unfortunate," and referred to her as a militant feminist.

To effectively deal with harassment and bullying, schools should have a central place to keep a record of all complaints of which they are aware. Ask your district if they keep track of this information and what they do with it. The Title IX Coordinator should ensure such record storage exists and is monitored with complete records identifying the outcome of each complaint. Without access to the records, it is almost impossible for schools to monitor and evaluate pervasive patterns of harassment and bullying when different school officials are aware of different complaints, and those complaints are not placed in a central location. This is particularly important when it appears as though one incident does not rise to the level of sexual harassment, yet, when referring to the stored records, it is evident that the one incident is actually one of several that the student has committed. This monitoring is critical to prevent ongoing misconduct that intensifies to illegal harassment. If the monitoring is done correctly, it will demonstrate what tactics were or were not effective in curtailing the misconduct. Sexual harassers are not likely to be a one-time perpetrator but rather repeat their misconduct with multiple classmates. Without the central database/record of complaints, even assuming that others documented and turned in the complaints to the appropriate school official, it would be difficult to monitor repeated harassment.

When a child tells you about her or his sexual harassment or bullying at school, it is sometimes a tough decision to determine the role to play—coach, mentor, advocate, or whistleblower, or all of these. Your most important role is to get all the facts from your child: who, what, when, where. Write it down; be specific even if the needed language bothers you. Get copies of the school's policies, and, when you talk to the school, keep detailed notes. Realize that your child may start showing signs that this incident is impacting his or her emotional and physical health and school work and attendance. The school district is required to stop the behavior—your job is to protect your child.

⑬

CONCLUSION

This was an emotional book to write. It was difficult writing about sexual harassment and bullying of students in our schools. It was probably difficult for many of you to read about it as well. The solutions to the problems of the misconduct are not simple. They require strong leadership, firm commitment, caring, and passion to delve into what is required to change the school's culture. Some progress has been made—state anti-bullying legislation, U.S. Supreme Court decisions, new case law regarding sexual harassment, school policies, and curricula have had some impact on students, schools, and parents. But, we have a long way to go.

Because the school includes society's mores of patriarchy, the problem of sexual (and other protected class) harassment and bullying is broader than just a school problem. School districts require assistance to "fix" this problem; they can't do it alone. Parents, faculty, administrators, community members, and other stakeholders of our children's well-being, have the responsibility to teach about, and to model, the behaviors of empathy, civility, equality, respect, integrity, peace, courtesy, and honesty. In addition, we must fuel an appreciation for the differences among us, including religion, gender, social status, race, and disability, among others, and embrace human worth and dignity for all. After all, we are citizens of the human race.

A multidisciplinary approach involving faith communities, public health, policy makers, parents, schools, and students must address the nexus of sexual harassment, bullying, and other forms of violence and gender violence. Sexual harassment and bullying in our schools are representative of larger societal issues in which we are all immersed. Our society shapes who we are, and provides alternatives in which to live. We were born into patriarchy, and can't avoid being entwined within it, but we do have a choice as to how to challenge and change its hold on us. As Archbishop Desmond Tutu said, "Our humanity is caught up in that of all others. We are human because we belong. We are made for community, for togetherness, for family, to exist in a delicate network of interdependence. . . . We are sisters and brothers of one another whether we like it or not, and each of us is a precious individual."[1]

NOTES

CHAPTER I

1. "Insights in Ink," *Star Tribune*, Newspaper on Education Program, Minneapolis, MN, 1992.

2. Kate Snow and Kelly Hagen, "Teen Girls Hazed on NJ High School 'Slut List,'" ABC Good Morning America, September 23, 2009. Accessed January 28, 2011 from abcnews.go.com/GMA/teen-girls-hazed-slut-list/story?id=8649050.

3. U.S. Department of Education, Office for Civil Rights, *Revised Sexual Harassment Guidance: Sexual Harassment of Students by School Employees, Other Students, or Third Parties.* Washington, DC: U.S. Department of Education, January 19, 2001. Accessed July 7, 2007 from www2.ed.gov/about/offices/list/ocr/docs/shguide.html.

4. U.S. Department of Education, *Revised Sexual Harassment Guidance.*

5. Susan Fineran and Larry Bennett, "Gender and Power Issues of Peer Sexual Harassment Among Teenagers," *Journal of Interpersonal Violence* 14, no. 6 (1999): 626–41.

6. Debbie Epstein, "Keeping Them in Their Place: Hetero/sexist Harassment, Gender and the Enforcement of Homosexuality," in *Sexual Harassment: Contemporary Feminist Perspectives*, ed. Alison M. Thomas and Celia Kitzinger, 154–71 (Buckingham: Open University Press, 1997).

7. Elina Lahelma, "Gendered Conflicts in Secondary School: Fun or Enactment of Power?" *Gender and Education* 14, no. 3 (2002): 295–306.

8. June Larkin, "Walking Through Walls: The Sexual Harassment of High School Girls," *Gender and Education* 3 (June 1994): 263–80.

9. Epstein, "Keeping Them in Their Place."

10. Ann Phoenix, "Youth and Gender: New Issues, New Agenda," *Young* 3 (1997): 2–19. Accessed February 4, 2011 from Sage database.

11. Jane Kenway and Lindsay Fitzclarence, "Masculinity, Violence, and Schooling: Challenging Poisonous Pedagogies," *Gender and* Education 9 (1997): 117–33. Accessed May 29, 2008 from EBSCO database.

12. Michael S. Kimmel, "Masculinity as Homophobia: Fear, Shame, and Silence in the Construction of Gender Identity," in *Theorizing Masculinities*, ed. Harry Brod and Michael Kaufman, 119–41. Thousand Oaks, CA: Sage, 1994.

13. Kenway and Fitzclarence, "Masculinity, Violence, and Schooling."

14. Catherine Hill and Holly Kearl, Crossing the Line: Sexual Harassment at School. (Washington, DC: American Association of UniveristyWomen, 2011).

15. American Association of University Women Educational Foundation, *Hostile Hallways: AAUW Survey on Sexual Harassment in American Schools* (Washington, DC: AAUW, 2001).

16. Education for All Global Monitoring Report Team, *Gender and Education for All: The Leap to Equality Summary Report* (Paris: UNESCO, 2003). Accessed March 29, 2009 from unesdoc.unesco.org/images/0013/001325/132550e.pdf.

17. Nicola Jones, Karen Moore, Eliana Villar-Marquez, and Emma Broadbent, "Painful Lessons: The Politics of Preventing Sexual Violence and Bullying at School," working paper 295 (London: Overseas Development Institute, October 2008). Accessed February 28, 2009 from www.odi.org.uk/resources/download/2429.pdf.

18. Ibid.

19. Education For All Global Monitoring Report Team, *Gender and Education for All*.

20. Judith Mirsky, "Beyond Victims and Villains: Addressing Sexual Violence in the Education Sector," report no. 47 (London: The Panos Institute, 2003). Accessed March 22, 2011 from www.panos.org.uk/?lid=250.

21. Etienne G. Krug, Linda L. Dahlberg, James A. Mercy, Anthony B. Zwi, and Rafael Lozano, eds., *World Report on Violence and Health* (Geneva: World Health Organization, 2002). Accessed March 25, 2009 from whqlibdoc.who.int/publications/2002/9241545615_eng.pdf.

22. Jeanne Ward and Jackie Kirk, "Violence Against Girls in School," in *Broken Bodies Broken Dreams: Violence Against Women Exposed*, ed. Lisa Ernst, 73–81 (Nairobi: United Nations, 2005). Accessed January 30, 2009 from www.irinnews.org/IndepthMain.aspx?IndepthId=59&ReportId=72831.

23. Fiona Leach and Sara Humphreys, "Gender Violence in Schools: Taking the 'Girl-as-Victims' Discourse Forward," *Gender & Development* 15 (2007): 51–65. Accessed January 12, 2009 from EBSCO database.

24. American Association of University Women, *Hostile Hallways*.

25. Fionnuala Ni Aolain, University of Minnesota law professor, personal communication, International Women's Day Celebration: Transforming the World Through Women's Voices, March 14, 2009 in Minneapolis, MN.

26. United Nations, *UN Declaration on the Elimination of Violence Against Women*, Resolution No. A/RES/48/104 (New York: United Nations, December 1993). Accessed January 28, 2009 from www.un.org/documents/ga/res/48/a48r104.htm.

27. Education for all Global Monitoring Team, "Gender and Education for All."

28. Jo Becker, *Easy Targets: Violence Against Children Worldwide* (New York: Human Rights Watch, 2001). Accessed January 19, 2009 from www.hrw.org/legacy/reports/2001/children/index.htm.

29. Ibid.

30. Krug, *World Report on Violence and Health*.

31. United Nations 2015 Millennium Goals. Accessed February 27, 2009 from un.org/millenniumgoals/gender.shtml.

32. Education For All Global Monitoring Team, *Gender and Education for All*.

33. Muta Kazue, "Sexual Harassment and Empowerment of Women in Japan," *NiASnytt: Asia Insights* 1 (2004): 12–13. Retrieved March 17, 2009 from www.nias.ku.dk/nytt/2004_1/2004_11.pdf.

34. Paulo S. Pinhiero, "Violence Against Children in Schools and Educational Settings," in *World Report on Violence Against Children*, 109–143 (Geneva: United Nations, 2006). Accessed March 25, 2009 from www.crin.org/docs/UNVAC_World_Report_on_Violence_against_Children.pdf.

35. Ward, "Violence Against Girls in School."

36. Fiona Leach, "Gender Violence in Schools in the Developing World," in *Combating Gender Violence in and around Schools*, ed. Fiona Leach and Claudia Mitchell, 23–29 (Sterling, VA: Trentham Books, 2006).

37. *Meritor Savings Bank v. Vinson*, 477 U.S. 57 (1986).

38. *Franklin v. Gwinnett Cty. Public Schools*, 911 F.2d 617 (CA11 1990).

39. *Davis v. Monroe County Board of Educ.*, 526 U.S. 629 (1999). A fifth-grade girl was touched on her breasts and genitals by a male classmate for months. Her teachers refused to let her move her seat away from him, and the principal refused to meet with her and other female students who were troubled by him.

40. U.S. Equal Employment Opportunity Commission, Policy Guidance on Current Issues of Sexual Harassment (Washington, DC: U.S. Dept. of Education, 2001). Accessed June 26, 2008 from www2.ed.gov/about/offices/list/ocr/docs/shguide.html.

41. Russlyn Ali, *Dear Colleague Letter: Harassment and Bullying* (Washington, DC: U.S. Department of Education, October 26, 2010). Accessed from www2.ed.gov/about/offices/list/ocr/letters/colleague-201010.html.

42. *Davis v. Monroe County Board of Educ.*, 526 U.S. 629 (1999)

43. *Gebser v. Lago Vista Indep. School District*, 524 U.S. 274 (1998). A high school girl sued her school district alleging that her social studies teacher (age fifty-one), with whom she had a lengthy relationship since the age of fourteen, that ended when the two were found having sex, used his authority to entice her, and her school district not only failed to define sexual harassment but failed to provide any redress for complaints.

44. U.S. Department of Education, *OCR's Revised Sexual Harassment Guidance.*

45. Ibid.

46. Ibid.

47. Ibid.

48. Ali, *Dear Colleague.*

49. U.S. Department of Education, *OCR's Revised Sexual Harassment Guidance.*

50. Ali, *Dear Colleague.*

51. U.S. Department of Education, *OCR's Revised Sexual Harassment Guidance.*

52. *Gebser v. Lago Vista Indep. School District*, 524 U. S. 274 (1998).

53. *Davis v. Monroe County Board of Educ.*, 526 U.S. 629 (1999).

54. U.S. Department of Education, *OCR's Revised Sexual Harassment Guidance.*

55. *DOE v. Dallas Independent School District et al.*, 220 F.3d 380 (5th Cir. 2000).

56. *Jackson Baynard v. Catherine Malone and Craig J. Lawson; Alexandria City School Board, et al.*, 268 F. 3d 228 (4th Cir. 2001).

57. *Theno v. Tonganoxie Unified Sch. Dist. No. 464*, 377 F. Supp. 2d 952 (2005 U.S. Dist).

58. *Milligan v. Board of Trustees, Southern Illinois University*, No. 9-cv-320-jpg-cjp, 2010 WL 2649917, June 30, 2010.

59. Elsa Cole, "Troubleshooting Tips: Section 1983 vs. Title IX," *Educator's Guide to Controlling Sexual Harassment* 18, no. 5 (2011): 4.

60. *Mary v. Pittsburgh Public Schools*, 2010 W. L. 562909 (W.D. Pa. Feb. 17, 2010).

61. *Price Waterhouse v. Hopkins*, 490 U.S. 228 (1989).

62. U.S. Department of Education, *OCR's Revised Sexual Harassment Guidance*.

63. Ali, *Dear Colleague*.

CHAPTER 2

1. Kenneth A. Mines, *Letter of Finding: (S) Eden Prairie Schools (Minn)* (OCR 05-92-1174) (Chicago: U.S. Department of Education, Office for Civil Rights, May 1992), 39.

2. Lisa M. Kelsey, "Note: Kids with Kissies and Schools with the Jitters: Finding a Reasonable Solution to the Problem of Student-To-Student Sexual Harassment in Elementary Schools," *The Boston University Public Interest Law Journal* 8 (Fall 1998): 119–44.

3. Susan Strauss, "Sexual Harassment at an Early Age," *Principal* (Sept. 1994): 6–29.

4. American Association of University Women Educational Foundation, *Hostile Hallways: Bullying, Teasing and Sexual Harassment in School* (Washington, DC: AAUW, 2001).

5. Minnesota Attorney General's Office, *Minnesota Attorney General's Report on Sexual Harassment in Minnesota Schools* (St. Paul: Minnesota Attorney General's Office, 1994).

6. JuJu Chang, et al. "First-Grader Labeled a Sexual Harasser: Has Zero Tolerance for Sexual Harassment in Schools Gone Too Far? (ABC Good Morning America, April 4, 2008). Accessed from abcnews.go.com/GMA/AsSeenOnGMA/story?id=4585388.

7. Sarah K. Murnen and Linda Smolak, "The Experience of Sexual Harassment Among Grade-School Students: Early Socialization of Female Subordination?" *Sex Roles* 43, no.1/2 (2000): 1–17.

8. Mines, *Letter of Finding*, 1992.

9. Strauss, "Sexual Harassment at an Early Age."

10. Andrew Marshall, "New York Targets Very Young for Sex Offences," *The Independent*, July 3, 2000. Accessed January 17, 2009 from www.independent.co.uk/news/world/americas/new-york-targets-very-young-for-sex-offences-707587.html.

11. Elaine Yaffe, "Expensive, Illegal, and Wrong: Sexual Harassment in Our Schools," *Kappan Special Report* (November 1995): 1–15.

12. Davis v. Monroe County *Bd. of Educ.*, 74 F.3d 1186, 1195 (11th Cir. 1996).

13. Dara Penn, "Comment: Finding the Standard of Liability Under Title IX for Student-Against-Student Sexual Harassment: Confrontation, Confusion, and Still No Conclusions," *Temple Law Review* 783 (Summer 1997).

14. Susan Strauss, "Sexual Harassment in K–12," in *Academic and Workplace Sexual Harassment: A Handbook of Cultural, Social Science, Management, and Legal Perspectives*, ed. Michele Paludi and Carmen A. Paludi, Jr., 105–45 (Westport, CT: Praeger, 2003).

15. Melinda Henneberger, "Now Sex and Violence Link at an Earlier Age," *New York Times*, July 4, 1993, 6.

16. Strauss, "Sexual Harassment in K–12."

17. Melinda Henneberger, "Younker School 'Game': or Hiding Sex Abuse?" *New York Times*, June 25, 1993.

18. Henneberger, "Now Sex and Violence Link at an Earlier Age."

19. Kurt Chandler, "Experts Report Increase in Child Sex Play: Culture, Abuse May Be Factor," *Star Tribune*, August 6, 1995.

20. Ibid.

21. Ellie Young, Melissa L. Allen, and Betty Y. Ashbaker, "Responding to Sexual Harassment in Special Education Settings," *Teaching Exceptional Children* 36, no. 4 (March/April 2004): 62–67; Ellie Young, Melissa L. Allen, and Betty Y. Ashbaker, "Sexual Harassment Handout for Helping Children at Home and School II," *Handouts For Families and Educators*, vol. 2 (National Association of School Psychologists, July 2004), 99–102.

22. Susan Fineran, "With Disabilities and Peer Sexual Harassment: School Policy and Practice Implications," paper presented at the Family Violence Research Conference, Durham, New Hampshire, August 2002.

23. Mines, *Letter of Finding*.

24. Harilyn Rousso and Michael Wehmeyer, eds., *Double Jeopardy: Addressing Gender Equity in Special Education* (Albany: State University of New York Press, 2001).

25. Harilyn Rousso and Michael Wehmeyer, eds., *Double Jeopardy: Addressing Gender Equity in Special Education* (Albany: State University of New York Press, 2001).

26. Paul Secunda, "At the Crossroads of Title IX and a New 'Idea': Why Bullying Need Not be 'a Normal Part of Growing Up' for Special Education Children," *Duke Journal of Gender Law & Policy* 12 (2005): 1–31.

27. U.S. Department of Education, Office of Special Education Programs (OSEP), IDEA website. idea.ed.gov/explore/home

28. Ibid.

29. Secunda, "At the Crossroads of Title IX."

CHAPTER 3

1. Joseph G. Kosciw, Emily A. Greytak, Elizabeth M. Diaz, and Mark J. Bartkiewicz, *The 2009 National School Climate Survey: The Experiences of Lesbian, Gay, Bisexual and Transgender Youth in Our Nation's Schools* (New York: GLSEN, 2010). Accessed from www.glsen.org/binary-data/GLSEN_ATTACHMENTS/file/000/001/1675-1.pdf.

2. *William Wolfe v. Fayetteville Arkansas School District*, No-2570 (8th Cir. July 14, 2010).

3. Dana Rudolph, "Fed to Schools: Law Requires Actions Against Bullying," *Keen News Service*, October 26, 2010. Accessed from www.keennewsservice.com/2010/10/26/fed-to-schools-law-requires-actions-against-bullying).

4. Kosciw et al., *The 2009 National School Climate Survey*.

5. *Theno v. Tonganoxie Unified School District No. 464*, 377 F.Supp. 2d 952.

6. Paul Secunda, "At the Crossroads of Title IX and a New 'Idea': Why Bullying Need Not Be a 'Normal Part of Growing Up' for Special Education Children," *Duke Journal of Gender Law and Policy* 12 (2005): 1–52.

7. Allan Johnson, *The Gender Knot: Unraveling Our Patriarchal Legacy* (Philadelphia: Temple University Press, 1997).

8. Ibid.

9. Michelle R. Davis, "Questions About Transgender Student Protections On the Rise, Schools Must Consider Ramifications," *Educator's Guide to Controlling Sexual Harassment* 16, no. 5 (2009): 6–7.

10. Elizabeth Meyer, *Gender, Bullying and Harassment: Strategies to End Sexism and Homophobia in Schools* (New York: Teachers College Press Columbia University, 2009).

11. *Doe v. Brockton Sch. Comm.*, 2000 WL 33342399 (Mass. App. Ct. 2000).

12. *Shore Regional High School Bd. of Educ. v. P.S.*, 381 F.3d 194, 198 (3rd Cir. 2004).

13. California Safe Schools Coalition, *Safe Place to Learn: Consequences of Harassment Based on Actual or Perceived Sexual Orientation and Gender Non-Conformity and Steps for Making Schools Safe* (Davis: University of California Press, 2004).

14. Michael Bochenek and A. Widney Brown, *Hatred in the Hallways: Violence and Discrimination Against Gay, Lesbian, Bisexual and Transgender Students in U.S. Schools* (New York: Human Rights Watch, 2001).

15. Kosciw et al., *The 2009 National School Climate Survey*.

16. Kathryn E. W. Himmelstein and Hannah Brückner, "Criminal Justice and School Sanctions Against Nonheterosexual Youth: A National Longitudinal

Study. *Pediatrics* (December 6, 2010); accessed January 4, 2011, from http://pediatrics.aappublications.org/content/early/2010/12/06/peds.2009-2306.full/pdf

17. ACLU, *The Cost of Harassment: A Fact Sheet for Lesbian, Gay, Bisexual, and Transgender High School Students* (ACLU, February 9, 2007). Accessed from www.aclu.org/lgbt-rights_hiv-aids/cost-harassment-fact-sheet-lesbian-gay-bisexual-and-transgender-high-school-stu.

18. *Nabozny v. Podlesny*, 92 F.3d 446 (7th Cir. 1996).

19. *Doe v. Southeastern Greene School District.*

CHAPTER 4

1. http://thinkexist.com/quotations

2. Hannah Arendt, "A Special Supplement: Reflections on Violence," *The New York Review of Books*. February 27, 1969. Accessed November 17, 2010, from www.nybooks.com/articles/archives/1969/feb/27/a_special_supplement_reflection_on_violence/

3. Ian Rivers, Neil Duncan, and Valerie E. Besag, *Bullying: A Handbook for Educators and Parents* (Lanham, MD: Rowman and Littlefield, 2009).

4. Barbara Coloroso, *The Bully, The Bullied, and the Bystander* (Toronoto: HarperCollins, 2006).

5. Nan Stein, "Bullying or Sexual Harassment: The Missing Discourse of Rights in an Era of Zero Tolerance," *Arizona Law Review* 45, no. 3 (2003): 783–99.

6. Renae D. Duncan, "Peer and Sibling Aggression: An Investigation of Intra and Extra-Familial Bullying," *Journal of Interpersonal Violence* 14 (1999): 871–886. Accessed November 17, 2010, from Sage Database.

7. Dorothy L. Espelage and Melissa K. Holt, "Bullying and Victimization During Early Adolescence: Peer Influence and Psychosocial Correlates," in *Bullying Behavior: Current Issues, Research and Interventions*, eds. Robert A. Geffner, Marti Loring, and Corinna Young (New York: Haworth Press, 2011).

8. Linda Jeffrey, DeMond Miller, and Margaret Linn, "Middle School Bullying as a Context for the Development of Passive Observers to the Victimization of Others," in *Bullying Behavior: Current Issues, Research and Interventions*, ed. Robert A. Geffner, Marti Loring, and Corinna Young, 143–56 (New York: Haworth, 2001).

9. Suellen Fried and Paula Fried, *Bullies and Victims: Helping Your Child Through the Schoolyard Battlefield* (New York: Evans, 1996).

10. Dan Olweus, *Core Program Against Bullying and Antisocial Behavior: A Teacher Handbook* (Bergen, Norway: Olweus, 2001).

11. Ellen DeLara, "Bullying and Violence in American Schools," in *Handbook of Children, Culture, and Violence*, ed. Nancy E. Dowd, Dorothy G. Singer, and Robin Fretwell Wilson, 333–54 (Thousand Oaks, CA: Sage, 2006).

12. Stein, "Bullying or Sexual Harassment."

13. Coloroso, *The Bully, the Bullied, and the Bystander.*

14. James Gruber and Susan Fineran, "Comparing the Impact of Bullying and Sexual Harassment Victimization on the Mental and Physical Health of Adolescents," *Sex Roles* 58 (2008): 13–14. Accessed March 13, 2010, from Proquest database.

15. Nan Stein, "Commentary: Sexual Harassment Left Behind: What the 'Bullying' Framework is Doing to Civil Rights Laws and Framework," *Research & Action Report* 32, Boston: Wellesley Center for Women, 6–7.

16. David Finkelhor, Richard Ormrod, Heather Turner, and Sherry Hamby, "The Victimization of Children and Youth," *Child Maltreatment* 10 (2005): 5–25. Accessed March 13, 2010, from the Sage database.

17. Ibid.

18. Tonja R. Nansel, Mary E. Overpeck, R. S. Pilla, W. June Ruan, B. Simons-Morton, and Peter Scheidt, "Bullying Behaviors Among U.S. Youth: Prevalence and Association with Psychosocial Adjustment," *Journal of the American Medical Association* 285 (2001): 2094–100.

19. George Batsche and Howard M. Knoff, "Bullies and Their Victims: Understanding a Pervasive Problem in the Schools," *School Psychology Review* 23, no. 2 (1994): 165–74. Accessed from EBSCO database.

20. Michael Shear and Jacqueline L. Salmon, "An Education in Taunting; Schools Learning Dangers of Letting Bullies Go Unchecked," *Washington Post* online, May 2, 1999. Accessed April 12, 2010 from www.nldine.com/washingt2.htm.

21. Coloroso, *The Bully, the Bullied, and the Bystander.*

22. Ibid.

23. James Garbarino and Ellen DeLara, *And Words Can Hurt Forever: How to Protect Adolescents from Bullying, Harassment, and Emotional Violence* (New York: Simon & Schuster/The Free Press, 2002).

24. Stopbullying.org.

25. Stein, "Sexual Harassment Left Behind."

26. Ibid.

27. Olweus, *Core Program Against Bullying.*

28. Nansel, "Bullying Behaviors Among U.S. Youth."

29. Ibid.

30. "Bruised Inside: What Our Children Say About Youth Violence, What Causes It and What We Need to do About it." Washington Attorney General Christine Gregoire's Presidential Initiative on Our Children in the New Millennium. Michigan: A Report of the National Attorneys General, 2000. Accessed from www.michigan.gov/documents/bruised_inside_38596_7.pdf.

31. Finkelhor, "The Victimization of Children and Youth."

32. Patricia C. Duttweiler, "Who's at Risk? Gay and Lesbian Youth," *The Journal of At-Risk Issues* 3, no. 2 (1997). Accessed January 1, 2011 from www.dropoutprevention.org/statistics/gay-lesbian-youth.

33. Ellen DeLara, "Peer Predictability: An Adolescent Strategy for Enhancing a Sense of Safety at School," *Journal of School Violence* 1, no. 3 (2002): 31–56.

34. Ellen DeLara and James Garbarino, *An Educator's Guide to School-Based Interventions*, edited series, ed. J. M. Cooper (Boston, MA: Houghton Mifflin, 2003).

35. Susan M. Swearer, Dorothy L. Espelage, Tracy Vaillancourt, and Shelley Hymel, "What Can Be Done About School Bullying? Linking Research to Educational Practice," *Educational Researcher* 39, no. 1 (2010): 38.

36. Dorothy Espelage and Melissa K. Holt, "Bullying and Victimization during Early Adolescence: Peer Influences and Psychosocial Correlates," in *Bullying Behavior: Current Issues, Research, and Interventions*, ed. Robert A. Geffner, Marti Loring, and Corinna Young, 123–42 (New York: Haworth Press, 2006).

37. "Hatred in the Hallways: Violence and Discrimination Against Lesbian, Gay, Bisexual, and Transgender Students in U.S. Schools" (Human Rights Watch, 2001). Accessed July 3, 2009 from www.hrw.org/legacy/reports/2001/uslgbt/.

38. Miriam K. Ehrensaft, Patricia K. Cohen, Jocelyn Brown, Elizabeth Smailes, Henian Chen, and Jeffrey G. Johnson, "Intergenerational Transmission of Partner Violence: A 20-Year Prospective Study," *Journal of Consulting and Clinical Psychology* 71 (2003): 741–53. Accessed May 21, 2010 from EBSCO database.

39. Susan Limber, "Addressing Youth Bullying Behaviors," in *Educational Forum on Adolescent Health: Youth Bullying*, ed. M. Fleming and K. Towey (Chicago: American Medical Association, May 2002): 5–16.

40. "Life Lessons: Addressing School Bullying," CBS News. www.cbsnews.com/stories/2011/01/09/Sunday/main7227783.shtml.

41. Nansel, "Bullying Behaviors Among U.S. Youth," 2094–100.

42. Wendy M. Craig, "The Relationship Among Bullying, Victimization, Depression, Anxiety, and Aggression in Elementary School Children," *Personality and Individual Differences* 24 (1998): 123–30.

43. Leonard D. Eron, L. Rowell Huesman, Eric Dubow, Richard Romanoff, and Patty W. Yarmel. "Aggression and its Correlates over 22 Years," in *Childhood Aggression and Violence: Sources of Influence, Prevention, and Control*, ed. David H. Crowell, Ian M. Evans, and Clifford R. O'Donnell, 249–62 (New York: Plenum, 1987).

44. Richard J. Hazler, "Bullying Breeds Violence. You Can Stop It," *Learning* 22 (1994): 38–41.

45. Renae Duncan, "Peer and Sibling Aggression: An Investigation of Intra- and Extra-Familial Bullying," *Journal of Interpersonal Violence* 14, no. 8 (1999): 871–86. Accessed December 3, 2010 from Sage database.

46. Irene Whitney and Peter K. Smith, "A Survey of the Nature and Extent of Bullying in Junior/Middle and Secondary Schools," *Educational Research* 35 (1993): 3–25.

47. Limber, "Addressing Youth Bullying Behaviors."

48. Nansel, "Bullying Behaviors Among U.S. Youth."

49. Pamela Paul, "The Playground Gets Even Tougher," *New York Times*, Oct. 8, 2010. www.nytimes.com/2010/10/10/fashion/10cultural.html ?pagewanted-print.

50. Lyn Mikel Brown, *Girlfighting: Betrayal and Rejection Among Girls* (New York: New York University Press, 2003).

51. Ibid.

52. Ibid.

53. Stephanie DeLuca and James E. Rosenbaum, "Are Dropout Decisions Related to Safety Concerns, Social Isolation, and Teacher Disparagement?" Institute for Policy Research, IPR Working Papers, WP-00-18, Northwestern University, 2001. Accessed September 1, 2010 from www.northwestern.edu/ipr/publications/workingpapers/wpabstracts00/wp0018.html.

54. Gwendolyn Cartledge and Carolyn T. Johnson, "School Violence and Cultural Sensitivity," in *School Violence Intervention: A Practical Handbook* (2nd ed.), ed. J. C. Conoley and A. P. Goldstein, 441–82 (New York: Guilford, 2004).

55. Nansel, "Bullying Behaviors Among U.S. Youth."

56. Sandra Graham and Jaana Juvonen, "Ethnicity, Peer Harassment, and Adjustment in Middle School: An Exploratory Study," *Journal of Early Adolescence* 22, no. 2 (2002): 173–99. Accessed August 5, 2010 from Sage database.

57. "Life's Lessons," CBS News.

58. Coloroso, *The Bully, the Bullied, and the Bystander*.

59. Ellen DeLara, "Peer Predictability: An Adolescent Strategy for Enhancing a Sense of Safety at School," *Journal of School Violence* 1, no. 3 (2002): 31–56.

60. Nansel, "Bullying Behaviors Among U.S. Youth."

61. Susan Limber, "Peer Victimization: The Nature and Prevalence of Bullying Among Children and Youth," in *Handbook of Children, Culture, and Violence*, ed. Nancy E. Dowd, Dorothy G. Singer, and Robin Fretwell Wilson, 313–33 (Thousand Oaks, CA: Sage). This book is a wonderful compilation of book chapters written by a variety of authors on the topics of bullying and children's violence. Each chapter is rich in discussing the research on the topics.

62. Susan Limber, "Addressing Youth Bullying Behaviors," in *Educational Forum on Adolescent Health: Youth Bullying*, ed. Missy Fleming and Kelly Towey, 5–16 (Chicago: American Medical Association, May 2002).

63. Nansel, "Bullying Behaviors Among U.S. Youth."

64. Limber, "Peer Victimization."

65. Ibid.

66. Cynthia Liu, "The Neuroscience of Bullying," December 27, 2010. Accessed January 3, 2011 from www.care2.com/causes/education/blog/the -neuroscience-of-bullying/. This site provides links to various studies about the impact of bullying on the brain.

67. Frank W. Putnam, "Beyond Sticks and Stones," *American Journal Psychiatry* 167, no.12 (December 2010): 1422–24. Accessed February 13, 2011 from ajp.psychiatryonline.org/cgi/reprint/167/12/1422?maxtoshow=&hits=10& RESULTFORMAT=1&author1=f+putnam&andorexacttitle=and&andorexact titleabs=and&andorexactfulltext=and&searchid=1&FIRSTINDEX=0&sortsp ec=relevance&resourcetype=HWCIT.

68. Swearer, "What Can be Done About School Bullying?"

69. Coloroso, *The Bully, the Bullied, and the Bystander.*

70. Ibid.

71. Nansel, "Bullying Behaviors Among U.S. Youth."

72. Jaana Juvonen, Sandra Graham, and Mark A. Schuster, "Bullying Among Young Adolescents: The Strong, the Weak, and the Troubled," *Pediatrics* 112, no. 6 (2003): 1231–37.

73. Renae Duncan, "Peer and Sibling Aggression: An Investigation of Intra- and Extra-Familial Bullying," *Journal of Interpersonal Violence* 14, no. 8 (1999): 871–86. Accessed October 18, 2010 from Sage database.

74. Coloroso, *The Bully, the Bullied, and the Bystander.*

75. Anthony Pellegrini and Jeffrey D. Long, "Part of the Solution and Part of the Problem: The Role of Peers in Bullying, Dominance, and Victimization During the Transition from Primary School Through Secondary School," in *Bullying in American Schools: A Social-Ecological Perspective on Prevention and Intervention*, ed. Dorothy L. Espelage and Susan M. Swearer, 107–17 (Mahway, NJ: Erlbaum, 2004).

76. Coloroso, *The Bully, the Bullied, and the Bystander*.

77. Ibid.

78. Linda R. Jeffrey, DeMond Miller, and Margaret Linn, "Middle School Bullying as a Context for the Development of Passive Observers to the Victimization of Others," in *Bullying Behavior: Current Issues, Research, and Interventions*, ed. Robert A. Geffner, Marti Loring, and Corinna Young, 143–56 (New York: Haworth Press, 2001).

79. "Witnesses to Bullying May Suffer Most of All," *U.S. News: Health*, December 17, 2020. Accessed December 27, 2009 from health.usnews.com/health-news/family-health/brain-and-behavior/articles/2009/12/17/witnesses-to-bullying-may-suffer-most-of-all.

80. Coloroso, *The Bully, the Bullied, and the Bystander*.

81. Ibid.

82. Anthony D. Pellegrini, "Bullying, Victimization, and Sexual Harassment During the Transition to Middle School," *Educational Psychologist* 37 (2002): 151–63.

83. Swearer, "What Can be Done About School Bullying?"

84. Tracy Vaillancourt, Shelley Hymel, and Peter McDougal, "Bullying is Power: Implications for School-Based Intervention Strategies," *Journal of Applied School Psychology* 19, no. 2 (2003): 157–76.

85. Melissa K. Holt and Melissa A. Keys, "Teachers' Attitudes Toward Bullying," in *Bullying in American Schools: A Social-Ecological Perspective on Prevention and Intervention*, ed. Dorothy L. Espelage and Susan M. Swearer, 121–140 (Mahway, NJ: Erlbaum 2004).

86. Michael J. Boulton, "Teachers' Views on Bullying: Definitions, Attitudes, and Ability to Cope," *British Journal of Educational Psychology* 67 (1997): 223–33.

87. Ibid.

88. Ron Astor, Heather Meyer, and William Behre, "Unowned Places and Times: Maps and Interviews About Violence in High Schools," *American Education Research Journal* 36 (1999): 3–42. Accessed August 5, 2010 from Sage database.

89. Ellen DeLara, "Peer Predictability."

90. Larry Richardson, "A Safer Ride on the Bus: Many High School Students Prefer to Drive, at Greater Risk," *The Post Standard*, Syracuse, New York, September 22, 2002.

91. Debra Pepler and Wendy Craig, "A Peek Behind the Fence: Naturalistic Observations of Aggressive Children with Remote Audiovisual Recording," *Developmental Psychology* 31, no. 4 (1995): 548–53. Accessed September 17, 2010 from EBSCO database.

92. Wendy Craig and Debra Pepler, "Observations of Bullying and Victimization in the School Yard," *Canadian Journal of School Psychology* 13 (1997): 41–59.

93. Coloroso, *The Bully, the Bullied, and the Bystander*.

94. Swearer, "What Can be Done About School Bullying?"

95. "Kids with ADHD May be More Likely to Bully," MSNBC.com. Accessed January 4, 2011 from www.msnbc.msn.com/id/22813400/ns/health -kids_and_parenting/.

96. Dorothy Espelage and Christine S. Asidao, "Conversations With Middle School Students About Bullying and Victimization: Should We Be Concerned?" in *Bullying Behavior: Current Issues, Research, and Interventions*, ed. Robert A. Geffner, Marti Loring, and Corinna Young, 49–62 (New York: Haworth Press, 2001).

97. Swearer, "What Can be Done About School Bullying?"

98. Rachel C. Vreeman and Aaron A. Carroll, "A Systematic Review of School-Based Interventions to Prevent Bullying," *Archives of Pediatric and Adolescent Medicine* 16 (2007): 78–88.

99. Kenneth W. Merrell, Barbara A. Gueldner, Scott W. Ross, and Duane M. Isava, "How Effective are School Bullying Intervention Programs? A Meta-Analysis of Intervention Research," *School Psychology Quarterly* 23 (2008): 26–42.

100. Maria M. Ttofi, David P. Farrington, and Anna C. Baldry, *Effectiveness of Programmes to Reduce School Bullying*. Swedish Council for Crime Prevention, Information, and Publications (2008. Accessed December 23, 2010, from www.crim.cam.ac.uk/people/academic_research/maria_ttofi/s08 .pdf

101. Swearer, "What Can Be Done About School Bullying?"

102. Susan Swearer and Janice Delucia-Waack, "How to Curb School Bullying in Massachusetts," *Newsweek*, June 28 and July 5, 2010, 12.

103. Kenneth W. Merrell, Barbara A. Gueldner, Scott W. Ross, and Duane M. Isava, "How Effective Are School Bullying Intervention Programs? A Meta-Analysis of Intervention Research," *School Psychology Quarterly* 23 (2008): 26–42.

104. Michelle Davis, "State Antibullying Laws Appear Mostly Ineffective, But Local Programs Can Be Valuable, Experts Say," *Employer's Guide to Controlling Sexual Harassment* 17, no. 2 (2009): 8–9.

105. Ibid.

106. Bully Police USA, www.bullypolice.org/.

107. Kathleen Conn, "Schools' Legal Responsibility for Sexting."

108. www.bullypolice.org.

109. Davis, "State Antibullying Laws Appear Mostly Ineffective."

CHAPTER 5

1. Nan Stein, "Commentary: Sexual Harassment Left Behind: What the 'Bullying' Framework is Doing to Civil Rights Laws and Framework," *Research and Action Report*, Wellesley Centers for Women, 32 (2010):6–7.

2. Jessie Klein, "An Invisible Problem: Everyday Violence Against Girls in Schools," *Theoretical Criminology* 10, no. 147 (2006): 147–77.

3. Ibid., 148.

4. Ibid.

5. Eunice Oh, "Rutgers Student Commits Suicide After Secret Sex Tape," *People*, September 30, 2010. Accessed October 15, 2020 from www.people.com/people/article/0,,20430783,00.html.

6. Jill Smolowe, Steve Helling, Daniel S. Levy, and Diane Herbst, "I Was Bullied Because . . . ," *People*, October 18, 2010, 66–9.

7. Nan Stein, "Bullying or Harassment? The Missing Discourse of Rights in an Era of Zero Tolerance," *Arizona Law Review* 45, no. 3. (2003): 783–99.

8. Russlyn Ali, *Dear Colleague Letter: Harassment and Bullying* (Washington, DC: U.S. Department of Education, Office for Civil Rights, October 26, 2010). www2.ed.gov/about/offices/list/ocr/letters/colleague-201010.html.

9. Ibid.

10. Ibid.

11. Stein, "Bullying or Harassment?"

12. Stein, "Commentary: Sexual Harassment Left Behind."

13. Liz McNeil, Diane Herbst, Kristen Mascia, and Monique Jessen, "Bullied to Death," *People*, February 22, 2010, 63–65.

14. Nancy Gibbs, "When Bullying Goes Criminal," *Time.com*, April 19, 1010. Accessed September 14, 2010 from www.time.com/time/printout/0,8816,1978773,99.html.

15. Anna Briare, "Massachusetts Attorney Claims State Bullying Law Has No Teeth," *Masslive.com*, January 11, 2011. Accessed January 23, 2011 from www.masslive.com/bullying/index.ssf/2011/01/massachusetts_attorney_abigail_williams claims_state_bullyin.html.

16. Ibid.

17. Jack Flynn, "Phoebe Prince's Parents Settle With South Hadley School System on Discrimination Complaint," December 14, 2010. Accessed December

18, 2010 from www.masslive.com/news/index.ssf/2010/12/phoebe_prince_
parents_settle_south_hadley_discrimination.html.

18. James E. Gruber and Susan Fineran, "Comparing the Impact of Bullying and Sexual Harassment Victimization on the Mental and Physical Health
of Adolescents," *Sex Roles* 58 (2008): 13–14. Accessed August 5, 2010 from
Proquest database.

19. Elizabeth Meyer, *Gender, Bullying and Harassment: Strategies to End
Sexism and Homophobia in Schools* (New York: Teachers College Press Columbia University, 2009), 11.

20. Ali, *Dear Colleague*.

CHAPTER 6

1. Joy Powell, "Stalkers and Harassers Plunge into Social Media," *Star Tribune*, Minneapolis, MN, January 15, 2011, 7.

2. Denise M. Dalaimo, "Electronic Sexual Harassment," in *Sexual Harassment on Campus*, ed. Bernice R. Sandler and Robert J. Shoop, 85–103 (Needham Heights, MA: Allyn & Bacon, 1997).

3. Jeremy Olson, "'Defriending' Latest Form of Adolescent Cyberbullying," *Star Tribune*, October 22, 2010.

4. Amanda Lenhart, Kristen Purcell, Aaron Smith and Kathryn Zickuhr,
"Social Media & Mobile Internet Use Among Teens and Young Adults," Pew
Internet and American Life, 2010. Accessed January 2, 1011 from pewinternet
.org/~/media//Files/Reports/2010/PIP_Social_Media_and_Young_Adults_
Report_Final_with_toplines.pdf.

5. Amanda Lenhart, Rich Ling, Scott Campbell, and Kristen Purcell,
"Teens and Mobile Phones," PEW Research Center (Washington, DC, April
20, 2010).

6. Patricia Agatston, "Staff, Students, and Parents Need Education Programs to Prevent Cyberbullying, Increase Digital Literacy," *Educator's Guide
to Controlling Sexual Harassment* 17 (2009): 8.

7. Lenhart, Ling, Campbell, and Purcell, "Teens and Mobile Phones."

8. "Sex and Tech: Results from a Survey of Teens and Young Adults," The
National Campaign to Protect Teen and Unplanned Pregnancy. 2008, Accessed
from www.thenationalcampaign.org/sextech/pdf/sextech_summary.pdf.

9. Powell, "Stalkers and Harassers."

10. Kathleen Conn, "Cyberbullying and Cyberharassment in American
Schools: Cautionary Tales from the Courts," *Educator's Guide to Controlling
Sexual Harassment* (October 2009): Tab 700, 27–41.

11. "Sexting Girls Facing Porn Charge Sue D.A.," CBS News.com, March 27, 2009. www.cbsnews.com/stories/2009/03/27/earlyshow/main4896577.shtml.

12. Ibid.

13. bid.

14. Deborah Feyerick and Sheila Steffen, "'Sexting' Lands Teen on Sex Offenders List," CNN.com, April 9, 2009. Accessed March 17, 2011.

15. Mike Celizic, "Her Teen Committed Suicide over 'Sexting,'" Today.com, March 8, 2009. Accessed November 4, 2010, from today.msnbc.msn.com/id/29546030/ns/today-parenting/.

16. *Requa v. Kent School District. No. 415*, 492 F. Supp. 2d 1272, 222 Ed. Law Rep. 178 (W.D. Wash. 2007).

17. Ibid.

18. Michelle R. Davis, "Higher Levels of Depression Found Among Victims of Cyberbullying Than Other Bullying, Study Says," *Educator's Guide to Controlling Sexual Harassment* 18, no. 2 (2010): 10.

19. Joe Pinchot, "Update: Court Rules Student's Rights Violated: *Layshock* Case Called Free-Speech Victory," *The Herald*, February 5, 2010. Accessed from sharonherald.com/local/x295329063/UPDATE-Court-rules-student-s-rights-violated-Layshock-case-called-free-speech-victory.

20. Duffy Trager, "New Tricks for Old Dogs: The Tinker Standard Applied to Cyber-bullying," *Journal of Law and Education* (July 2009). Accessed January 5, 2011 from findarticles.com/p/articles/mi_qa3994/is_200907/ai_n35628076/.

21. David L. Hudson, Jr., "Cyberspeech," K–12 Public School Student Expression, First Amendment Center.org. Accessed January 5, 2011, from www.firstamendmentcenter.org/speech/studentexpression/topic.aspx?topic=cyberspeech.

22. Kathleen Conn, "Schools' Legal Responsibility for Sexting: Upcoming Decision Could Offer Framework," *Educator's Guide To Controlling Sexual Harassment* 18, no. 3 (2010): 9–11.

23. "Two Student Speech Rulings Seemingly Conflict, But May Instead Offer Blueprint for Administrators," *Educator's Guide to Controlling Sexual Harassment* 17, no. 6 (2010): 2, 4, 9.

24. Michelle R. Davis, "Districts Taking Steps to Address, Prevent 'Sexting' Incidents at School," *Educator's Guide to Controlling Sexual Harassment* 16, no. 12 (2009): 5, 7.

25. Ikuko Aoyama, Tony Talbert, Lucy Barnard-Brak, "Cyberbullying and Victimization Among High School Students: Cluster Analysis of Age and Sex Differences," *International Journal of Cyber Behavior, Psychology, and Learning*, In press, 2010.

26. Conn, "Cyberbullying and Cyberharassment," 35.

27. Talbert, "Cyberbullying and Victimization."

28. Joy Powell, "Stalkers and Harassers."

CHAPTER 7

1. American Association of University Women Educational Foundation, *Hostile Hallways: Bullying, Teasing and Sexual Harassment in School* (Washington, DC: AAUW, 2001).

2. James E. Gruber and Susan Fineran, "The Impact of Bullying and Sexual Harassment on Middle School and High School Girls," *Violence Against Women* 13, no. 2 (2007): 627–43.

3. James E. Gruber and Susan Fineran, "Comparing the Impact of Bullying and Sexual Harassment Victimization on the Mental and Physical Health of Adolescents," *Sex Roles* 58 (2008): 13–14.

4. American Association of University Women Educational Foundation, *Hostile Hallways: AAUW Survey on Sexual Harassment in American Schools* (Washington, DC: AAUW, 2001).

5. American Association of University Women, "Hostile Hallways."

6. Ibid.

7. Catherine Hill and Holly Kearl, *Crossing the Line: Sexual Harassment at School* (Washington, DC: American Association of Univeristy Women, 2011).

8. Nan Stein, "Sexual Harassment in School: The Public Performance of Gendered Violence," *Harvard Educational Review* 65 (1995): 145–62.

9. Fiona Leach, "Gender Violence in Schools in the Developing World," in *Combating Gender Violence in and around Schools*, ed. Fiona Leach and Claudia Mitchell, 23–29 (Sterling, VA: Trentham Books, 2006).

10. Hill and Kearl, *Crossing the Line*, p. 16.

11. American Association of University Women, "Hostile Hallways."

12. Susan Fineran and Larry Bennett, "Gender and Power Issues of Peer Sexual Harassment Among Teenagers," *Journal of Interpersonal Violence* 14, no. 6 (1999): 626–41.

13. Anna C. O'Donahue, "Sexual Harassment and PTSD: Is Sexual Harassment a Diagnosable Trauma?" *Journal of Trauma Stress*, 15 (2002): 69–75.

14. Strauss, "Sexual Harassment in K–12."

15. Becky Henry, *Just Tell Her to Stop: Family Stories of Eating Disorders* (Minneapolis: Infinite Hope Publishing, 2011).

16. Strauss, "Sexual Harassment in K–12."

17. Rebecca Jones, "Courting Controversy," *The American School Board Journal* (October, 1996): 26–30.

CHAPTER 8

1. "Insights in Ink," *Star Tribune*, Newspaper in Education Programs, Minneapolis, MN, 1992.

2. Susan Strauss, *Sexual Harassment and Teens: A Program for Positive Change* (Minneapolis, MN: Free Spirit Publishing, 1992).

3. "McCoy Receives High Grades," *Eden Prairie News*, May 20, 1993.

4. Russlyn Ali, *Dear Colleague Letter: Harassment and Bullying* (Washington, DC: U.S. Department of Education, Office for Civil Rights, October 26, 2010). Accessed from www2.ed.gov/about/offices/list/ocr/letters/colleague-201010.html.

5. Charol Shakeshaft and Audrey Cohan, "Sexual Abuse of Students by School Personnel," *Phi Delta Kappan* (March 1995): 513–19.

6. Ibid.

7. Ibid.

8. Ibid.

9. Caroline Hendrie, "Sex with Students: When Employees Cross the Line," *Education Week* (December 2, 1998): 1, 12–14.

10. Caroline Hendrie, "'Passing the Trash' by School Districts Frees Sexual Predators to Hunt Again," *Education Week* 18, no. 3 (1998): 16–17.

11. Erika Fitzpatrick, "Stronger Laws Needed to Protect Students from Sexual Predators," *Educator's Guide to Controlling Sexual Harassment* 18, no. 6 (2011): 5–6.

12. Charol Shakeshaft, *Educator Sexual Misconduct: A Synthesis of Existing Literature* (Washington, DC: U.S. Department of Education of the Under Secretary, 2004).

13. Erika Fitzpatrick, "Public Schools Could Soon Be Required to Check Criminal Histories," *Educator's Guide to Controlling Sexual Harassment* 18, no. 5 (2011): 10–11.

14. *Dyess ex rel. Dyess v. Tehachapi Unified School Dist.*, 2010 WL 3154013 and 2010 WL 3154083.

15. Alice Charach, D. J. Pepler, and Suzanne Ziegler, "Bullying at School," *Education Canada* 35 (Spring 1995): 12–18.

16. Bernice R. Sandler and Harriett M. Stonehill, *Student-to-Student Sexual Harassment K–12: Strategies and Solutions for Educations to Use in the Classroom, School and Community* (Lanham, MD: Rowman & Littlefield, 2005).

17. American Association of University Women Educational Foundation, *Hostile Hallway: Bullying, Teasing and Sexual Harassment in School* (Washington, DC: AAUW, 2001).

18. Ibid.

19. Elizabeth J. Meyer, "Gendered Harassment in Secondary Schools: Understanding Teachers' (Non) Interventions," *Gender and Education* 20, no. 6 (November 2008): 555–70.

20. Ibid.

21. Ibid.

22. Gloria Jones, "Site-Based Voices: Dilemmas of Educators Who Engage in Activism Against Student Sexual Harassment," paper presented at the American Educational Research Association, Montreal, 2005.

23. Meyer, "Gendered Harassment in Secondary Schools."

24. Ibid.

25. Ibid.

26. Ibid.

27. Ibid.

28. Ibid.

29. Ibid.

30. Kerry H. Robinson, "Reinforcing Hegemonic Masculinities Through Sexual Harassment: Issues of Identity, Power, and Popularity in Secondary Schools," *Gender and Education* 17 (2005): 19–37.

31. Jane Kenway, Sue Willis, Jill Blackmore, and Leonie Rennie, *Answering Back: Girls, Boys and Feminism in Schools in Sydney* (New York: Routledge, 1997).

32. Meyer, "Gendered Harassment in Secondary Schools."

33. Ibid.

34. Center for Disease Control and Prevention, *Teen Dating Violence*. Accessed December 14, 2010, from www.cdc.gov/ViolencePrevention/intimate-partnerviolence/teen_dating_violence.html.

35. Dorothea Anagnostopoulos, NiCole T. Buchanan, Christine Pereira, and Lauren F. Lichty, "School Staff Responses to Gender-Based Bullying as Moral Interpretation: An Exploratory Study," *Educational Policy* 23 (2009): 519–53. Accessed from Sage database.

36. Ibid.

37. Meyer, "Gendered Harassment in Secondary Schools."

38. Anagnostopoulos, "School Staff Responses to Gender-Based Bullying."

39. Ibid.

40. Ibid.

41. Meyer, "Gendered Harassment in Secondary Schools."

42. Michael D. Shear and Jacqueline L. Sunday, "An Education in Taunting: Schools Learning Dangers of Letting Bullies Go Unchecked," *Washington Post*, May 2, 1999. Accessed December 20, 2010, from www.nldline.com/washingt2.htm.

43. Michele R. Davis, "In-Depth Training Needed for Top Administrators on How to Handle Sexual Harassment Complaints," *Educator's Guide to Controlling Sexual Harassment* 17, no. 6 (2010): 7, 10.

44. Michelle Davis, "Schools Have Far to Go in Properly Instituting Title IX Harassment Policies that Protect Students, Employees," *Educator's Guide to Controlling Sexual Harassment* 16, no. 9 (2009): 4–5, 7, 11.

45. Lauren Lichty, Jennifer M. C. Torres, Maria Valenti, and NiCole T. Buchanan, "Sexual Harassment Policies in K–12 Schools: Examining Accessibility to Students and Content," *Journal for School Health* 78, no. 11 (2008): 607–14.

46. Nan Stein, "Bullying or Harassment? The Missing Discourse of Rights in an Era of Zero Tolerance," *Arizona Law Review* 45, no. 3 (2003): 783–99.

CHAPTER 9

1. "Insights in Ink," *Star Tribune*, Newspaper in Education Program, Minneapolis, MN, 1992.

2. Ibid.

3. Ms. Foundation for Women, "Youth, Gender and Violence: Building a Movement for Gender Justice," New York, September 2008, 11.

4. Ibid., 644.

5. Allan Johnson, *The Gender Knot: Unraveling Our Patriarchal Legacy* (Philadelphia: Temple University Press, 1997), 87.

6. Ibid., 87.

7. Mike Donaldson, "What is Hegemonic Masculinity? Theory and Society," *Masculinities* 22, no. 5 (1993, special issue): 643–57.

8. Joelle Schmitz, "Women in Politics? The U.S. is Failing," *USA Today*. Accessed February 26, 2011 from www.usatoday.com/news/opinion/forum/2010 -10-13-column13_ST_N.htm.

9. Sylvia Ann Hewlett, "Sponsors and the Glass Ceiling," *Miami Herald*, December 3, 2010. Accessed January 5, 2011 from www.miamiherald com/2010/12/03/1956219/sponsors-and-the-glass-ceiling.html.

10. American Association of University Women, *AAUW Women and Leadership Brochure* (Washington, DC: AAUW, 2011).

11. Jing Zhao Cesarone, "Number of U.S. Women CEOs, Board Members Still Far Below Men," CRIEnglish.com. Accessed February 25, 2011 from english.cri.cn/6826/2010/03/08/1601s554839.htm

12. Johnson, *The Gender Knot*, 7.

13. Deborah Tannen, *Talking 9 to 5: Women and Men in the Workplace: Language, Sex and Power* (New York: Avon, 1994).

14. Johnson, *The Gender Knot.*

15. Ibid.

16. Ibid.

17. Ibid.

18. "Insights in Ink," 1992.

19. Mike Donaldson, "What is Hegemonic Masculinity?"

20. Paul Kivel, *Boys Will Be Men: Raising Our Sons for Courage, Caring and Community* (British Columbia, Canada: New Society Publishers, 1999).

21. Kivel, *Boys will be Men.*

22. Ms. Foundation, "Youth, Gender and Violence."

23. Bob Herbert, "Misogyny is America's True National Pastime," *New York Times*, January 17, 2008. Accessed November 27, 2010 from www.nytimes .com/2008/01/15/opinion/15herbert.html?hp=&pagewanted=print.

24. Ms. Foundation, "Youth, Gender and Violence."

25. Fiona Leach, "Gender Violence in Schools in the Developing World," in *Combating Gender Violence in and around Schools*, ed. Fiona Leach and Claudia Mitchell, 23–29 (Sterling, VA: Trentham Books, 2006).

26. Leach, "Gender Violence in Schools."

27. Ms. Foundation, "Youth, Gender and Violence."

28. Centers for Disease Control and Prevention, *CDC Sexual Violence Fact Sheet* (Washington, DC: CDC, April 19, 2007). Accessed November 12, 2010 from cdc.gov/ncipc/factsheets/syfacts.htm.

29. Ms. Foundation, "Youth, Gender and Violence."

30. Ibid.

31. National Teen Dating Violence Prevention Initiative, American Bar Association. Accessed January 5, 2011 from www.americanbar.org/groups/public_ education/initiatives_awards/national_teen_dating_violence_prevention_ initiative.html.

32. Gigi Durham, *The Lolita Effect: The Media Sexualization of Young Girls and What We Can Do About It* (New York: Overlook Press, 2008).

33. Ms. Foundation, "Youth, Gender and Violence."

34. Jane Kenway and Lindsay Fitzclarence, "Masculinity, Violence, and Schooling: Challenging 'Poisonous Pedagogies,'" *Gender & Education* 9 (1997): 117–34.

35. "Insights in Ink," 1992.

36. Ibid.

37. American Psychological Association, Task Force on the Sexualization of Girls, *Report of the APA Task Force on the Sexualization of Girls* (2010). Retrieved from www.apa.org/pi/women/programs/girls/report-full.pdf.

38. Andrea Canning and Jessica Hoffman, "Toddlers and Tiaras, Little Divas Make their Entrance," ABC News Good Morning America, July 21, 2009. Accessed November 29, 2010 from abcnews.go.com/GMA/story?id= 8128371&page=1.

39. Suzanne Smalley, "This Could be Your Child," *Newsweek*, August 18, 2003. Accessed October 30, 2010 from www.newsweek.com/2003/08/17/this -could-be-your-kid.html.

40. Durham, *The Lolita Effect*.

41. American Psychological Association, *Sexualization of Girls*.

42. John Briere and Diana M. Elliot, "Prevalence and Psychological Sequelae of Self-Reported Childhood Physical and Sexual Abuse in a General Population Sample of Men and Women," *Child Abuse and Neglect* 27 (2003): 1205–22.

43. Bella English, "The Disappearing Tween Years: Bombarded by Sexualized Forces, Girls Are Growing Up Faster than Ever," *Boston Globe*, March 12, 2005. Accessed December 23, 2010 from www.boston.com/ae/media/ articles/2005/03/12/the_disappearing_tween_years?pg=full.

44. "Tesco's 'Toy' Pole Dance Kit," *Birmingham Post* (UK), Oct 25, 2006. Accessed December 23, 2010 from www.mirror.co.uk/news/top-stories/ 2006/10/23/tesco-s-toy-pole-dance-kit-115875-17976652/.

45. Olinka Koster, "What Possessed BHS to Sell 'Provocative' Underwear for Girls as Young as Seven?" *Daily Mail* (London), March 26, 2003.

46. Katie Zezima, "Not All are Pleased at Plan to Offer Birth Control at Maine Middle School," *New York Times*, October 21, 2007. Accessed October 21, 2010 from www.nytimes.com/2007/10/21/us/21portland.html.

47. Diane Levin and Jean Kilbourne. *So Sexy So Soon* (New York: Random House, 2009).

48. English, "The Disappearing Tween Years."

49. Karen R. Brooks, "Corporate Kidnapping," *Sydney's Child*, December 2005/January 2006, 19.

50. American Psychological Association, *Sexualization of Girls*.

51. Leach, "Gender Violence in Schools."

52. Margaret Stockdale, "The Sexual Harassment of Men: Articulating the Approach-Rejection Theory of Sexual Harassment," in *In the Company of Men: Male Dominance and Sexual Harassment*, ed. James Gruber and Phoebe Morgan, 117–42 (Boston: Northeastern University Press, 2005).

53. Kenway, "Masculinity, Violence and Schooling."

54. Jonathan Salisbury and David Jackson, *Challenging Macho Values: Practical Ways of Working with Adolescent Boys* (London: Falmer Press, 1996).

55. Alice Miller, *For Your Own Good: The Roots of Violence in Child-Rearing* (London: Virago Press, 1987).

56. Myra Sadker and David Sadker, *Failing at Fairness: How America's Schools Cheat Girls* (New York: Scribner, 1994).

57. Peter K. Smith, ed., *Violence in Schools: The Response in Europe* (New York: Routledge, 2003).

58. Gary L. Bowen, "Social Organizations in Schools: A General Systems Theory Perspective," in *Social Work Services in Schools* (4th ed), ed. Paula Allen-Meares (Boston: Pearson, 2004): 50–503.

59. Durham, *The Lolita Effect*.

60. Diane Levin and Jean Kilbourne, *So Sexy So Soon* (New York: Random House, 2009).

61. American Psychological Association, *Sexualization of Girls*.

62. Levin, *So Sexy So Soon*.

63. Barbara Wilson and Nicole Martins, "Impact of Violent Music on Youth," in *Handbook of Children, Culture, and Violence*, ed. Nancy E. Dowd, Dorothy G. Singer, and Robin Fretwell Wilson, 179–202 (Thousand Oaks, CA: Sage, 2006).

64. American Psychiatric Association, "Psychiatric Effects of Media Violence," accessed February 23, 2011 from www.psych.org/public_info/media_violence.cfm.

65. Kaiser Family Foundation, "Key Facts on TV Violence," Report 3335, Spring 2003. Accessed February 23, 2011 from www.kff.org/entmedia/upload/Key-Facts-TV-Violence.pdf.

66. Ibid.

67. American Psychiatric Association, "Psychiatric Effects of Media Violence."

68. Durham, *The Lolita Effect*.

69. Dale Kunkel, Erica Biely, Karen Eyal, Kirstie Cope-Farral, Edward Donnerstein, and Rena Randrich, *Sex on TV 2003* (Santa Barbara: University of CA: Kaiser Family Foundation, 2003). Accessed October 26, 2010 from www.kff.org/entmedia/upload/Sex-on-TV-3.pdf.

70. American Psychological Association, *Sexualization of Girls*.

71. Dale Kunkel, Karen Eyal, Keli Finnerty, Erica Biely, and Edward Donnesrstein, *Sex on TV 2003* (Menlo Park, CA: Kaiser Family Foundation, 2005). Accessed December 3, 2010 from www.kff.org/entmedia/upload/Sex-on-TV-4-Full-Report.pdf.

72. Durham, *The Lolita Effect*.

73. American Psychological Association, *Sexualization of Girls*.

74. Wilson, "Impact on Violent Music."

75. American Psychological Association, *Sexualization of Girls*.

76. Tom Zeller, Jr., "Link by Link; Defending Cruelty: It's Only a Game," *New York Times*, February 20, 2006. Accessed November 3, 2010 from query. nytimes.com/gst/fullpage.html?res=9D04E7DD113EF933A15751C0A9609 C8B63.

77. "Grand Theft Auto: Vice City," *Financial Times*, Nov. 26, 2002.

78. Durham, *The Lolita Effect*.

79. Stacy Smith and Marc Choueiti, *Gender Disparity on Screen and Behind the Camera in Family Films* (Geena Davis Institutue of Gender in Media, 2009). Accessed March 5, 2011 from www.thegeenadavisinstitute.org/research .php.

80. The Children's Defense Fund. *Each Day in America 2009*. Accessed December 3, 2010, from www.childrensdefense.org/child-research-data-publi-cations/each-day-in-america.htmlfound.

81. Lucille Glicklick-Rosenberg, "Violence and Children: A Public Health Issue," *Psychiatric Times* 13, no 3. (1996): 45–7.

82. Brett Brown and Sharon Bzostek, "Violence in the Lives of Children," *Cross Currents* (August 2003). Accessed October 4, 2010 from www.catalyst forchildren.org/pdf/Violence.pdf.

83. "Youth Victims and Perpetrators," ChildStats.gov. Accessed December 13, 2010 from www.childstats.gov/search/?as_sitesearch=www.childstats.gov/ americaschildren09&output=xml_no_dtd&client=childstats&site=childstats& q=youth+victims+and+perpetrators&ie=UTF-8&ip=192.168.132.61&access= p&sort=date:D:L:d1&entqr=3.

84. Jose I. Concepcion, "Understanding Preadolescent Sexual Offenders: Can These Children Be Rehabilitated to Stem the Tide of Adult Predatory Behaviors?" *Florida Bar Journal* 78 (2007): 30–7.

85. Maia Szalavitz, "How Not to Raise a Bully: The Early Roots of Empa-thy," *Time*, Apr. 17, 2010. Accessed October 16, 2010 from www.time.com/ time/health/article/0,8599,1982190,00.html#ixzz157IYzVZq.

86. Ibid.

87. Ibid.

88. Kathleen C. Basile, Dorothy L. Espelage, Ian Rivers, Pamela M. Mc-Mahon, and Thomas R. Simon, "TheTheoretical and Empirical Links Between Bullying Behavior and Male Sexual Violence Perpetration," *Aggression and Violent Behavior* 14, no. 5 (2009): 336–47. Accessed December 15, 2002 from Science Direct database. This is a superb reference that summarizes a variety of studies dealing with bullying, homophobic bullying, sexual violence, theory, anger and hostility, empathy, manipulation, sex, and more.

89. "Insights in Ink," *Star Tribune*.

90. Levin, *So Sexy So Soon*.

91. Jessica Pieklo, "Minnie Mouse Gets a Makeover." Accessed February 15, 2010 from www.care2.com/causes/womens-rights/blog/minnie-mouse-gets -a-makeover/.

92. Caroline Heldman, "Disney Ride Makes Light of Sex Slavery," *Sociological Images*. Accessed January 28, 2011 from thesocietypages.org/ socimages/2010/11/10/guest-post-disney-ride-still-makes-light-of-sex-slavery/.

93. Dawn C. Chmielewski and Claudia Eller, "Disney Animation is Closing the Book on Fairy Tales," *Los Angeles Times*, Nov. 21, 2010. Accessed January 5, 2011 from articles.latimes.com/2010/nov/21/entertainment/la-et-1121 -tangled-20101121.

CHAPTER 10

1. American Bar Association, "Part I: What is the Rule of Law?" (n.d.), 6. Accessed February 5, 2011, www.americanbar.org/content/dam/aba/migrated/ publiced/features/PartIDialogueROL.autheheckdam.pdf

2. U.S. Equal Employment Opportunity Commission, *Policy Guidance on Current Issues of Sexual Harassment*, March 1990. Accessed from www.eeoc .gov/policy/docs/currentissues.html.

3. Ibid., 186.

4. *Theno v. Tonganoxie Unified School District*, 377 F.Supp.3d 952 (D. Kansas 2005).

5. *Price Waterhouse v. Hopkins*, 490 U.S. 228 (1989).

6. "42 U.S.C. Section 1983: U.S. Code—Section 1983: Civil Action for Deprivation of Rights," FindLaw for Legal Professionals. Accessed from codes. lp.findlaw.com/uscode/42/21/I/1983.

7. Elsa Cole, "Troubleshooting Tips: Section 1983 vs. Title IX," *Educator's Guide to Controlling Sexual Harassment* 18, no. 5 (2011): 4.

8. "Qualified Immunity Law and Legal Definition," USLegal.com. Accessed from definitions.uslegal.com/q/qualified-immunity/.

9. Michelle R. Davis, "Plaintiffs Can Pursue Action Under Section 1983 and Title IX, Supreme Court Says in Recent Landmark Ruling," *Educator's Guide to Controlling Sexual Harassment* 16, no. 6 (2009): 2, 5, 10.

10. Ibid.

11. Michelle R. Davis, "Schools Can Face Lawsuits in Sexual Assault Cases for Damages to the Parent-Child Relationship," *Educator's Guide to Controlling Sexual Harassment* 16, no. 11 (2009): 3, 6.

12. *Doe v. Dickenson*, 2009 WL 1211812 (D. Ariz., April 30, 2009).

13. *Thelma D. v. Board of Ed., City of St. Louis*, 934 F.2d 929 (8th Cir. 1991).

14. Elsa Cole, "Troubleshooting Tips For Section 1983 Claims," *Educator's Guide to Controlling Sexual Harassment* 16, no. 6 (2009): 6.

15. "Educating to Eliminate Hazing," Stophazing.org.

16. Elizabeth Meyer, "Hazing and High School Gendered Rites of Group Membership," *Psychology Today*, PsychologyToday.com (January 15, 2010). Accessed from www.insidehazing.com/headlines.php?headlines2PageSize=50 &idno=1415&headlines2Page=3.

17. Ibid.

18. "Qualified Immunity," 'Lectric Law Library. Accessed from www.lect-law.com/def2/q063.htm.

19. Michelle R. Davis, "Student-Teacher Sex Relationships Not Consensual, Even if the Student is Over 18 Years Old, Court Says," *Educator's Guide to Controlling Sexual Harassment* 18, no. 2 (2010): 3, 8, 11.

20. U.S. Department of Education, *The Family Educational Rights and Privacy Act: Guidance for Eligible Students*, February 2011. Accessed from www2.ed.gov/policy/gen/guid/fpco/ferpa/for-eligible-students.pdf.

21. *Tinker v. Des Moines Independent Community School District*, 393 U.S. 503 (1969)

22. *Bethel School District v. Fraser, 478 U.S. 675 (1986)*

23. Susan Strauss, "Sexual Harassment in K–12," in *Academic and Workplace Sexual Harassment: A Handbook of Cultural, Social Science, Management, and Legal Perspectives,* eds. Michele Paludi and Carmen A. Paludi, Jr. 105–45. Westport: Praeger, 2003.

24. "Judge Lifts School Ban on Teen's Shirt," *Star Tribune* (May 19, 2001): B3.

25. "Circuit Courts Send Mixed Messages on Clothing; Schools May Choose to Ban All T-Shirt Slogans," *Educator's Guide to Controlling Sexual Harassment* 17 no. 4 (2010): 3, 6.

26. Nancy Willard, "Educator's Guide to Cyberbullying and Cyberthreats," Center for Safe and Responsible Use of the Internet April 2007. Accessed January 5, 2011 from www.cyberbully.org/cyberbully/docs/cbcteducator.pdf.

CHAPTER 11

1. BookBrowse, BookBrowse Favorite Quotes; www.bookbrowse.com/quotes/detail/index.cfm?quote_number=88.

2. Dave Ulrich, *Human Resource Champions: The Next Agenda for Adding Value and Delivering Results* (Boston: Harvard Business School Press, 1997).

3. Ibid.

4. Ibid.

5. Russlyn Ali, *Dear Colleague Letter: Harassment and Bullying* (Washington, DC: U.S. Department of Education, Office for Civil Rights, October 26, 2010). Accessed from www2.ed.gov/about/offices/list/ocr/letters/colleague-201010.html.

6. Sibylle Artz and Ted Riecken, "What, So What, Then What: The Gender Gap in School Based Violence and Its Implications for Child and Youth Care Practice," *CYC Forum* 26, no. 4 (1997): 291–303.

7. Ron Avi Astor, Heather Anne Meyer, and William Behre, "Unowned Places and Times: Maps and Interviews About Violence in High Schools," *American Educational Research Journal* 36 (1999): 3–42.

8. Ellen Delara and James Garbarino, *An Educator's Guide to School-Based Interventions* (Boston: Houghton Mifflin, 2003).

9. "Title IX Coordinator's Role and Responsibilities: Local School Districts." Accessed January 7, 2011 from dese.mo.gov/divcareered/Civil_Rights/Title_IX_Coordinator_Roles_and_Responsibilities.pdf.

10. Joseph G. Kosciw, Emily A. Greytak, Elizabeth M. Diaz, and Mark J. Bartkiewicz, *The 2009 National School Climate Survey: The Experiences of Lesbian, Gay, Bisexual and Transgender Youth in Our Nation's Schools* (New York: GLSEN, 2010). Accessed January 7, 2011 from www.glsen.org/binary-data/GLSEN_ATTACHMENTS/file/000/001/1675-1.pdf.

11. www.dayofsilence.org.

12. www.nonamecallingweek.org.

13. Anthony D. Pellegrini and Maria Bartini, "An Empirical Comparison of Methods of Sampling Aggression and Victimization in School Settings," *Journal of Educational Psychology* 92 (2000): 360–66.

14. James Garbarino and Ellen Delara, *And Words Can Hurt Forever: How to Protect Adolescents from Bullying, Harassment, and Emotional Violence* (New York: Simon & Shuster/The Free Press, 2002).

15. Derek Glover, Gerry Gough, Michael M. Johnson, and Netta Cartwright, "Bullying in 25 Secondary Schools: Incidence, Impact and Intervention," *Educational Research* 42, no. 2 (2000): 141–56.

16. Garbarino, *And Words Can Hurt Forever.*

17. Nancy Willard, "Educator's Guide to Cyberbullying and Cyberthreats," Center for Safe and Responsible Use of the Internet, April 2007. Accessed January 5, 2011 from www.cyberbully.org/cyberbully/docs/cbcteducator.pdf).

18. Carol Greta, "Cyberbullying: Doing Something About it Lawfully," Iowa Department of Education, nd. Accessed January 8, 2011 from iowa.gov/educate/index.php?option=com_content&view=article&id=1718:cyberbullying-guidance&catid=411:legal-lessons&Itemid=2656.

19. The information in this section was adapted from the following two sources:

Dave Doty and Susan Strauss, "Prompt & Equitable: The Importance of Student Sexual Harassment Policies in Public Schools," *West's Education Law Reporter* (November 28, 1996): 1–29; and Bernice R. Sandler and Harriett M. Stonehill, *Student-To-Student Sexual Harassment K–12: Strategies and Solutions for Educators to Use in the Classroom, School, and Community* (Lanham, MD: Rowman & Littlefield Education, 2005). This is a fantastic resource outlining what schools must do to minimize the sexual harassment in their districts. It is a must-read for parents and school officials.

CHAPTER 12

1. "Insights in Ink," *Star Tribune*, Newspaper on Education Programs, Minneapolis, MN, 1992.

2. U.S. Department of Education, Office for Civil Rights, *Revised Sexual Harassment Guidance: Sexual Harassment of Students by School Employees, Other Students, and Third Parties.* January 19, 2001. Accessed October 30, 2008 from www2.ed.gov/about/offices/list/ocr/docs/shguide.html

3. Russlyn Ali, "Dear Colleague Letter: Harassment and Bullying," U. S. Department of Education, Office for Civil Rights. (Washington, DC: U. S. Department of Education, October 26, 2010). Accessed October 30, 2010, from www2.ed.gov/about/offices/list/ocr/letters/colleague-201010.html

CHAPTER 13

1. Desmond Tutu, "Reconcilliation," The Desmond Tutu Peace Foundation, n.d.; accessed March 3, 2011, www.tifandgif.com/tutu/pdfs/tutu_3rd.pdf

BIBLIOGRAPHY

"A Thin Line: 2009 AP-MTV Digital Abuse Study." MTV, 2009. Accessed February 4, 2011 from www.athinline.org/MTV-AP_Digital_Abuse_Study_Executive_Summary.pdf.

ACLU. "The Cost of Harassment: A Fact Sheet for Lesbian, Gay, Bisexual, and Transgender High School Students." ACLU, February 9, 2007. Accessed October 30, 2010 from www.aclu.org/lgbt-rights_hiv-aids/cost-harassment-fact-sheet-lesbian-gay-bisexual-and-transgender-high-school-stu.

Agatston, Patricia. "Staff, Students, and Parents Need Education Programs to Prevent Cyberbullying, Increase Digital Literacy." *Educator's Guide to Controlling Sexual Harassment* 17 (2009): 8.

Ali, Russlyn. *Dear Colleague Letter: Harassment and Bullying.* Washington, DC: U.S. Department of Education, Office for Civil Rights, 2010. Accessed October 30, 2010, from www2.ed.gov/about/offices/list/ocr/letters/colleague-201010.html.

American Association of University Women Educational Foundation. *Hostile Hallways: Bullying, Teasing and Sexual Harassment in School.* Washington, DC: AAUW, 2001.

American Association of University. Women, Women and Leadership (brochure). Washington, DC: AAUW, 2010.

American Bar Association. "Part I: What is the Rule of Law," (n.d.): 6. Accessed February 5, 2011, from www.americanbar.org/content/dam/aba/migrated/publiced/features/PartIDialogueROL.authcheckdam.pdf

American Psychological Association, Task Force on the Sexualization of Girls. *Report of the APA Task Force on the Sexualization of Girls.* 2010. Accessed December 23, 2010 from www.apa.org/pi/women/programs/girls/report-full .pdf.

Anagnostopoulos, Dorothea, NiCole T. Buchanan, Christine Pereira, and Lauren F. Lichty. "School Staff Responses to Gender-Based Bullying as Moral Interpretation: An Exploratory Study." *Educational Policy* 23 (2009): 519–553. Accessed October 28, 2010 from Sage database.

Anti-Defamation League. *Using Children's Literature to Increase Empathy and Help Students Cope with Bullying: Annotated Bibliography of Children's Fiction on Bullying.* 2005. Accessed January 4, 2011 from www.adl .org/education/curriculum_connections/winter_2005/bibliography.asp?cc_ section=biblio.

Aoyama, Ikuko, Tony Talbert, and Lucy Barnard-Brak. "Cyberbullying and Victimization Among High School Students: Cluster Analysis of Age and Sex Differences." *International Journal of Cyber Behavior, Psychology, and Learning* (in press, 2010).

Arendt, Hannah, "A Special Supplement: Reflections on Violence," The New York Review of Books, February 27, 1969. Accessed November 17, 2010 from www.nybooks,com/articles/archives/1969/Feb/27/a-special-supplfement -reflections-on-violence/

Artz, Sibylle, and Ted Riecken. "What, So What, Then What: The Gender Gap in School Based Violence and Its implications for Child and Youth Care Practice." *CYC Forum* 26, no. 4 (1997): 291–303.

Astor, Ron, Heather Meyer, and William Behre. "Unowned Places and Times: Maps and Interviews About Violence in High Schools." *American Education Research Journal* 36 (1999): 3–42. Accessed August 5, 2010 from Sage database.

Basile, Kathleen C., Dorothy L. Espelage, Ian Rivers, Pamela M. McMahon, and Thomas R. Simon. "The Theoretical and Empirical Links Between Bullying Behavior and Male Sexual Violence Perpetration." *Aggression and Violent Behavior* 14, no. 5 (2009): 336–347. Accessed December 15, 2020 from Science Direct database.

Batsche, George, and Howard M. Knoff. "Bullies and Their Victims: Understanding a Pervasive Problem in the Schools." *School Psychology Review* 23, no. 2 (1994): 165–74. Accessed December 15, 2010 from EBSCO database.

Baynard v. Lawson, 112 F. Supp. 2d 524 (2000).

Becker, Jo. *Easy Targets: Violence Against Children Worldwide.* New York: Human Rights Watch, 2001. Accessed January 19, 2009 from www.hrw.org/ legacy/reports/2001/children/index.htm.

Bennett, Larry, and Susan Fineran. "Sexual and Severe Physical Violence among High School Students: Power Beliefs, Gender and Relationship." *American Journal of Orthopsychiatry* 67, no. 4 (1998): 645–52.

Bethel School District v. Fraser, 478 U.S. 675 (1986).

Bibby v. Philadelphia Coca-Cola Bottling Co., 260 F.3d 257 (3d Cir. 2001).

Bochenek, Michael, and A. Widney Brown. *Hatred in the Hallways: Violence and Discrimination Against Gay, Lesbian, Bisexual and Transgender Students in U.S. Schools*. New York: Human Rights Watch, 2001. Accessed November 17, 2010 from www.hrw.org/legacy/reports/2001/uslgbt/toc.htm.

BookBrowse, Bookbrowse Favorite Quotes. Accessed September 2, 2011, from www.bookbrowse.com/quotes/detail/index.cfm?quote_number=88

Boulton, Michael J. "Teachers' Views on Bullying: Definitions, Attitudes, and Ability to Cope." *British Journal of Educational Psychology* 67 (1997): 223–33.

Bowen, Gary L. "Social Organizations in Schools: A General Systems Theory Perspective." In *Social Work Services in Schools* (4th ed.), ed. Paula Allen-Meares, 50–53. Boston: Pearson, 2004.

Briare, Anna. "Massachusetts Attorney Claims State Bullying Law Has No Teeth," *Masslive.com*, January 11, 2011. Accessed January 23, 2011 from www .masslive.com/bullying/index.ssf/2011/01/massachusetts_attorney_abigail_ williams claims_state_bullyin.html _.

Briere, John, and Diana M. Elliot. "Prevalence and Psychological Sequelae of Self-Reported Childhood Physical and Sexual Abuse in a General Population Sample of Men and Women." *Child Abuse and Neglect* 27 (2003): 1205–22. Accessed November 18, 2010 from Science Direct database.

Brown, Brett, and Sharon Bzostek. "Violence in the Lives of Children." *Cross Currents* (August 2003). Accessed October 4, 2010 from www.catalystfor-children.org/pdf/Violence.pdf.

Brown, Lyn Mikel. *Girlfighting: Betrayal and Rejection Among Girls*. New York: New York University Press, 2003.

Brown, Lyn Mikel, Meda Chesney-Lind, and Nan Stein. "Patriarchy Matters: Toward a Gendered Theory of Teen Violence and Victimization." *Violence Against Women* 13, no. 12 (2007): 1249–73.

"Bruised Inside: What Our Children Say About Youth Violence, What Causes It and What We Need to do About it." Washington Attorney General Christine Gregoire's Presidential Initiative on Our Children in the New Millennium. Michigan: A Report of the National Attorneys General, 2000. Accessed January 5, 2010 from www.michigan.gov/documents/bruised_in-side_38596_7.pdf.

Bully Police USA, www.bullypolice.org/.

California Safe Schools Coalition. *Safe Place to Learn: Consequences of Harassment Based on Actual or Perceived Sexual Orientation and Gender Non-Conformity and Steps for Making Schools Safe*. Davis: University of California Press, 2004.

Canning, Andrea, and Jessica Hoffman. "Toddlers and Tiaras, Little Divas Make their Entrance." ABC News Good Morning America, July 21, 2009. Accessed November 29, 2010 from abcnews.go.com/GMA/story?id =8128371&page=1.

Cartledge, Gwendolyn, and Carolyn T. Johnson. "School Violence and Cultural Sensitivity." In *School Violence Intervention: A Practical Handbook* (2nd ed.), ed. Jane C. Conoley and Arnold P. Goldstein, 441–82. New York: Guilford, 2004.

Cedello, Sylvia. *Peer Sexual Harassment: A Texas-Size Problem*. Austin: Texas Civil Rights Project, 1997.

Celizic, Mike. "Her Teen Committed Suicide over 'Sexting.'" Today.com, March 8, 2009. Accessed from today.msnbc.msn.com/id/29546030/ns/today -parenting/.

Centers for Disease Control and Prevention. *CDC Sexual Violence Fact Sheet*. Washington, DC: CDC, April 19, 2007. Accessed November 12, 2010 from www.cdc.gov/ncipc/factsheets/syfacts.htm.

———. *Teen Dating Violence*. Accessed January 5, 2011 from www.cdc.gov/ ViolencePrevention/intimatepartnerviolence/teen_dating_violence.html.

Chandler, Kurt. "Experts Report Increase in Child Sex Play: Culture, Abuse May Be Factor." *Star Tribune*, August 6, 1995, 1, 14.

Chang, JuJu, Alisha Davis, Cole Kazdin, and Olivia Sterns. "First-Grader Labeled a Sexual Harasser: Has Zero Tolerance for Sexual Harassment in Schools Gone Too Far?" ABC Good Morning America, April 4, 2008. Accessed March 18, 2011 from abcnews.go.com/GMA/AsSeenOnGMA/ story?id=4585388.

Charach, Alice, D. J. Pepler, and Suzanne Ziegler. "Bullying at School." *Education Canada* 35 (1995): 12–18.

Children and Watching TV. American Academy of Child and Adolescent Psychiatry, 2001. Accessed December 18, 2011 from www.aacap.org/cs/root/ facts_for_families/children_and_watching_tv.

The Children's Defense Fund. *Each Day in America*. 2009. Accessed December 3, 2010 from www.childrensdefense.org/child-research-data -publications/each-day-in-america.htmlfound.

Chmielewski, Dawn C., and Claudia Eller. "Disney Animation is Closing the Book on Fairy Tales." *Los Angeles Times*, Nov. 21, 2010. Accessed January 5, 2011 from articles.latimes.com/2010/nov/21/entertainment/la-et-1121 -tangled-20101121.

"Circuit Courts Send Mixed Messages on Clothing; Schools May Choose to Ban All T-Shirt Slogans." *Educator's Guide to Controlling Sexual Harassment* 17, no. 4 (2010): 3, 6.

Cole, Elsa. "Troubleshooting Tips For Section 1983 Claims." *Educator's Guide to Controlling Sexual Harassment* 16, no. 6 (2009): 6.

———. "Troubleshooting Tips: Section 1983 vs. Title IX." *Educator's Guide to Controlling Sexual Harassment* 18, no. 5 (2011): 4.

Coloroso, Barbara. *The Bully, the Bullied, and the Bystander*. Toronto: Harper Collins, 2006.

Concepcion, Jose I. "Understanding Preadolescent Sexual Offenders: Can These Children Be Rehabilitated to Stem the Tide of Adult Predatory Behaviors?" *Florida Bar Journal* 78 (2007): 30–37.

Conn, Kathleen. "Cyberbullying and Cyberharassment in American Schools: Cautionary Tales from the Courts." *Educator's Guide to Controlling Sexual Harassment* (October 2009): Tab 700, 27–41.

———. "Schools' Legal Responsibility for Sexting: Upcoming Decision Could Offer Framework." *Educator's Guide To Controlling Sexual Harassment* 18, no. 3 (2010): 9–11.

Craig, Wendy M. "The Relationship Among Bullying, Victimization, Depression, Anxiety, and Aggression in Elementary School Children." *Personality and Individual Differences* 24 (1998): 123–30.

Craig, Wendy, and Debra Pepler. "Observations of Bullying and Victimization in the School Yard." *Canadian Journal of School Psychology* 13 (1997): 41–59.

Dalaimo, Denise M. "Electronic Sexual Harassment." In *Sexual Harassment on Campus*, ed. Bernice R. Sandler and Robert J. Shoop, 85–103. Needham Heights, MA: Allyn & Bacon, 1997.

Davis v. Monroe County Bd. of Educ., 74 F.3d 1186, 1195 (11th Cir. 1996).

Davis, Michelle R. "Districts Taking Steps to Address, Prevent 'Sexting' Incidents at School." *Educator's Guide to Controlling Sexual Harassment* 16, no. 12 (2009): 5, 7.

———. "Higher Levels of Depression Found Among Victims of Cyberbullying Than Other Bullying, Study says." *Educator's Guide to Controlling Sexual Harassment* 18., no. 2 (2010): 10.

———. "In-Depth Training Needed for Top Administrators on How to Handle Sexual Harassment Complaints." *Educator's Guide to Controlling Sexual Harassment* 17, no. 6 (2010): 7, 10.

———. "Plaintiffs Can Pursue Action Under Section 1983 and Title IX, Supreme Court Says in Recent Landmark Ruling." *Educator's Guide to Controlling Sexual Harassment* 16, no. 6 (2009): 2, 5, 10.

———. "Questions About Transgender Student Protections On the Rise, Schools Must Consider Ramifications." *Educator's Guide to Controlling Sexual Harassment* 16, no. 5 (2009): 6–7.

———. "Schools Can Face Lawsuits in Sexual Assault Cases for Damages to the Parent-Child Relationship." *Educator's Guide to Controlling Sexual Harassment* 16, no. 11 (2009): 3, 6.

———. "Schools Have Far to Go in Properly Instituting Title IX Harassment Policies that Protect Students, Employees." *Educator's Guide to Controlling Sexual Harassment* 16, no. 9 (2009):4–5,7, 11.

———. "State Antibullying Laws Appear Mostly Ineffective, But Local Programs Can Be Valuable, Experts Say." *Employer's Guide to Controlling Sexual Harassment* 17, no. 2 (2009): 8–9.

———. "Student-Teacher Sex Relationships Not Consensual, Even if the Student is Over 18 Years Old, Court Says." *Educator's Guide to Controlling Sexual Harassment* 18, no. 2 (2010): 3, 8, 11.

www.dayofsilence.org

DeLara, Ellen. "Bullying and Violence in American Schools." In *Handbook of Children, Culture, and Violence*, ed. Nancy E. Dowd, Dorothy G. Singer and Robin Fretwell Wilson, 333–354. Thousand Oaks, CA: Sage, 2006.

———. "Peer Predictability: An Adolescent Strategy for Enhancing a Sense of Safety at School." *Journal of School Violence* 1, no. 3 (2002): 31–56. Accessed August 3, 2010 from EBSCO database.

DeLara, Ellen, and James Garbarino. *An Educator's Guide to School-Based Interventions.* Boston: Houghton Mifflin, 2003.

DeLuca, Stephanie, and James E. Rosenbaum. "Are Dropout Decisions Related to Safety Concerns, Social Isolation, and Teacher Disparagement?" Institute for Policy Research, IPR Working Papers, WP-00-18, Northwestern University, 2001. Accessed September 1, 2010 from www.northwestern.edu/ipr/publications/workingpapers/wpabstracts00/wp0018.html.

Doe v. Brockton Sch. Comm., 2000 WL 33342399 (Mass. App. Ct. 2000).

Doe v. Dallas Independent School District et al., 220 F.3d 380 (5th Cir. 2000).

Doe v. Dickenson, 2009 WL 1211812 (D. Ariz., April 30, 2009).

Doe v. Southeastern Green School District, 2006 U.S. Dist. LEXIS 12790 (W.D. Pa. 2006).

Doty, Dave, and Susan Strauss. "Prompt & Equitable: The Importance of Student Sexual Harassment Policies in Public Schools." *West's Education Law Reporter*, November 28, 1996, 1–29.

Dowd, Nancy, Dorothy G. Singer, and Robin Fretwell Wilson, eds. *Handbook of Children, Culture, and Violence.* Thousand Oaks, CA: Sage, 2006.

Duncan, Renae. "Peer and Sibling Aggression: An Investigation of Intra- and Extra-Familial Bullying." *Journal of Interpersonal Violence* 14, no. 8 (1999): 871–86. Accessed October 18, 2010 from Sage database.

Durham, Gigi. *The Lolita Effect: The Media Sexualization of Young Girls and What We Can Do About It.* New York: Overlook Press, 2008.

Duttweiler, Patricia C. "Who's at Risk? Gay and Lesbian Youth." *The Journal of At-Risk Issues* 3, no. 2 (1997). Accessed December 29, 2010 from www.dropoutprevention.org/statistics/gay-lesbian-youth.

Dyess v. Tehachapi Unified School Dist., 2010 WL 3154013 and 2010 WL 3154083.

"Educating to Eliminate Hazing." Stophazing.org.

Education for All Global Monitoring Report Team. Gender and Education for All: The Leap to Equality Summary Report. Paris: UNESCO, 2003. Accessed March 29, 2009 from unesdoc.unesco.org/images/0013/001325/132550e .pdf.

Ehrensaft, Miriam K., Patricia K. Cohen, Jocelyn Brown, Elizabeth Smailes, Henian Chen, and Jeffrey G. Johnson. "Intergenerational Transmission of Partner Violence: A 20-Year Prospective Study." *Journal of Consulting and Clinical Psychology* 71 (2003): 741–53. Accessed October 23, 2010 from EBSCO database.

English, Bella. "The Disappearing Tween Years: Bombarded by Sexualized Forces, Girls are Growing up Faster than Ever." *Boston Globe*, March 12, 2005. Accessed December 23, 2010 from www.boston.com/ae/media/articles/2005/03/12/the_disappearing_tween_years?pg=full.

Epstein, Debbie. "Keeping Them in Their Place: Hetero/sexist Harassment, Gender and the Enforcement of Homosexuality." In *Sexual Harassment: Contemporary Feminist Perspectives*, ed. Alison M. Thomas and Celia Kitzinger, 154–71. Buckingham: Open University Press, 1997.

Eron, Leonard D., L. Rowell Huesmann, Eric Dubow, Richard Romanoff, and Patty W. Yarmel. "Aggression and its Correlates over 22 Years." In *Childhood Aggression and Violence: Sources of Influence, Prevention, and Control*, ed. David H. Crowell, Ian M. Evans, and Clifford R. O'Donnell, 249–262. New York: Plenum, 1987.

Espelage, Dorothy, and Christine S. Asidao. "Conversations With Middle School Students About Bullying and Victimization: Should We Be Concerned?" In *Bullying Behavior: Current Issues, Research, and Interventions*, ed. Robert A. Geffner, Marti Loring, and Corinna Young, 49–62. New York: Haworth Press, 2001.

Espelage, Dorothy, and Melissa K. Holt. "Bullying and Victimization during Early Adolescence: Peer Influences and Psychosocial Correlates." In *Bullying Behavior: Current Issues, Research, and Interventions*, ed. Robert A. Geffner, Marti Loring, and Corinna Young, 123–42. New York, Haworth Press, 2006.

Feyerick, Deborah, and Sheila Steffen. "'Sexting' Lands Teen on Sex Offenders List." CNN.com, April 9, 2009. Accessed March 17, 2011 from articles. cnn.com/2009-04-07/justice/sexting.busts_1_phillip-alpert-offender-list-offender-registry?_s=PM:CRIME.

Fineran, Susan. "With Disabilities and Peer Sexual Harassment: School Policy and Practice Implications." Paper presented at the Family Violence Research Conference, Durham, New Hampshire, Aug. 2002.

Fineran, Susan, and Larry Bennet. "Gender and Power Issues of Peer Sexual Harassment Among Teenagers." *Journal of Interpersonal Violence* 14, no. 6 (1999): 626–41.

Fineran, Susan, and Robert M. Bolen. "Risk Factors for Peer Sexual Harassment in Schools." *Journal of Interpersonal Violence* 21 (2006): 1169–90.

Finkelhor, David, Richard Ormrod, Heather Turner, and Sherry Hamby. "The Victimization of Children and Youth." *Child Maltreatment* 10 (2005): 5–25. Accessed November 3, 2010 from the Sage database.

Fitzpatrick, Erika. "Stronger Laws Needed to Protect Students from Sexual Predators." *Educator's Guide to Controlling Sexual Harassment* 18, no. 6 (2011): 5–6.

——. "Public Schools Could Soon be Required to Check Criminal Histories." *Educator's Guide to Controlling Sexual Harassment* 18, no. 5 (2011): 10–11.

——. "ED Releases Examples of State Anti-Bullying Policies." *Educator's Guide to Controlling Sexual Harassment* 18, no. 5 (2011): 11.

Flynn, Jack. "Phoebe Prince's Parents Settle With South Hadley School System on Discrimination Complaint." December 14, 2010. Accessed December 18, 2010 from www.masslive.com/news/index.ssf/2010/12/phoebe_prince_parents_settle_south_hadley_discrimination.html.

"42 U.S.C. Section 1983: U.S. Code—Section 1983: Civil Action for Deprivation of Rights." FindLaw for Legal Professionals. Accessed at codes. lp.findlaw.com/uscode/42/21/I/1983.

Franklin v. Gwinnett Cty. Public Schools, 911 F.2d 617 (CA11 1990).

Fraser v. Bethel School District No. 403, 478 U.S. 675 (1986).

Fried, SuEllen, and Paula Fried. *Bullies and Victims: Helping Your Child Through the Schoolyard Battlefield*. New York: Evans, 1996.

Garbarino, James, and Ellen DeLara. *And Words Can Hurt Forever: How to Protect Adolescents from Bullying, Harassment, and Emotional Violence*. New York: Simon and Schuster/The Free Press, 2002.

"Gay Students Receive Harsher Punishments in School, Study Says." *Huffington Post.* Accessed December 12, 2010 from www.huffingtonpost.com/2010/12/06/gay-students-punished-more-than-straight-peers_n_792628.html.

Gebser v. Lago Vista Indep. School District, 524 U.S. 274 (1998).

Gibbs, Nancy. "When Bullying Goes Criminal." *Time.com,* April 19, 1010. Accessed September 14, 2010 from www.time.com/time/printout/0,8816,1978773,99.html.

Geffner, Robert, Marti Loring, and Corinna Young. *Bullying Behavior: Current Issues, Research and Interventions.* New York, Haworth Press, 2001.

Glicklick-Rosenberg, Lucille. "Violence and Children: A Public Health Issue." *Psychiatric Times* 13, no 3. (1996): 45–7.

Glover, Derek, Gerry Gough, Michael M. Johnson, and Netta Cartwright. "Bullying in 25 Secondary Schools: Incidence, Impact and Intervention." *Educational Research,* 42 no. 2 (2000): 141–56.

Graham, Sandra, and Jaana Juvonen. "Ethnicity, Peer Harassment, and Adjustment in Middle School: An Exploratory Study." *Journal of Early Adolescence* 22, no. 2 (2002): 173–99. Accessed August 5, 2010 from Sage database.

Greta, Carol. "Cyberbullying: Doing Something About it Lawfully." Iowa Department of Education, nd. Accessed January 8, 2011 from iowa .gov/educate/index.php?option=com_content&view=article&id=1718:cyber bullying-guidance&catid=411:legal-lessons&Itemid=2656.

Gruber, James E., and Susan Fineran. "Comparing the Impact of Bullying and Sexual Harassment Victimization on the Mental and Physical Health of Adolescents." *Sex Roles* 58 (2008): 13–14. Accessed August 5, 2010 from Proquest database.

———. "The Impact of Bullying and Sexual Harassment on Middle School and High School Girls." *Violence Against Women* 13, no. 2 (2007): 627–43.

Hazler, Richard J. "Bullying Breeds Violence: You Can Stop It." *Learning* 22 (1994): 38–41.

Heldman, Caroline. "Disney Ride Makes Light of Sex Slavery." *Sociological Images.* Accessed January 28, 2011 from thesocietypages.org/socimages/2010/11/10/guest-post-disney-ride-still-makes-light-of-sex-slavery/.

Hendrie, Caroline. "Abuse by Women Raises its Own Set of Problems." *Education Week* (December 2, 1998): 1, 14–15, 17.

———. "Cost is High When Schools Ignore Abuse." *Education Week* (December 9, 1998): 1, 14–16.

———. "'Passing the Trash' by School Districts Frees Sexual Predators to Hunt Again." *Education Week* 18, no. 3. (1998): 16–17.

———. "Sex with Students: When Employees Cross the Line." *Education Week* (December 2, 1998): 1, 12–14.

Henneberger, Melinda. "Now Sex and Violence Link at an Earlier Age." *New York Times*, July 4, 1993, 6.

———. "Younker School 'Game': or Hiding Sex Abuse?" *New York Times*, June 25, 1993, A16.

Henry, Becky. *Just Tell Her to Stop: Family Stories of Eating Disorders*. Minneapolis: Infinite Hope Publishing, 2011.

Herbert, Bob. "Misogyny is America's True National Pastime." *New York Times*, January 17, 2008. Accessed November 27, 2010 from www.nytimes .com/2008/01/15/opinion/15herbert.html?hp=&pagewanted=print.

Hill, Catherine and Holly Kearl. *Crossing the Line: Sexual Harassment at School*. Washington, DC: American Association of University Women, 2001.

Himmelstein, Kathryn E. W., and Hannah Brucker, "Criminal Justice and School Sanctions Against Non-heterosexual Youth: A National Longitudinal Study," Pediatrics (December 6, 2010). Accessed January 4, 2011, from http://pediatrics.aapplublications.org/content/early/2010/12/06/peds.2009 -2306.full.pdf+html

Holt, Melissa K., and Melissa A. Keys. "Teachers' Attitudes Toward Bullying." In *Bullying in American Schools: A Social-Ecological Perspective on Prevention and Intervention*, eds. Dorothy L. Espelage and Susan M. Swearer, 121–140. Mahway, NJ: Lawrence Erlbaum 2004.

Hudson, David, L. Jr. "Cyberspeech." K–12 Public School Student Expression. First Amendment Center.org. Accessed February 23, 2011 from www .firstamendmentcenter.org/speech/studentexpression/topic.aspx?topic= cyberspeech.

"Insights in Ink." *Star Tribune*, Newspaper in Education Program (Minneapolis, MN), 1992.

Jackson Baynard v. Catherine Malone and Craig J. Lawson; Alexandria City School Board, et al., 268 F3d 228 (4th Cir. 2001).

Jeffrey, Linda, DeMond Miller, and Margaret Linn. "Middle School Bullying as a Context for the Development of Passive Observers to the Victimization of Others." In *Bullying Behavior: Current Issues, Research and Interventions*, ed. Robert A. Geffner, Marti Loring, and Corinna Young, 143–56. New York: Haworth, 2001.

Johnson, Allan. *The Gender Knot: Unraveling Our Patriarchal Legacy*. Philadelphia: Temple University Press, 1997.

Jones, Gloria. "Site-Based Voices: Dilemmas of Educators who Engage in Activism Against Student Sexual Harassment." Paper presented at the American Educational Research Association, Montreal, 2005.

Jones, Nicola, Kim Moore, Eliana Villar-Marquez, and Emma Broadbent. "Painful Lessons: The Politics of Preventing Sexual Violence and Bullying at School." Working paper 295. London: Overseas Development Institute, October 2008. Accessed February 28, 2009 from www.odi.org.uk/resources/download/2429.pdf.

Jones, Rebecca, "Courting Controversy." *The American School Board Journal* (October 1996): 26–30.

"Judge Lifts School Ban on Teen's Shirt." *Star Tribune*, May 19, 2001.

Juvonen, Jaana, Sandra Graham, and Mark A. Schuster. "Bullying Among Young Adolescents: The Strong, the Weak, and the Troubled." *Pediatrics* 112, no. 6 (2003): 1231–37.

Kaiser Family Foundation. "Key Facts on TV Violence." Report 3335, Spring 2003. Accessed February 23, 2011 from www.kff.org/entmedia/upload/Key -Facts-TV-Violence.pdf.

Kelsey, Lisa M. "Note: Kids with Kissies and Schools with the Jitters: Finding a Reasonable Solution to the Problem of Student-To-Student Sexual Harassment in Elementary Schools." *The Boston University Public Interest Law Journal* 8 (Fall 1998):119–44.

Kenway, Jane, and Lindsay Fitzclarence. "Masculinity, Violence, and Schooling: Challenging Poisonous Pedagogies." *Gender and Education* 9 (1997): 117–33. Accessed May 29, 2008 from EBSCO database.

Kenway, Jane, Sue Willlis, Jill Blackmore, and Leonie Rennie. *Answering Back: Girls, Boys and Feminism in Schools in Sydney*. Routledge: New York, 1997.

"Kids with ADHD May be More Likely to Bully." MSNBC.com. Accessed January 4, 2011 from www.msnbc.msn.com/id/22813400/ns/health-kids_ and_parenting/.

Kimmel, Michael S. "Masculinity as Homophobia: Fear, Shame, and Silence in the Construction of Gender Identity." In *Theorizing Masculinities*, ed. Harry Brod and Michael Kaufman, 119–41. Thousand Oaks, CA: Sage, 1994.

Kivel, Paul. *Boys Will Be Men: Raising Our Sons for Courage, Caring, and Community*. British Columbia, Canada: New Society Publishers, 1999.

Kivel, Paul. *Men's Work: How to Stop the Violence that Tears Our Lives Apart*. Center City, MN: Hazelden: 1992.

Klein, Jessie. "An Invisible Problem: Everyday Violence Against Girls in Schools." *Theoretical Criminology* 10, no. 147 (2006): 147–77.

Kosciw, Joseph G., Emily A. Greytak, Elizabeth M. Diaz, and Mark J. Bartkiewicz. *The 2009 National School Climate Survey: The Experiences of Lesbian, Gay, Bisexual and Transgender Youth in Our Nation's Schools*. New York: GLSEN, 2010. Accessed March 1, 2011 from www.glsen.org/binary-data/ GLSEN_ATTACHMENTS/file/000/001/1675-1.pdf.

Koster, Olinka. "What Possessed BHS to sell 'Provocative' Underwear for Girls as Young as Seven?" *Daily Mail* (London), March 26, 2003.

Krug, Etienne G., Linda L. Dahlberg, James A. Mercy, Anthony B. Zwi, and Rafael Lozano, eds. *World Report on Violence and Health*. Geneva: World Health Organization, 2002. Accessed March 25, 2009 from whqlibdoc.who.int/publications/2002/9241545615_eng.pdf.

Kunkel, Dale, Erica Biely, Keren Eyal, Kirstie Cope-Farral, Edward Donnerstein, and Rena Randrich. *Sex on TV 2003*. Santa Barbara: University of California, Kaiser Family Foundation, 2003. Accessed October 26, 2010 from www.kff.org/entmedia/upload/Sex-on-TV-3.pdf.

Kunkel, Dale, Keren Eyal, Keli Finnerty, Erica Biely, and Edward Donnerstein. *Sex on TV 2004*. Menlo Park, CA: Kaiser Family Foundation, 2005. Accessed December 3, 2010 from www.kff.org/entmedia/upload/Sex-on-TV 4-Full-Report.pdf.

Lahelma, Elina. "Gendered Conflicts in Secondary School: Fun or Enactment of Power?" *Gender and Education* 14, no. 3 (2002): 295–306.

Larkin, June. "Walking Through Walls: The Sexual Harassment of High School Girls." *Gender and Education* 3 (June 1994): 263–80.

Leach, Fiona. "Gender Violence in Schools in the Developing World." In *Combating Gender Violence in and Around Schools*, ed. Fiona Leach and Claudia Mitchell, 23–29. Sterling, VA: Trentham Books, 2006.

Leach, Fiona, and Sara Humphreys. "Gender Violence in Schools: Taking the 'Girl-as-Victims' Discourse Forward." *Gender & Development* 15 (2007): 51–65. Accessed January 12, 2009 from EBSCO database.

Lee, Valerie E., Robert G. Croninger, Eleanor Linn, and Chen Xianglei. "The Culture of Sexual Harassment in Secondary Schools." *American Educational Research Journal* 2 (1996): 383–415.

Lenhart, Amanda, Kristen Purcell, Aaron Smith, and Kathryn Zickuhr. "Social Media & Mobile Internet Use Among Teens and Young Adults." Pew Internet and American Life, 2010. Accessed from pewinternet.org/~/media//Files/Reports/2010/PIP_Social_Media_and_Young_Adults_Report_Final_with_toplines.pdf.

Levin, Diane, and Jean Kilbourne. *So Sexy So Soon*. New York: Random House, 2009.

Lichty, Lauren, Jennifer M. C. Torres, Maria Valenti, and NiCole T. Buchanan. "Sexual Harassment Policies in K–12 Schools: Examining Accessibility to Students and Content." *Journal for School Health* 78, no. 11 (2008): 607–14.

"Life Lessons: Addressing School Bullying." CBS News. Accessed from www.cbsnews.com/stories/2011/01/09/Sunday/main7227783.shtml.

Limber, Susan. "Addressing Youth Bullying Behaviors." In *Educational Forum on Adolescent Health: Youth Bullying*, ed. M. Fleming and K. Towey, 5–16. Chicago: American Medical Association, May 2002.

———. "Peer Victimization: The Nature and Prevalence of Bullying Among Children and Youth." In *Handbook of Children, Culture, and Violence*, ed. Nancy E. Dowd, Dorothy G. Singer, and Robin Fretwell Wilson, 313–33. Thousand Oaks, CA: Sage, 2006.

Liu, Cynthia. "The Neuroscience of Bullying." December 27, 2010. Accessed January 3, 2011 from www.care2.com/causes/education/blog/the -neuroscience-of-bullying/. This site provides links to various studies about the impact of bullying on the brain.

Lovell v. Poway Unified School District, 90 F.3d 367 (9th Cir. 1996).

Mann, Judy. *The Difference: Growing Up Female in America*. New York: Warner Books, 1994.

Marshall, Andrew. "New York Targets Very Young for Sex Offences." *The Independent*, July 3, 2000. Accessed January 17, 2009 from www.independent.co.uk/news/world/americas/new-york-targets-very-young-for-sex-offences-707587.html.

Mary v. Pittsburgh Public Schools, 2010 W.L. 562909 (W.D. Pa. Feb. 17, 2010).

Meritor Savings Bank v. Vinson, 477 U.S. 57 (1986).

"McCoy Receives High Grades." *Eden Prairie News*, May 20, 1993, 9.

McNeil, Liz, Diane Herbst, Kristen Mascia, and Monique Jessen. "Bullied to Death." *People*, February 22, 2010, 63–5.

Merrell, Kenneth W., Barbara A. Gueldner, Scott W Ross, and Duane M. Isava. "How Effective Are School Bullying Intervention Programs? A Meta-Analysis of Intervention Research." *School Psychology Quarterly* 23 (2008): 26–42.

Meyer, Elizabeth. *Gender, Bullying and Harassment: Strategies to End Sexism and Homophobia in Schools*. New York: Teachers College Press Columbia University, 2009.

———. "Gendered Harassment in Secondary Schools: Understanding Teachers' (Non) Interventions." *Gender and Education* 20, no. 6 (November 2008): 555–70.

———. "Hazing and High School Gendered Rites of Group Membership." *Psychology Today*, PsychologyToday.com, January 15, 2010. Accessed from. www.insidehazing.com/headlines.php?headlines2PageSize=50&idno=1415 &headlines2Page=3.

Miedzian, Myriam. *Boys Will Be Boys: Breaking the Link Between Masculinity and Violence*. New York: Doubleday 1991.

Miller, Alice. *For Your Own Good: The Roots of Violence in Child-Rearing.* London: Virago Press, 1987.

Milligan v. Board of Trustees, Southern Illinois University, No. 9-cv-320-jpg -cjp, 2010 WL 2649917 (June 30, 2010).

Mines, Kenneth A. *Letter of Finding: (S) Eden Prairie Schools (Minn) (OCR 05-92-1174).* Chicago, IL: U.S. Department of Education, Office for Civil Rights, May 1992, 39.

Minnesota Attorney General's Office, *Minnesota Attorney General's Report on Sexual Harassment in Minnesota Schools.* St. Paul: Minnesota Attorney General's Office, 1994.

————. *Sexual Harassment in Minnesota Elementary Schools.* St. Paul: Minnesota Attorney General's Office, 1994.

Mirsky, Judith. *Beyond Victims and Villains: Addressing Sexual Violence in the Education Sector. Report no. 47.* London: The Panos Institute, 2003. Accessed March 22, 2011 from www.panos.org.uk/?lid=250.

Ms. Foundation for Women. "Youth, Gender and Violence: Building a Movement for Gender Justice." New York, September 2008.

Murnen, Sarah K., and Linda Smolak. "The Experience of Sexual Harassment Among Grade-School Students: Early Socialization of Female Subordination?" *Sex Roles* 43, no.1/2 (2000): 1–17.

Muta, Kazue. "Sexual Harassment and Empowerment of Women in Japan." *NiASnytt: Asia Insights 1* (2004): 12–13. Retrieved March 17, 2009 from www.nias.ku.dk/nytt/2004_1/2004_11.pdf.

Nabozny v. Podlesny, 92 F.3d 446 (7th Cir. 1996).

Nansel, Tonja R., Mary E. Overpeck, R. S. Pilla, W. June Ruan, B. Simons-Morton, and Peter Scheidt. "Bullying Behaviors Among U.S. Youth: Prevalence and Association with Psychosocial Adjustment." *Journal of the American Medical Association* 285 (2001): 2094–100.

National Teen Dating Violence Prevention Initiative, American Bar Association. Accessed January 5, 2011 from www.americanbar.org/groups/ public_education/initiatives_awards/national_teen_dating_violence_ prevention_initiative.html.

Ni Aolain, Fionnuala. University of Minnesota law professor. Personal communication. International Women's Day Celebration: Transforming the World Through Women's Voices, March 14, 2009 in Minneapolis, MN.

www.nonamecallingweek.org.

O'Donahue, Anna C. "Sexual Harassment and PTSD: Is Sexual Harassment a Diagnosable Trauma?" *Journal of Trauma Stress* 15 (2002): 69–75.

Oh, Eunice. "Rutgers Student Commits Suicide After Secret Sex Tape." *People*, September 30, 2010. Accessed October 15, 2020 from www.people.com/ people/article/0,,20430783,00.html.

Olson, Jeremy. "'Defriending' Latest Form of Adolescent Cyberbullying." *Star Tribune*, October 22, 2010, B1.

Olweus, Dan. *Core Program Against Bullying and Antisocial Behavior: A Teacher Handbook*. Bergen, Norway: Olweus, 2001.

Orenstein, Peggy. *School Girls: Young Women, Self-esteem, and the Confidence Gap*. New York: Doubleday, 1994.

Paul, Pamela. "The Playground Gets Even Tougher." *The New York Times*, October 8, 2010. Accessed January 6, 2010 from www.nytimes.com/2010/10/10/fashion/10cultural.html?pagewanted-print.

Pellegrini, Anthony. "Bullying, Victimization, and Sexual Harassment During the Transition to Middle School." *Educational Psychologist* 37 (2002): 151–63.

Pellegrini, Anthony, and Jeffrey D. Long. "Part of the Solution and Part of the Problem: The Role of Peers in Bullying, Dominance, and Victimization During the Transition from Primary School Through Secondary School." In *Bullying in American Schools: A Social-Ecological Perspective on Prevention and Intervention*, ed. Dorothy L. Espelage and Susan M. Swearer, 107–17. Mahway, NJ: Erlbaum, 2004.

Pellegrini, Anthony, and Maria Bartini. "An Empirical Comparison of Methods of Sampling Aggression and Victimization in School Settings." *Journal of Educational Psychology* 92 (2000): 360–66.

Pellegrini, Anthony, Maria Bartini, and Fred Brooks. "School Bullies, Victims, and Aggressive Victims: Factors Relating To Group Affiliation and Victimization in Early Adolescence." *Journal of Educational Psychology* 9, no. 2 (1999): 216–24. Accessed January 4, 2011 from EBSCO database.

Penn, Dara. "Comment: Finding the Standard of Liability Under Title IX for Student-Against-Student Sexual Harassment: Confrontation, Confusion, and Still No Conclusions." *Temple Law Review* 783 (Summer 1997).

Pepler, Debra, and Wendy Craig. "A Peek Behind the Fence: Naturalistic Observations of Aggressive Children Remote Audiovisual Recording." *Developmental Psychology* 31, no. 4 (1995): 548–53. Accessed August 6, from EBSCO database.

Phoenix, Ann. "Youth and Gender: New Issues, New Agenda." *Young* 3 (1997): 2–19. Accessed February 4, 2011 from Sage database.

Pinchot, Joe. "Update: Court Rules Student's Rights Violated: *Layshock* Case Called Free-Speech Victory." The Herald, Sharonherald.com, February 5, 2010. Accessed from sharonherald.com/local/x295329063/UPDATE-Court-rules-student-s-rights-violated-Layshock-case-called-free-speech-victory.

Pinhiero, Paulo S. "Violence Against Children in Schools and Educational Settings." In *World Report on Violence Against Children*, 109–143. Geneva:

United Nations, 2006. Accessed March 25, 2009 from www.crin.org/docs/UNVAC_World_Report_on_Violence_against_Children.pdf.

Pipher, Mary. *Reviving Ophelia: Saving the Selves of Adolescent Girls*, New York: Anchor 1994.

Powell, Joy. "Stalkers and Harassers Plunge into Social Media," *Star Tribune*, January 15, 2011.

Price Waterhouse v. Hopkins, 490 U.S. 228 (1989).

Putnam, Frank W. "Beyond Sticks and Stones," *American Journal Psychiatry* 167, no.12 (December 2010): 1422–24. Accessed February 13, 2011 from ajp.psychiatryonline.org/cgi/reprint/167/12/1422?maxtoshow=&hits=10&RESULTFORMAT=1&author1=f+putnam&andorexacttitle=and&andorexacttitleabs=and&andorexactfulltext=and&searchid=1&FIRSTINDEX=0&sortspec=relevance&resourcetype=HWCIT.

"Qualified Immunity Law and Legal Definition." USLegal.com. Accessed from definitions.uslegal.com/q/qualified-immunity/.

Quesada, Emmalena K. "Note: Innocent Kiss or Potential Legal Nightmare: Peer Sexual Harassment and the Standard for School Liability Under Title IX." *Cornell Law Review* 83 (1998): 1014–67.

Requa v. Kent School District. No. 415, 492 F. Supp. 2d 1272 222 Ed. Law Rep. 178 (W.D. Wash. 2007).

Richardson, Larry. "A Safer Ride on the Bus: Many High School Students Prefer to Drive, at Greater Risk." *The Post Standard* (Syracuse, New York), September 22, 2002.

Rivers, Ian, Neil Duncan, and Valerie E. Besag. *Bullying: A Handbook for Educators and Parents*. Lanham, MD: Rowman & Littlefield, 2009.

Robinson, Kerry H. "Reinforcing Hegemonic Masculinities Through Sexual Harassment: Issues of Identity, Power, and Popularity in Secondary Schools." *Gender and Education* 17 (2005): 19–37.

Rousso, Harilyn, and Michael Wehmeyer, eds. *Double Jeopardy: Addressing Gender Equity in Special Education*. Albany: State University of New York Press, 2001.

Rudolph, Dana. "Fed to Schools: Law Requires Actions Against Bullying." *Keen News Service*, October 26, 2010. Accessed from www.keennewsservice.com/2010/10/26/fed-to-schools-law-requires-actions-against-bullying.

Sadker, Myra, and David Sadker. *Failing at Fairness: How America's Schools Cheat Girls*. New York: Scribner, 1994.

Salisbury, Jonathan, and David Jackson. *Challenging Macho Values: Practical Ways of Working with Adolescent Boys*. London: Falmer Press, 1996.

Sandler, Bernice R., and Harriett M. Stonehill. *Student-to-Student Sexual Harassment K–12: Strategies and Solutions for Educations to Use in the*

Classroom, School and Community. Lanham, MD: Rowman & Littlefield Education, 2005.

Secunda, Paul. "At the Crossroads of Title IX and a New 'Idea': Why Bullying Need Not Be a 'Normal Part of Growing Up' for Special Education Children." *Duke Journal of Gender Law and Policy* 12 (2005): 1–52.

Sex and Tech: Results from a Survey of Teens and Young Adults. National Campaign to Prevent Teen and Unplanned Pregnancy, 2008. Accessed from www.thenationalcampaign.org/sextech/pdf/sextech_summary.pdf.

"Sexting Girls Facing Porn Charge Sue D.A." CBS News.com, March 27, 2009. Accessed from www.cbsnews.com/stories/2009/03/27/earlyshow/main4896577.shtml).

Shakeshaft, Charol. *Educator Sexual Misconduct: A Synthesis of Existing Literature.* U. S. Department of Education of the Under Secretary, 2004.

Shakeshaft, Charol, and Audrey Cohan. "Sexual Abuse of Students by School Personnel." *Phi Delta Kappan* (March 1995): 513–19.

She Should Run. Women's Campaign Forum. Accessed January 1, 2011 from www.wcfonline.org/pages/programs/she-should-run.html.

Shear, Michael D., and Jacqueline L. Sunday. "An Education in Taunting: Schools Learning Dangers of Letting Bullies Go Unchecked." *Washington Post*, May 2, 1999. Accessed from www.nldline.com/washingt2.htm.

Shore Regional High School Bd. of Educ. v. P.S., *381* F.3d 194, 198 (3rd Cir. 2004).

Smalley, Suzanne. "This Could be Your Child." *Newsweek* August 18, 2003. Accessed October 30, 2010 from www.newsweek.com/2003/08/17/this-could-be-your-kid.html.

Smith, Peter K., ed. *Violence in Schools: The Response in Europe.* New York: Routledge, 2003.

Smith, Stacy, and Marc Choueiti. "Gender Disparity on Screen and Behind the Camera in Family Films." Geena Davis Institute of Gender in Media 2009. Accessed March 5, 2011 from www.thegeenadavisinstitute.org/research.php.

Smolowe, Jill, Steve Helling, Daniel S. Levy, and Diane Herbst. "I Was Bullied Because...." *People*, October 18, 2010, 66–9.

Snow, Kate, and Kelly Hagen. "Teen Girls Hazed on NJ High School 'Slut List.'" ABC Good Morning America, September 23, 2009. Accessed January 28, 2011 from abcnews.go.com/GMA/teen-girls-hazed-slut-list/story?id=8649050.

Stein, Nan. "Bullying or Harassment? The Missing Discourse of Rights in an Era of Zero Tolerance." *Arizona Law Review* 45, no. 3 (2003): 783–99.

———. "Commentary: Sexual Harassment Left Behind: What the 'Bullying' Framework is Doing to Civil Rights Laws and Framework." *Research & Action Report* 32. Boston: Wellesley Center for Women, 6–7.

————. "Sexual Harassment in School: The Public Performance of Gendered Violence." *Harvard Educational Review* 65 (1995): 145–62.

Stein, N., N. L. Marshall, and L. R. Tropp. *Secrets in Public: Sexual Harassment in Our Schools.* Wellesley, MA: Wellesley College Center for Research on Women, 1993.

Stockdale, Margaret S. "The Sexual Harassment of Men: Articulating the Approach-Rejection Theory of Sexual Harassment." In *In the Company of Men: Male Dominance and Sexual Harassment,* ed. James E. Gruber and Phoebe Morgan, 117–42. Boston: Northeastern University Press, 2005.

Stopbullying.org.

Strauss, Susan. *Sexual Harassment and Teens: A Program for Positive Change.* Minneapolis, MN: Free Spirit Publishing Inc., 1992.

————. "Sexual Harassment at an Early Age." *Principal* (September, 1994): 6–29.

————. "Sexual Harassment in K–12." In *Academic and Workplace Sexual Harassment: A Handbook of Cultural, Social Science, Management, and Legal Perspectives,* ed. Michele Paludi and Carmen A. Paludi, Jr., 105–45. Westport, CT: Praeger, 2003.

————. "Sexual Violence to Girls and Women in Education Around the World." In *Feminism and Women's Rights Worldwide,* vol. 1, ed. Michele A. Paludi. Santa Barbara, CA: Praeger, 2010.

Strauss, Susan, Sue Sattel, Becky Montgomery, Katia Petersen, and Steven Petersen. *Girls and Boys Getting Along: Teaching Sexual Harassment Prevention in the Elementary Classroom.* Minneapolis: Minnesota Department of Education, 1993.

Swearer, Susan, and Janice Delucia-Waack. "How to Curb School Bullying in Massachusetts." *Newsweek,* June 28 and July 5, 2010, 12.

Swearer, Susan M., Dorothy L. Espelage, Tracy Vaillancourt, and Shelley Hymel. "What Can be Done About School Bullying?" Linking Research to Educational Practice 39, no. 1 (2010): 38–47.

Szalavitz, Maia, "How Not to Raise a Bully: The Early Roots of Empathy." Time, April 17, 2010. Accessed October 16, 2010 from www.time.com/time/health/article/0,8599,1982190,00.html#ixzz157IYzVZq.

Tannen, Deborah. *Talking 9 to 5: Women and Men in the Workplace: Language, Sex and Power.* New York: Avon, 1994.

"Tesco's 'Toy' Pole Dance Kit." *Birmingham Post* (UK), October 25, 2006. Accessed December 23, 2010 from www.mirror.co.uk/news/top-stories/2006/10/23/tesco-s-toy-pole-dance-kit-115875-17976652/.

"The Phoebe Prince 'Bullycide' Trial: An Instant Guide." *The Week,* September 16, 2010. Accessed October 30, 2010 from theweek.com/article/index/207125/the-phoebe-prince-bullycide-trial-an-instant-guide.

Thelma D. v. Board of Ed., City of St. Louis, 934 F.2d 929 (8th Cir. 1991).

Theno v. Tonganoxie Unified School District, 377 F.Supp.3d 952 (D. Kansas 2005).

Thinkexist.com/quotations

Thompson Publishing Group. *Educator's Guide to Controlling Sexual Harassment*. Washington, DC: Thompson Publishing Group, March 2003, Tab 200, 4.

Tinker v. Des Moines Independent Community School District, 393 U.S. 503 (1969).

Title IX Coordinator's Role and Responsibilities: Local Districts. Accessed January 7, 2011 from dese.mo.gov/divcareered/Civil_Rights/Title_IX_Coordinator_Roles_and_Responsibilities.pdf.

Trager, Duffy. "New Tricks for Old Dogs: The *Tinker* Standard Applied to Cyber-bullying." *Journal of Law and Education* (July 2009). Accessed from findarticles.com/p/articles/mi_qa3994/is_200907/ai_n35628076/.

Tutu, Desmond, "Reconcilliation," The Desmond Tutu Peace Foundation, n.d., accessed March 3, 2011, from www.tifandgif.com/tutu/pdfs/tutu_3rd .pdf

"Two Student Speech Rulings Seemingly Conflict, But May Instead Offer Blueprint for Administrators." *Educator's Guide to Controlling Sexual Harassment* 17, no. 6 (2010): 2, 4, 9.

Ulrich, Dave. *Human Resource Champions: The Next Agenda for Adding Value and Delivering Results*. Boston: Harvard Business School Press, 1997.

United Nations. *UN Declaration on the Elimination of Violence Against Women. Resolution No. A/RES/48/104*. New York: United Nations, December 1993. Accessed January 28, 2009 from www.un.org/documents/ga/res/48/a48r104.htm.

United Nations. *2015 Millennium Goals*. Accessed February 27, 2009 from un.org/millenniumgoals/gender.shtml.

Unnever, James D., and Dewey G. Cornell. "The Culture of Bullying in Middle School." *Journal of School Violence* 2, no. 2 (2003): 5–27.

U.S. Department of Education. *Dear Colleague Letter: First Amendment*. 2003. www.ed.gov/about/offices/list/ocr/firstamend.html.

———. *Dear Colleague Letter: Prohibited Disability Harassment*. 2000. www .ed.gov/about/offices/list/ocr/docs/disabharassltr.html.

———. *Dear Colleague Letter: Religious Discrimination*. 2004. www2.ed.gov/ about/offices/list/ocr/religious_rights2004.html.

———. *The Family Educational Rights and Privacy Act: Guidance for Eligible Students*. February 2011. www2.ed.gov/policy/gen/guid/fpco/ferpa/for -eligible-students.pdf.

——. Office of Special Education Programs (OSEP), *OSEP's Idea Website*. idea.ed.gov/explore/home.

——. *Racial Incidents and Harassment Against Students at Educational Institutions: Investigative Guidance*. 59 Fed. Reg. 11,448 (Mar. 10, 1994). www.ed.gov/about/offices/list/ocr/docs/race394.html.

——. *Revised Sexual Harassment Guidance: Harassment of Students by School Employees, Other Students, or Third Parties*. January 19, 2001. www.ed.gov/about/offices/list/ocr/docs/shguide.html.

——. *Sexual Harassment: It's Not Academic* (Revised 2008): www.ed.gov/about/offices/list/ocr/docs/ocrshpam.html.

U.S. Department of Education, Office for Civil Rights, and National Association of Attorneys General. *Protecting Students from Harassment and Hate Crime: A Guide for Schools*. January, 1999.

U.S. Equal Employment Opportunity Commission. *Policy Guidance on Current Issues of Sexual Harassment*. March 1990. Accessed June 26, 2008 from www.eeoc.gov/policy/docs/currentissues.html.

Vaillancourt, Tracy, Shelley Hymel, and Peter McDougal. "Bullying is Power: Implications for School-Based Intervention Strategies." *Journal of Applied School Psychology* 19, no. 2 (2003): 157–76.

Ward, Jeanne, and Jackie Kirk. "Violence Against Girls in School," In *Broken Bodies, Broken Dreams: Violence Against Women Exposed*, ed. Lisa Ernst, 73–81. Nairobi: United Nations, 2005. Accessed January 30, 2009 from www.irinnews.org/IndepthMain.aspx?IndepthId=59&ReportId=72831.

Whitney, Irene L., and Peter K. Smith. "A Survey of the Nature and Extent of Bullying in Junior/Middle and Secondary Schools." *Educational Research* 35 (1993): 3–25.

Willard, Nancy. *Educator's Guide to Cyberbullying and Cyberthreats*. Center for Safe and Responsible Use of the Internet, April 2007. Accessed January 5, 2011 from www.cyberbully.org/cyberbully/docs/cbcteducator.pdf.

William Wolfe v. Fayetteville Arkansas School District, No. 10-2570 (8th Cir. July 14, 2010).

Wilson, Barbara, and Nicole Martins. "Impact of Violent Music on Youth." In *Handbook of Children, Culture, and Violence*, ed. Nancy E. Dowd, Dorothy G. Singer, and Robin Fretwell Wilson. Thousand Oaks, CA: Sage, 2006, 179–202.

"Witnesses to Bullying May Suffer Most of All." *U.S. News: Health*, December 17, 2020. Accessed December 27, 2009 from health.usnews.com/health-news/family-health/brain-and-behavior/articles/2009/12/17/witnesses-to-bullying-may-suffer-most-of-all.

Yaffe, Elaine. "Expensive, Illegal, and Wrong: Sexual Harassment in Our Schools. " *Kappan Special Report* (November 1995): 1–15.

Young, Ellie, Melissa L. Allen, and Betty Y. Ashbaker. "Responding to Sexual Harassment in Special Education Settings." *Teaching Exceptional Children* 36, no. 4 (March/April 2004): 62–67.

———. "Sexual Harassment Handout for Helping Children at Home and School II, Handouts For Families and Educators." *National Association of School Psychologists* 2 (2004): 99–102.

"Youth Victims and Perpetrators." ChildStats.gov. Accessed December 13, 2010 from www.childstats.gov/search/?as_sitesearch=www.childstats.gov/americaschildren09&output=xml_no_dtd&client=childstats&site=childsta ts&q=youth+victims+and+perpetrators&ie=UTF-8&ip=192.168.132.61& access=p&sort=date:D:L:d1&entqr=3.

Zeller, Jr., Tom. "Link by Link; Defending Cruelty: It's Only a Game." *New York Times*, February 20, 2006. Accessed Nov. 3, 2010 from query.nytimes .com/gst/fullpage.html?res=9D04E7DD113EF933A15751C0A9609C8B63.

Zezima, Katie. "Not All are Pleased at Plan to Offer Birth Control at Maine Middle School." *New York Times*, October 21, 2007. Accessed October 21, 2010 from www.nytimes.com/2007/10/21/us/21portland.html.

GLOSSARY OF TERMS

Bisexual: Those who are attracted to both sexes to varying degrees

Bullying: Repeated abusive acts over time with the intent to control, have power over, or intimidate another

Case law: Law based on court rulings rather than on already existing statutes

Compensatory damages: Restitution; pay

Cyberbully: An individual who bullies another online; it may be a friend, an acquaintance, or a stranger, and may be anonymous

Cyberbullying: Bullying, by use of the Internet or other digital/electronic technology

Cyberharassment: Sexual harassment by using the Internet or other digital/electronic technology

Digital/electronic technology: Cell phones, laptops, Facebook, MySpace, e-mail, chat rooms, instant messaging (IM), texting, Internet discussion groups

Empathy: Placing ourselves in another's shoes; emotional reaction to another's emotional state

Equal Protection: Fourteenth Amendment of the Constitution; a commitment to the nation that certain rights would not be violated by state and local governments. Without the availability of Section

1983, much of the promise of the Fourteenth Amendment would be betrayed

Exclusion: Intentionally excluding someone from a group, including an online group

***Fraser* standard**: Legal standard stating that controversial views may be expressed, but not if the school perceives those views as vulgar or lewd

Gay: One who is attracted to a person of the same sex; homosexual; sometimes refers only to male homosexuals

Gay-Straight Alliance (GSA): A student club for lesbian, gay, bisexual, transgender, and straight (heterosexual) youth

Gender: Socially set behavioral norms based on masculinity or femininity

Gender expression: How an individual displays his or her masculinity or femininity including by dress, speech, mannerisms, and social interactions

Gender harassment: Harassment as a form of punishment because an individual doesn't fit the traditional norms of masculinity or femininity; a form of nonsexualized harassment directed toward a female or male because of their gender

Gender identity: A person's internal sense of being male or female or something other than male or female

Gender nonconformity: Expressions of gender (masculinity and femininity) that do not conform to the dominant gender norms of Western culture

Gender violence: Refers to violence against women and girls

Gender role: The behaviors, attitudes, values, beliefs, and so on that a particular cultural group considers appropriate for males and females on the basis of their biological sex

GLBT: Acronym for gay, lesbian, bisexual, and transgender individuals; at times, the acronym reads "GLBTQ," with "Q" indicating that an individual is questioning their sexual orientation or gender identity

Heterosexism: An assumption that all people are heterosexual and that heterosexuality is superior or more desirable than homosexuality or bisexuality

Heterosexual: "Straight"; attracted to people of the opposite sex

Homosexual: Attracted to a person of the same sex; most GLBT persons in the United States prefer the terms *lesbian* and *gay*

Injunctive relief: A court order for something to happen or to stop happening

Lesbian: A female sexually attracted to another female

Oppression: A system of inequality between groups where one group dominates and benefits from the exploitation and subordination of the other group; the oppressed group unavoidably colludes in their own oppression

Patriarchy: Refers to a system/society that is male identified, male centered, and male dominated; includes oppression and hatred of women

Plaintiff: Someone who initiates a lawsuit

Protected class: A characteristic of groups of people protected from discrimination and harassment

Punitive damages: Monetary compensation awarded to an injured party to compensate the individual for losses, and that is intended to punish the wrongdoer

Qualified immunity: Qualified immunity protects public officials from being sued for damages unless they violated "clearly established" law of which a reasonable official in his or her position would have known

Sex: Being male or female as determined by reproductive function

Sex bias: Treating people unfairly because they are women or because they are men

Sexism: An ideology that depicts women as inferior to men

Sexualization: A person's value comes only from his or her sex appeal or behavior, to the exclusion of other characteristics; equates physical attractiveness with sexiness; is sexually objectified (see the APA report on sexualization of children)

Sexual orientation: Attraction to the opposite sex, the same sex, or both sexes

Sex role: Shared expectations that people hold about the characteristics women and men should have based on their sex

Sex role stereotype: Cultural beliefs about what the gender roles should be. It differs from gender role in that it tends to be the way people feel "others" should behave

Sexting: (1) The act of sending pictures of a sexual nature between cell phones or over other electronic media such as the Internet. (2) Houston Independent School District defines sexting as using a cell phone or other personal communication device to send text or e-mail messages or possessing text or e-mail messages containing images reasonably interpreted as indecent or sexually suggestive while at school or at a school-related function

Sexts: The sexual pictures sent electronically from one person to another

Sexual violence: Sexual assault; rape or attempted rape, as well as any unwanted sexual contact or threats

Straight: Heterosexual; attracted to the opposite sex

***Tinker* Standard**: States that for schools to ban disruptive speech/ expression, they must prove that it would cause a "reasonable" disruption of education and/or violate the rights of other students

Transgender: One whose identity or behavior falls outside of stereotypical gender norms

Transsexual: An individual who has undergone sex reassignment surgery so that one's physical sex matches to one's gender identity. Female-to-male transsexual people were born with female bodies but with a male gender identity; male-to-female transsexual people were born with male bodies but with a female gender identity

WEBSITE RESOURCES

BULLYING[1]

1. Centers for Disease Control and Prevention—School and Workplace Bullying

   www.cdc.gov/search.do?q=bullying&sort=date%3AD%3AL%3Ad1&ud=1&oe=UTF-8&ie=UTF-8

2. Bullying for K–12 and the Workplace

   awesomelibrary.org/bullying.html

3. Comprehensive Guide and Resources on Bullying

   www.guidetohealthcareschools.com/library/bullying

4. "Protecting Students from Harassment and Hate Crimes, A Guide for Schools," by the Association of Attorneys General

   www.ed.gov/pubs/harassment

5. U.S. Department of Justice—Bullying in Schools

   www.cops.usdoj.gov/pdf/e12011405.pdf

---

1. Because there is not a consistent definition of bullying, some of these links include examples of sexual harassment, including GLBT harassment, yet label it as bullying, which it is not.)

6. Bullying information website provides information on a variety of bullying issues for parents, teachers, and kids

    www.findyouthinfo.gov/topic_bullying.shtml?utm_source=BullyingInfo.org&utm_medium=Redirect&utm_campaign=BullyingSummitt

7. CNN Video: Bullying Victims Speak Out (includes students sexually and religiously harassed)

    ac360.blogs.cnn.com/2010/10/06/video-bullying-victims-speak-out/

8. CNN Teen Bullying Video

    www.popcrunch.com/anderson-cooper-teen-bullying-special-oct-8/

9. Bullying: Help Your Child Handle a School Bully—Mayo Clinic

    www.mayoclinic.com/health/bullying/MH00126

10. Pacer Center's Kids Against Bullying

    www.pacerkidsagainstbullying.org/

11. Pacer Center's Teens Against Bullying

    www.pacerteensagainstbullying.org/

12. National Institutes of Health: Numerous resources/website links about bullying

    www.nlm.nih.gov/medlineplus/bullying.html

13. Bullying and Cyberbullying Prevention for Kids and Teens

    stompoutbullying.org/

CYBERBULLYING AND CYBERHARASSMENT

1. An Educator's Guide to Cyberbullying and Cyberthreats

    www.cyberbully.org/cyberbully/docs/cbcteducator.pdf

2. Cyberbullying Research Center

    www.cyberbullying.us

3. Resources for youth for "digital drama" or cyberbullying

    www.athinline.org/

4. National Conference on State Legislatures: Information on Cyberstalking, Cyberharassment, and Cyberbullying Laws

   www.ncsl.org/default.aspx?tabid=13495

5. Dr. Strauss' Blog Interview on Cyberbullying/Cyberharassment

6. Cyberbullying: Doing Something About It, Lawfully (Iowa Department of Education)

   www.google.com/search?sourceid=navclient&ie=UTF-8&rlz=1T4GGLL_enUS316

SEXTING

1. New Law Proposed to Specifically Cover "Sexting" (Video)
   www.wlwt.com/video/19167023/detail.html

2. Teens Facing Charges in Brown County "Sexting" Probe (Video)
   www.wlwt.com/video/19123709/detail.html

3. Friends Hope Teen's Death Warns Others Against "Sexting" (Video)
   www.wlwt.com/video/18874100/detail.html

4. Mom Loses Daughter Over "Sexting," Demands Accountability (Video)
   www.wlwt.com/news/18866515/detail.html

5. How To Talk To Your Children About "Sexting" (Video)
   www.wlwt.com/video/18869406/detail.html

6. Teenagers Charged in Mason "Sexting" Case (Video)
   www.wlwt.com/video/18858368/detail.html

7. Teen Unwilling Participant in "Sexting," Prosecutor Says
   www.wlwt.com/news/18864984/detail.html

8. Two Mason Teenagers Charged in "Sexting" Case
   www.wlwt.com/news/18855563/detail.html

9. Teen Trend: Exchanging Nude Cell Phone Photos
   www.wlwt.com/news/16350682/detail.html

10. CBS News Videos on "Sexting" and the Law
    www.youtube.com/results?search_query=cbs+sexting+videos
    &aq=f
11. National Conference on State Legislatures: Information on Sexting
    www.ncsl.org/default.aspx?tabid=19696

SEXUAL HARASSMENT

1. U.S. Department of Education, Office of Civil Rights (OCR):
   How to File a Discrimination or Harassment Complaint
   www.ed.gov/about/offices/list/ocr/docs/howto.html?src=rt
2. U.S. Department of Education, OCR: Sexual Harassment Guidance: Harassment of Students by School Employees, Other Students, or Third Parties
   www.ed.gov/about/offices/list/ocr/docs/sexhar01.html
3. Family Violence Prevention Fund: Toolkit for Working with Men
   and Boys
   toolkit.endabuse.org/Home.html
4. Working with Men and Boys to Prevent Gender-based Violence
   toolkit.endabuse.org/Home.html
5. U.S. Department of Education report on sexual harassment/
   abuse of students by educators
   www2.ed.gov/rschstat/research/pubs/misconductreview/report.
   pdf
6. S.E.S.A.M.E. (Stop Educator Sexual Abuse, Misconduct, and
   Exploitation)
   www.sesamenet.org/
7. AAUW—Harassment-Free Hallways: How to Stop Harassment
   in the Schools
   www.aauw.org/learn/research/upload/completeguide.pdf
8. AAUW—Hostile Hallways: Bullying, Teasing, and Sexual Harassment in Schools (2001)
   www.aauw.org/learn/research/upload/hostilehallways.pdf;

9. AAUW—Gender Gaps: Where Schools Still Fail Our Children
   www.aauw.org/learn/research/upload/GGES.pdf

10. AAUW—Beyond the Gender Wars: A Conversation about Girls, Boys, and Education
   www.aauw.org/learn/research/upload/BeyondGenderWar.pdf

11. Protecting Students from Harassment and Hate Crimes: A Guide for Schools
   www2.ed.gov/offices/OCR/archives/Harassment/index.html

12. How to Protect Students from Sexual Harassment: A Primer for Schools
   www.sde.ct.gov/sde/lib/sde/pdf/equity/title_ix/studentsfromsexual harassment.pdf

13. Sexual Misconduct: Effective Policies and Practices
   www.tolerance.org/activity/sexual-misconduct-effective-policies -and

14. National Association for Sport and Physical Education: Sexual Harassment in Athletic Settings
   www.aahperd.org/naspe/standards/upload/Sexual-Harassment -in-Athletic-Settings-2000.pdf

15. National Women's Law Center—Do the Right Thing: Understanding, Addressing, and Preventing Sexual Harassment in School
   www.nwlc.org

16. Educator's Guide to Controlling Sexual Harassment by Thompson Publishing
   www.thompson.com/public/offerpage.jsp?prod=SINK

GLBT YOUTH

1. Resource for GLBT youth in crisis
   www.thetrevorproject.org

2. Parents, Families and Friends of Lesbians and Gays
   www.pflag.org

3. Hatred in the Hallways: A Report by Human Rights Watch on Violence and Discrimination Against Gay, Lesbian, Bisexual, and Transgendered Youth in U.S. Schools

   www.hrw.org/reports/2001/uslgbt/toc.htm

4. Gay, Lesbian and Straight Education Network (GLSEN)

   www.glsen.org/cgi-bin/iowa/all/research/index.html

5. Human Rights Watch – Hatred in the Hallways (study of harassment of and discrimination against gay, lesbian, bisexual, and transgender students in school)

   www.hrw.org/reports/2001/uslgbt/toc.htm

6. YouTube videos of GLBT adults speaking to GLBT youth from Dan Savage's "It Gets Better" Project

   www.youtube.com/itgetsbetterproject

7. National Gay and Lesbian Task Force

   www.thetaskforce.org

8. Thirteen-year-old harassed because of perception of being gay, small boned, Buddhist, and the clothes he wore

   www.youtube.com/watch?v=Gm0Numi1PzM

OCR

1. U.S. Department of Education: How to File a Discrimination or Harassment Complaint

   www.ed.gov/about/offices/list/ocr/docs/howto.html?src=rt

2. U.S. Department of Education: Sexual Harassment Guidance: Harassment of Students by School Employees, Other Students, or Third Parties

   www.ed.gov/about/offices/list/ocr/docs/sexhar01.html

3. U.S. Department of Education report on sexual harassment/abuse of students by educators

   www2.ed.gov/rschstat/research/pubs/misconductreview/report.pdf

4. Sexual Harassment: It's Not Academic

   www.ed.gov/about/offices/list/ocr/docs/ocrshpam.html

5. Dear Colleague Letter: Sexual Harassment Issues

   www2.ed.gov/about/offices/list/ocr/letters/sexhar-2006.html

6. Dear Colleague Letter: Religious Discrimination

   www2.ed.gov/about/offices/list/ocr/religious-rights2004.html

7. Dear Colleague Letter: First Amendment

   www.ed.gov/about/offices/list/ocr/firstamend.html

8. Dear Colleague Letter: Prohibited Disability Harassment

   www.ed.gov/about/offices/list/ocr/docs/disabharassltr.html

9. Racial Incidents and Harassment Against Students

   www.ed.gov/about/offices/list/ocr/docs/race394.html

10. For information on OCR's bullying prevention resources, please visit the Office of Safe and Drug-Free Schools website at:

    www2.ed.gov/about/offices/list/osdfs/index.html

11. For the OCR Regional Office serving your state, please visit:

    wdcrobcolp01.ed.gov/CFAPPS/OCR/contactus.cfm

12. OCR surveys school districts in a variety of areas related to civil rights in education through its Civil Rights Data Collection (CRDC). School districts are required to collect and report information on allegations of harassment, policies regarding harassment, and discipline imposed for harassment. For more information about the CRDC data, please visit:

    www2.ed.gov/about/offices/list/ocr/whatsnew.html

13. Information about the OCR

    www2.ed.gov/about/offices/list/ocr/aboutocr.html

CONTACT INFORMATION FOR OFFICE FOR CIVIL RIGHTS, HEADQUARTERS AND COUNTRY DIVISIONS

HEADQUARTERS

U.S. Department of Education
400 Maryland Ave., SW
Washington, DC 20202-1100
(800) 421-3481
Fax: (202) 205-9862; TDD (877) 521-2172
E-mail: OCR@ed.gov
Web site: www.ed.gov.ocr

EASTERN DIVISION

Connecticut, Maine, Massachusetts, New Hampshire, Rhode Island, Vermont
Office for Civil Rights, Boston Office
U.S. Department of Education
5 Post Office Sq.
8th Floor
Boston, MA 02109-3921
(617) 289-0111

Fax: (617) 289-0150
E-mail: OCR.Boston@ed.gov

New Jersey, New York, Puerto Rico, Virgin Islands
Office for Civil Rights, New York Office
U.S. Department of Education
32 Old Slip, 26th Floor
New York, NY 10005-2500
(646) 428-3900
Fax: (646) 428-3843
E-mail: OCR.NewYork@ed.gov

Delaware, Kentucky, Maryland, Pennsylvania, West Virginia
Office for Civil Rights, Philadelphia Office
U.S. Department of Education
100 Penn Square East, Suite 515
Philadelphia, PA 19107
(215) 656-8541
Fax: (215) 656-8605; TDD (215) 656-8604
E-mail: OCR.Philadelphia@ed.gov

SOUTHERN DIVISION

Alabama, Florida, Georgia, Tennessee
Office for Civil Rights, Atlanta Office
U.S. Department of Education
61 Forsyth St. SW, Suite 19T70
Atlanta, GA 30303-8927
(404) 974-9406
Fax: (404) 974-9471; TDD (404) 331-7236
E-mail: OCR.Atlanta@ed.gov

Arkansas, Louisiana, Mississippi, Texas
Office for Civil Rights, Dallas Office
U.S. Department of Education
1999 Bryan Street, Suite 1620
Dallas, TX 75201-6810
(214) 661-9600

Fax: (214) 661-9587
E-mail: OCR.Dallas@ed.gov

North Carolina, South Carolina, Virginia, Washington, DC
Office for Civil Rights, District of Columbia Office
U.S. Department of Education
400 Maryland Ave. SW
Washington, DC 20202-1475
(202) 453-6020
Fax: (202) 453-6021; TDD (877) 521-2172
E-mail: OCR.DC@ed.gov

MIDWESTERN DIVISION

Illinois, Indiana, Iowa, Minnesota, North Dakota, Wisconsin
Office for Civil Rights, Chicago Office
U.S. Department of Education
Citigroup Center
500 W. Madison Street, Suite 1475
Chicago, IL, 60661
(312) 730-1560
Fax: (312) 730-1576
E-mail: OCR.Chicago@ed.gov

Michigan, Ohio
Office for Civil Rights, Cleveland Office
U.S. Department of Education
600 Superior Avenue East
Bank One Center, Suite 750
Cleveland, OH 44114-2611
(216) 522-4970
Fax: (216) 522-2573: TDD (877) 521-2172
E-mail: OCR.Cleveland@ed.gov

Kansas, Missouri, Nebraska, Oklahoma, South Dakota
Office for Civil Rights, Kansas City Office
U.S. Department of Education
8930 Ward Parkway, Suite 2037

Kansas City, MO 64114-3302
(816) 268-0550
Fax: (816) 823-1404; TDD (877) 521-2172
E-mail: OCR.KansasCity@ed.gov

WESTERN DIVISION

Arizona, Colorado, New Mexico, Utah, Wyoming
Office for Civil Rights, Denver Office
U.S. Department of Education
Caesar Chavez Memorial Building
1244 Speer Blvd., Suite 310
Denver, CO 80204-3582
(303) 844-5695;
Fax: (303) 844-4303; TDD (877) 521-2172
E-mail: OCR.Denver@ed.gov

California
Office for Civil Rights, San Francisco Office
U.S. Department of Education
50 Beale Street, Suite 7200
San Francisco, CA 94105-4912
(415) 486-5555
Fax: (415) 486-5570; TDD (807) 521-2172
E-mail: OCR.SanFrancisco@ed.gov

Alaska, Hawaii, Idaho, Montana, Nevada, Oregon, Washington, American Samoa, Guam, Mariana Islands
Office for Civil Rights, Seattle Office
U.S. Department of Education
915 Second Avenue, Room 3310
Seattle, WA 98174-1099
(206) 607-1600
Fax: (206) 607-1601; TDD (206) 607-1647
E-mail: OCR.Seattle@ed.gov

STATE-BY-STATE RESOURCES FOR STATE LAW AND STATUTES

Alabama
Attorney General's Office
(334) 242-7300
www.ago.state.al.us

Alaska
Alaska State Commission for Human Rights
(907) 274-4692; TTY/TDD: (907) 276-3177
www.gov.state.ak.us/aschr/aschr.htm

Arizona
Arizona Attorney General, Civil Rights Division
(602) 542-5263
www.ag.state.az.us

Arkansas
Office of the Attorney General, Civil Rights Division
(501) 682-2007
www.ag.state.ar.us

California
Department of Fair Employment and Housing
(916) 445-5523; Toll-free: (800) 884-1684
www.dfeh.ca.gov

Colorado
Colorado Civil Rights Division
(303) 894-2997; Toll-free: (800) 262-4845
www.dora.state.co.us/civil-rights

Connecticut
Connecticut Commission on Human Rights and Opportunity
(860) 541-3400; Toll-free: (800) 477-5737
www.state.ct.us/chro

Delaware
Office of Labor Law Enforcement
(302) 761-8200
www.delawareworks.com/divisions/industaffairs/law.enforcement.htm

District of Columbia
Office of Human Rights
(202) 727-4559
www.ohr.washingtondc.gov/main.shtm

Florida
Florida Commission on Human Relations
(850) 488-7082
fchr.state.fl.us

Georgia
Georgia Human Relations Commission
(404) 206-6320
No web site as of this writing

Hawaii
Hawaii Civil Rights Commission
(808) 586-8636
hawaii.gov/labor/hcre.

Idaho
Idaho Human Rights Commission
(208) 334-2873
www2.state.id.us/irhc/ihrchome.htm

Illinois
Illinois Department of Human Rights
(312) 814-6200
www.state.il.us/dhr

Indiana
Indiana Civil Rights Commission
(317) 232-2600
www.state.in.us/icrc

Iowa
Iowa Civil Rights Commission
(515) 281-4121
www.state.ia.us/government/crc

Kansas
Kansas Human Rights Commission
(785) 296-3206
www.khrc.net

Kentucky
Kentucky Commission on Human Rights
(502) 595-4024
www.state.ky.us/agencies2/kchr

Louisiana
Louisiana Commission on Human Rights, Governor's Office
(225) 342-6969
www.gov.state.la.us/depts/lchr.htm

Maine
Maine Human Rights Commission
(207) 624-6050
www.state.me.us/mhrc/index.shtml

Maryland
Maryland Commission on Human Relations
(410) 767-8600
www.mchr.state.md.us

Massachusetts
Massachusetts Commission Against Discrimination
(617) 994-6000
www.mass.gov/mcad

Michigan
Michigan Department of Civil Rights
(313) 456-3700
www.michigan.gov/mdcr

Minnesota
Minnesota Department of Human Rights
(651) 296-5663
www.humanrights.state.mn.us

Mississippi
Mississippi Attorney General's Office
(601) 359-3680
www.ago.state.ms.us

Missouri
Missouri Commission on Human Rights
(573) 751 3325
www.dolir.mo.gov/hr

Montana
Montana Human Rights Bureau
(406) 444-2884
erd.dli.mt.gov/humanrights/hrhome.asp

Nebraska
Nebraska Equal Opportunity Commission
(402) 471-2024
www.neoc.ne.gov

Nevada
Nevada Equal Rights Commission
(702) 486-7161
detr.state.nv.us/nerc_index.htm

New Hampshire
New Hampshire Commission for Human Rights
(603) 271-2767
www.nh.gov/hrc

New Jersey
New Jersey Division on Civil Rights
(609) 292-4605
www.state.nj.us/lps/dcr

New Mexico
New Mexico Human Rights Division (of DOL)
(505) 827-6838
www.dol.state.nm.us/dol_hrd.html

New York
New York State Division of Human Rights
(718) 741-8400
www.nysdhr.com

North Carolina
North Carolina Civil Rights Division
(919) 733-0431
www.oah.state.nc.us/civil

North Dakota
North Dakota Department of Labor
(701) 328-2660
www.state.nd.us/labor/services/human-rights

Ohio
Ohio Civil Rights Commission
(614) 466-2785
www.state.oh.us/crc

Oklahoma
Oklahoma Human Rights Commission
(405) 521-2360
www.onenet.net/~ohrc2

Oregon
Oregon Bureau of Labor & Industries, Civil Rights Division
(503) 731-4200, ext. 1
www.boli.state.or.us

Pennsylvania
Pennsylvania Human Relations Commission
(717) 787-9784
Sites.state.pa.us/PA_Exec/PHRC

Rhode Island
Rhode Island Commission for Human Rights
(401) 222-2661
www.richr.ri.gov/frames.html

South Carolina
South Carolina Human Affairs Commission
(803) 737-7800
www.state.sc.us/schac

South Dakota
South Dakota Department of Commerce, Division of Human Rights
(605) 773-4493
www.state.sd.us/dcr/hr/HR_HOM.htm

Tennessee
Tennessee Human Rights Commission
(615) 741-5825
www.state.tn.us/humanrights

Texas
Texas Commission on Human Rights
(512) 437-3450
www.twc.state.tx.us/customers/jsemp/jsempsubcrd.html

Utah

Utah Antidiscrimination and labor Division
(801) 530-6801
www.labor.state.ut.us

Vermont

Vermont Human Rights Commission
(800) 416-2010 or (800) 828-2481
www.hrc.state.vt.us

Virginia

Council on Human Rights
(804) 225-2292
chr.vipnet.org/index.html

Washington

Washington State Human Rights Commission
(360) 753-6770
www.wa.gov/hrc

West Virginia

West Virginia Human Rights Commission
(304) 558-2616
www.state.wv.us/wvhrc

Wisconsin

Wisconsin Equal Rights Davison, Civil Rights Bureau
(608) 266-6860
www.dwd.state.wi.us/er/equal_rights_division/default.htm

Wyoming

Wyoming Department of Employment, Labor Standards Office
(307) 777-7261
wydoe.state.wy.us/doe.asp?ID=3

INDEX

ABOUT THE AUTHOR

Susan L. Strauss is a national and international speaker, trainer, consultant, and a recognized expert on workplace and school harassment and bullying. She conducts harassment and bullying investigations and functions as a consultant to attorneys as well as an expert witness in harassment lawsuits. Her clients are from business, education, health care, law, and government organizations from both the public and the private sector. She is an associate faculty at the University of Phoenix and DeVry University.

Dr. Strauss has conducted research, written two books, book chapters, and journal articles on sexual harassment and related topics. She has been featured on *20/20, CBS Evening News*, and other television and radio programs as well as interviewed for newspaper and journal articles such as *Harvard Education Newsletter, Lawyers Weekly*, and *Times of London.*

Susan is the recipient of the *Excellence in Educational Equity Award* from the Minnesota Department of Education for her work in sexual harassment in education. She has spoken about sexual harassment at international conferences in Botswana, Egypt, Thailand, and the United States. She consulted with the Israeli Ministry of Education, as well as with educators from Israel, England, Australia, St. Maartin, and Canada. She traveled to Poland with the Minnesota Advocates for Human Rights and conducted research on sex discrimination and sexual harassment in Polish workplaces.

Susan has a doctorate in organizational leadership. She is a registered nurse, has a bachelor's degree in psychology and counseling, a master's degree in public health, and a professional certificate in training and development. She has been involved in the harassment arena since 1985.